INTEGRATED PRODUCTION SYSTEMS
DESIGN, PLANNING, CONTROL, AND SCHEDULING
FOURTH EDITION

INTEGRATED PRODUCTION SYSTEMS
DESIGN, PLANNING, CONTROL, AND SCHEDULING
FOURTH EDITION

VINCENT A. MABERT
F. ROBERT JACOBS
EDITORS

Industrial Engineering and Management Press
Institute of Industrial Engineers
Norcross, Georgia

Library of Congress Cataloging-in-Publication Data

Integrated production systems : design, planning, control, and
    scheduling / [edited by] F. Robert Jacobs, Vincent A. Mabert. -- 4th
    ed.
            p.   cm.
        Includes bibliographical references.
        ISBN 0-89806-119-9
        1. Production planning. 2. Inventory control. 3. Scheduling
    (Management)   I. Jacobs, F. Robert.   II. Mabert, Vincent A.
    TS176.I5518   1991
    658.5'03--dc20   91-31574

Additional copies may be obtained by contacting:
Institute of Industrial Engineers
Customer Service
25 Technology Park
Norcross, Georgia 30092 USA
1-404-449-0460 phone
1-404-263-8532 fax

Quantity discounts available.

TABLE OF CONTENTS

v

PREFACE

"Continuous improvement" and "adding value" are the watch words for manufacturing firms desiring to produce valued products. In the same spirit of continuous improvement and adding value, this book attempts to provide the reader with a greater understanding of the tools, techniques, and systems required for the effective management of today's complex manufacturing environment.

The first three editions were titled *Production Planning, Scheduling, and Inventory Control: Concepts, Techniques, and Systems* (1974, 1982, 1986) and we wish to recognize the valuable contributions of earlier authors, Douglas Montgomery, William Berry, and Colin Moodie, for the body of knowledge they identified and organized. The goal of the three books was to provide better understanding of the many building blocks that are part of managing production systems. For example, various topics like aggregate planning, forecasting techniques, dispatching priority rules, and order sizing logic were addressed. Such an approach was useful and informative, as indicated by positive feedback from readers.

However, this fourth edition shifts the focus to how to integrate these techniques, concepts and systems into an effective manufacturing system. Because of this goal, this edition's title has been altered to *Integrated Production Systems: Design, Planning, Control, and Scheduling*, reflecting the criteria that influenced the selection of the included articles. More attention is given to how product, process, and information decisions interplay with each other and affect performance of the manufacturing function.

The key is integration, not isolation! Past decisions and systems were implemented to solve local problems, with little concern on how they would impact other parts of the manufacturing process. The future requires looking at decisions in a holistic framework, being sensitive to suppliers, processes, quality, inventory levels, shipping schedules, etc. Within this framework, Wickham Skinner has stated five characteristics that are needed for effective manufacturing systems (from "The Taming of Lions: How Manufacturing Leadership Evolved, 1780-1984," in the *Uneasy Alliance,* edited by K. B. Clark, R. H. Hayes, and C. Lorenz, Harvard Business School Press, Boston, MA, 1985):

ix

1. Seeing the factory as a resource that can be used to create competitive advantage and leadership, rather than just as a financial investment.

2. Carrying out a primary role in the corporation as the architect and builder of new manufacturing systems structured to provide competitive and strategic advantage, rather than acting as custodian and housekeeper.

3. Emphasizing as key skills those managing technological and product change and building flexible, learning organizations, rather than acting as coordinator and stabilizer.

4. Becoming involved with and gaining the support and commitment of the work force, rather than considering labor as a cost and a disturbing element to be managed well down the organization.

5. Seeking maximum flexibility for product and volume change by choosing technology appropriate for the competitive market, rather than generally seeking maximum mechanization and the use of mass-production processes.

The spirit of Skinner's five characteristics guided our selection of articles for this book, and we hope you find them useful, informative, and maybe, provocative in what they mean to success.

F. ROBERT JACOBS
VINCENT A. MABERT
INDIANA UNIVERSITY
BLOOMINGTON, INDIANA

SECTION 1
INTRODUCTION

Manufacturing firms, both domestic and international, are facing intensified competition in the global marketplace. For many companies, it is an issue of survival. Firms successfully competing in the international market owe their success not so much to better product design or marketing ingenuity, but to something more difficult to duplicate: a world class manufacturing capability to produce high quality products on a timely basis.

What does world class manufacturing capability mean? In today's dynamic environment, world class manufacturing has four goals:

• produce high quality products
• maintain dependable delivery on a timely basis
• improve productivity to be cost competitive
• provide a flexible manufacturing structure

Effective manufacturing today requires the integration of numerous systems (machining, information, supply, etc.) that influence and control the production process, which affects the firm's ability to attain the above four goals. How these systems are selected, implemented, and managed ultimately determines the effectiveness of the firm.

The goal of this book is to provide a series of readings covering important process selection, planning, and control issues for integrated manufacturing systems (automated and manual) that are emerging in the factories of the future. While effective management covers a wide range of topics, this book concentrates upon the more technical aspects of designing and managing the production system, leaving many of the behavioral and work force motivational topics for other authors. Our attention will focus on system design using, in some cases, group technology and cellular manufacturing concepts. The evaluation of these systems is a critical phase in effective management, requiring the use of financial and non-financial yardsticks. Next, planning the use of these systems, like Computer Aided Process Planning (CAPP) or Material Requirements Planning (MRP), represents a major step to effective integration. Finally, interfacing Just-in-Time (JIT) with more traditional material systems as well as how they interact with manufacturing systems is discussed.

In the remaining parts of this section, we expand our discussion of world class manufacturing and its four elements to provide a basis for the three selected articles that follow the Introduction.

First, a *quality product* (or service) is the foundation of a successful business. And what is quality? It is the production of a product that meets the "expectations" of the customer! Reliability, durability, aesthetic appeal, usability, etc. are all important dimensions of quality that the manufacturing process must be prepared to support during the fabrication, assembly, and testing of a quality product.

Competing today requires that a company focus its attention and resources on what it needs to do to effectively support the marketplace. An example is the Copeland Corporation, which manufacturers compressors for industrial coolers and air conditioners (Ruwe and Skinner 1987). In the late 1970s the corporation realized that it needed to differentiate itself in the marketplace by producing high quality products for different market segments. To do this successfully with the broad product line they currently supported, they divided their compressor (hermetic, semi-hermetic and remanufacturing) businesses along specific market segments. This then defined the nature of the manufacturing task that needed to be implemented to support those markets which was the establishment of focused factories. For a high volume product line of hermetically sealed compressors for air conditioners, Copeland built a highly automated plant in Hartsville, Alabama. This plant employed state of the art machining systems to maintain tight tolerances, which were required for high quality production at a competitive price.

Second, today's customers expect *dependable delivery* of products, both new and mature. Firms need to design manufacturing systems, process and information support systems, that allow for the effective management of material flows from vendors through to customers, and which meet specified due dates. Interacting with vendors, ordering through material requirement planning, using computer aided process planning, employing flexible manufacturing systems, etc., are all important components in the drive to attain reliable delivery of products.

The Copeland Corporation manufactures customized large semi-hermetic compressors for the industrial refrigerator market; a market sensitive to reliable product delivery. These low volume/high variety products required a more traditional batch manufacturing approach. For this product line, the Shelby, Ohio plant managers focused their efforts on production planning systems for good material control. Since the assembly of a broad spectrum of product options was required, product support activities concentrated heavily on material ordering, component coordination, and training of the higher skilled work force to handle the product variety present in the plant.

Third, today's pressure for competitive product prices requires that manufacturing managers focus more of their attention on productivity improvement activities. For most hard-goods producing companies, the bulk of their labor force and assets are tied to the manufacturing group. Therefore, the cost of producing a product is directly influenced by how well the manufacturing function utilizes the resources under its control. The rationalizing of the production process through group technology concepts helps standardize product and systems to reduce flow time, lower work-in-process (WIP), minimize scrap, and increase quality, leading to better utilization of the existing asset base in many companies. The implementation of JIT principals for sequencing the receipt of materials from vendors reduces raw material inventory and obsolete inventory write-offs. (Section Five presents a number of approaches to more effectively manage the factory floor.)

In the early 1980s, Allen-Bradley (Blackburn 1991) was under significant competitive pressure for its electric contractors and relays because of foreign competition. They implemented their World Contactor One (WCI) project, which involved working with suppliers and the creation of a manufacturing system in the Milwaukee plant to produce over 600 variations of contractors and relays to meet the emerging international standards. By focusing on filling orders within twenty-four hours, in a make-to-order environment, management has been able to collapse part flow time, squeeze down work-in-progress inventory, and reduce costs by sixty percent making them the lowest cost producer in the world for this line of products.

Fourth, greater *flexibility* is expected from the manufacturing function to adapt to continuing changes in the market and the technologies that influence the firm's ability to produce competitive products. This means that manufacturing firms need to recognize that: new product introductions are a way of life; technological changes will introduce new manufacturing processes and materials; significant work force training will be required to handle the changes in technology and systems on the

3

shop floor; and management systems will adapt and change to improve planning and control of the manufacturing function.

Successful companies in the future will continuously introduce new products to the marketplace, with new product cycles being very short compared to historical experience. We can view the product introduction function as having two extremes. The first involves small incremental changes to existing products to maintain a competitive advantage in the marketplace; while the second concerns an innovative or radical change in the nature of the product. Such conditions are common and manufacturing processes need to be supportive of these product changes. Therefore, flexibility is a critical element for long-term success. Flexible Manufacturing Systems (FMS) are one way that manufacturing departments can quickly respond to the production of these new products.

For example, Cummins Engine Corporation (Columbus, Indiana) employs a number of computerized numerical control (CNC) cells and flexible manufacturing systems as a way of handling the significant product variety that exists in their business. With a significant part number base, currently over 100,000, and more coming on line, Cummins has turned to flexible manufacturing systems as a way to support the small volume and high variety options present in the diesel engine business (Venkatesan 1990).

They are also using flexible manufacturing systems to support some of their high volume business. In particular, they have found that flexible manufacturing systems dedicated to high volume production provides an excellent vehicle to support quick introduction of the next generation of products within a particular family. The key here is the significant lead time compression of the product development cycle because of flexible tooling, fixturing, and machining capabilities of these systems. The compression brake they produce for the diesel engine industry, which has been a very successful product for Cummins, is such an example. This new product line was quickly brought to the market and then incremental changes in product design were launched in very short order using FMS technology.

WORLD CLASS MANUFACTURING

Many firms today are struggling to be competitive and attain world class manufacturing status. This is not an easy task, since the evidence suggests there are as many failures as successes. Success seems to be routed in shifting the manufacturing organizational climate to focus on continuous improvement, rather than the purchase and/or implementation of a system or the adoption of a specific program.

The first article by Jeff Barrett ("IE's at CalComp are Integrating JIT, TQC and Employee Involvement for World Class Manufacturing"), provides an excellent case study of how the Display Products Division of CalComp moved forward to become a world class manufacturer. As noted in the article, this involved a number of projects focusing on JIT concepts, total quality control tasks, and employee involvement programs. The article provides a nice framework of what needs to be done to rationalize the material flow and production process. Barrett also discusses how to orchestrate and organize management, staff, and workers to effectively implement change on the factory floor.

As indicated earlier, quality is an important cornerstone for success in the world market. Television advertising, like Ford's Job #1 slogan, tells consumers that quality is high on the priority list. The big question is how does this theme get implemented in the factory? Hugh Harrington and Jack ReVelle describe (in "Hughes Aircraft Manages Total Quality Control in a DOD Environment") how Hughes Aircraft started a quality focus and the different programs that were initiated. It involved communicating a vision, setting goals, establishing milestones, and moving ahead in a positive manner.

It is nice to start with a clean slate when establishing a manufacturing facility or bringing online a new product, but such a situation is atypical. Greenfield plant projects are normally able to avoid many of the constraints that exist when one tries to revitalize an existing facility. However, most manufacturing firms must make their existing production facilities more responsive to current manufacturing practices. One well noted turnaround involves Harley-Davidson, a manufacturer of heavy weight motorcycles. In the final article of the introductory section ("Manufacturing Revitalization at Harley-Davidson Motor Co."), Mehran Sepehri describes the change process that took place at Harley-Davidson. He outlines the various programs like "materials as needed," employee involvement, inventory reduction, and set up time reduction that were utilized. This article is an excellent example of what needs to be done to remain competitive in today's dynamic world.

REFERENCES

Blackburn, Joseph D. *Time-Based Competition: The Next Battle Ground in American Manufacturing.* Homewood, IL: Business One Irwin, 1991.

Ruwe, Dean M. and Wickham Skinner. "Reviving a rust belt factory." *Harvard Business Review.* May-June, 1987. 70-76.

Venkatesan, Ravi. "Cummins Engine flexes its factory." *Harvard Business Review*. March-April, 1990. 120-127.

1

IES AT CALCOMP ARE INTEGRATING JIT, TQC AND EMPLOYEE INVOLVEMENT FOR "WORLD CLASS MANUFACTURING"

JEFF BARRETT

World class manufacturing techniques such as just-in-time, total quality control and employee involvement have received a considerable amount of attention in recent years. Many articles and seminars offer generalities about these concepts, but they rarely delve into the nuts and bolts of world class manufacturing (WCM) implementation.

This article uses a case study approach to describe the step-by-step process that the Display Products Division of CalComp Inc., a Lockheed company, has followed to begin a world class manufacturing transformation. This case study is offered as an integrated approach to WCM implementation that other manufacturers can use in their facilities.

The Display Products Division of CalComp, located in Hudson, NH, produces computer graphics systems. These systems come in ten basic models, each with up to 40 options. The process involves producing 400-500 printed circuit board assemblies per day and assembling them into the final product. Approximately 750 employees occupy the four-year-old, 250,000-sq-ft facility.

The initial drive to bring CalComp into the ranks of world class manufacturing came from top management's commitment to just-in-time (JIT) manufacturing. Roger Damphousse, vice president and general manager, showed commitment from the outset by providing the necessary resources and by assuring that management goals were in line with JIT philosophies.

From there, Jim Bell, director of operations, and Phil Insinga, director of operations engineering, selected a group of industrial engineers to champion change within the organization. The industrial engineers' systems perspective of manufacturing and its supporting areas made them an excellent choice to begin the change. A JIT steering committee comprised of operations manage-

Reprinted from *Industrial Engineering*, September 1988, vol. 9, no. 8; Norcross, GA: Institute of Industrial Engineers, 26-32.

ment was also established to provide vision and long range planning to the JIT movement.

INITIAL TRAINING

With management's commitment firmly established, the next step in the process was to learn what JIT production was all about. Seminars and books (see References) provided solid theory in WCM principles, while visiting other plants that had implemented JIT gave managers and industrial engineers the chance to study real world JIT applications. This exposure was key in the implementation process.

PILOT PROJECTS

JIT pilot projects are important for several reasons. First, a successful pilot project proves to everyone that JIT techniques really work and establishes a positive setting for further production improvements. Second, small scale pilot projects provide engineers and operators with hands-on training in applying JIT philosophies.

When choosing pilot areas for JIT implementation, management must be careful not to tackle too large an area. Projects initially perceived to be simple often turn out to be quite complex. Thus, small, simple assemblies containing few parts are the best candidates for successful pilot projects.

CalComp's industrial engineers started in Final Assembly and chose a simple keyboard unit for the first pilot project. The original process involved kitting, inspecting and issuing parts to the production area. Assemblers would then build batches of the assemblies and send their work to an inspector. This batch processing was characterized by large amounts of work-in-process (WIP) inventory and long cycle times. Also, inspection served mostly as a sorting process in which defective units were reworked and good units sent along.

Under the JIT philosophy of building what is needed when it is needed, inventory hides manufacturing problems. With this philosophy in mind, the original keyboard assembly process illustrated two major problems. First, although the assemblers were thought to be efficient or productive when they produced large quantities of keyboards, they were actually producing more than were needed by the next operation, which resulted in money tied up in keyboards that could not be used.

The second problem concerned quality. Specifically, problems in the assembly process were not being solved because feedback was nonexistent; defective inventory would already be built by the time quality problems were detected at inspection. This small keyboard assembly was typical of what occurred at the plant as a whole: kitting, inspection, large lots, long cycle times and high amounts of scrap and rework.

The JIT transformation of this area required a new streamlined layout which placed the required assembly operations adjacent to one another. The entire process of assembly and test was split into three fairly equal operations. Although the total labor to assemble the product remained the same, the organization of the work was changed to decrease cycle time, lower inventory and improve quality.

Production flow was controlled by placing yellow kanban squares between the operators. An empty kanban square signaled the upstream operator to build the required assembly while a full kanban square signaled that the next operator did not require any product. An empty kanban square was the only authorization to begin production.

At CalComp, touch labor is less than 5% of the product's total cost. As a result, labor efficiency is not considered the highest priority. Idle labor is permitted, provided there is no demand from the next work center; producing faster than necessary is considered waste.

Each operator inspected, as part of the process, material received from the previous operator. If found defective, it was returned immediately for repair. Large amounts of rework were eliminated since inventory was kept to a minimum and quality problems were addressed immediately. The constant feedback resulted in continual improvement of the assembly process. The formal inspection operation was eliminated since each operator was now responsible not only for his own work but for the previous operator's work as well.

The results of the first pilot project were promising. In two months, WIP was reduced by 80% and cycle time by 80%, and quality (determined by Final Test) improved by 30%. Everyone in the plant now saw that JIT really worked.

Four more pilot areas within Final Assembly were attacked by the team of industrial engineers and converted to JIT production within two months. All operators and supervisors who worked on the pilot projects were selected based on their attitudes as opposed to their assembly skills. Once trained in JIT philosophy, these enthusiastic and flexible operators made the pilot areas a showcase for the rest of the plant.

CONVERTED FINAL ASSEMBLY

The next step in the JIT implementation process was to apply the techniques mastered in the pilot areas to a major final assembly containing hundreds of parts.

Final Assembly's previous mode of operation involved a large carousel surrounded by work stations. Each work station functioned independently and used the carousel to obtain its raw material and store its WIP inventory.

Prior to JIT, it was not uncommon to have hundreds of subassemblies built and stored in the carousel.

The JIT approach in this area involved implementing a progressive assembly line where value is added to the product at each stage on the line. All the non-value-added activities such as queueing, moving, counting and storing were eliminated with the new layout.

Now, customer orders describing the specific model and options are assigned to units at the beginning of the line. As the units are pulled through the assembly line, each operation adds the appropriate subassemblies. All the subassemblies (except for circuit card assemblies) are built at feeder operations attached to the main assembly line.

The demand for each required sub-assembly is relayed via visible kanbans. Yellow squares and pigeonholes are used as kanban mechanisms; an empty square or pigeon hole tells the feeding work station to build a replacement. This simple kanban system communicates exactly what is needed, when it is needed, and has eliminated the need for production control.

Designing this JIT layout started with a cycle time analysis. Every operation on the line was designed to support the cycle time mandated by the average market demand. Planning the line for 80% capacity helped absorb schedule fluctuations and production problems and enabled the operators to meet daily to discuss process improvements. It was also important not to overkill the line balancing efforts as operators fine tuned the line once it was operational.

The results of this six-month effort were dramatic. Final assembly cycle time was reduced from three weeks to five days and final test yields improved by 33%.

JIT CIRCUIT CARD ASSEMBLY

While Final Assembly was undergoing all these improvements, the circuit card assembly (CCA) area was still producing by the traditional batch methods. This included kitting parts for large lots of PCB assemblies three weeks in advance of the scheduled production date. The basic CCA operations are automatic insertion, hand assembly, wave solder, post wave assembly and test.

The original layout included a state-of-the art transporter system that moved totes of circuit boards to these operations. The totes were stored between operations in a WIP flow rack area located at the end of the conveyor system. Since long machine setup times resulted in large lot sizes, the batch output of the CCA area often did not match what Final Assembly needed.

TRANSPORTERS REMOVED

The first step in the CCA area overhaul was removing the entire transporter and WIP storage area. This was an expensive job but showed management's commitment to the JIT philosophy. In CalComp's case, the transporter system was automated waste; the success in Final Assembly made everyone realize that the goal was to eliminate the waste, not automate it.

The new layout streamlined the assembly process by moving the required operations closer together in a U-shaped layout. This configuration allows for a continuous mix of boards to be pulled through each operation in small lot sizes. In addition, the U-shaped layout provides a fertile environment for immediate feedback between work centers.

HAND ASSEMBLY PASS ALONG

The hand assembly operation was redesigned, using cycle time analysis, into pass along lines where groups of operators work on a JIT assembly line. Kanban squares between the operators control the flow of product while red and yellow lights attached to each line are used by the operators to communicate process problems to supporting personnel. Yellow lights are used to highlight minor production problems, and red lights indicate that the line has stopped.

Each line is dedicated to several PCB types and all parts are stored at their point of use; thus, the set-up time has been reduced to virtually zero. This enables the lines to produce the mixed output of boards needed by Final Assembly.

Simple, color coded visual aids have replaced cumbersome process sheets. The color coding communicates to each operator what to inspect and what parts to insert. Each operator always inspects the previous operator's work (shown in yellow on the visual aid) before adding value to the board himself.

In the JIT environment, flexibility of both machines and people is critical. All the operators in the hand assembly area are cross trained to perform a variety of tasks. Floaters, or lead team members, keep all the hand assembly lines loaded with parts. They also fill in for absent operators when necessary.

AUTOMATIC INSERTERS

The same pass along or pull concept was applied in the auto-insertion area. Two lines, or cells, were established, each containing two DIP inserters and one axial inserter. The methods engineering group worked with the industrial engineers to balance the work load on each machine in the cell. A computer simulation of the proposed area was helpful in determining the kanban size required between machines. Kanbans of 20 PCBs were selected for the initial start-up. Since machine downtime was still a problem, kanbans of one PCB were unrealistic.

A major challenge in the autoinsertion area was set-up times and kitting. Set-ups were reduced by grouping boards into families based on common parts. Kitting was once again eliminated by storing all the necessary parts directly at the machines in master DIP storage units.

The streamlined layout JIT assembly techniques implemented in subassembly have reduced cycle time from six weeks to ten days.

SPC TRAINING

Now that large amounts of waste were being eliminated in the product flow, the world class manufacturing pursuit started to focus more on process control. All production workers attended weekly statistical process control (SPC) seminars conducted by CalComp's Quality Assurance Department. The training was followed by implementing SPC in key production areas, where operators were responsible for maintaining the SPC charts.

Many critical processes were greatly improved through SPC. Solder defects were reduced from 1,900 to 36 defects per million solder joints. The charts also highlighted problems with Auto-Insertion's preventive maintenance schedule which, once modified, resulted in a 15% reduction in unscheduled machine down time.

JIT SUPPORT TEAMS

With all the emphasis on eliminating waste and exposing problems, there came a need for problem solving support for the production floor. Management responded by assigning JIT support teams to each work center. These support teams consisted of an area supervisor along with a representative from quality assurance, manufacturing engineering and material planning. All the JIT support team members were assigned offices on the production floor.

Implementing JIT support teams has placed the majority of the problem solving effort where it belongs—on the production floor. The teams are held accountable for their work centers and treat the previous and following work centers as suppliers and customers respectively.

Training was critical in implementing the JIT support teams. Management hired a full time trainer to train all the support team members in communication and problem solving skills. This training helped smooth the transition from a culture of individualism to one of team problem solving and collaboration. Overlooking training requirements when considering world class manufacturing would prove disastrous.

EMPLOYEE INVOLVEMENT

No one is more familiar with the production processes than the operators who perform them. CalComp has tapped this valuable resource by implementing a system of employee involvement. Each working day, twenty minutes before the shift ends, production workers meet with their support teams to discuss and solve production problems.

Problems are usually selected by Pareto analysis and then analyzed using fishbone diagrams. Operators then develop action plans to improve the manufacturing process in question and measure their progress by using simple run charts and control charts posted within each work center.

Training was also critical in this area. The company trainer provided training not only in problem solving and the tools mentioned above, but also in areas such as conducting productive meetings.

Timely data collection is vital for process improvement. Defect data are collected by a personal computer data base program through a network of bar code readers. As defects are found, the type of defect and other critical attributes are entered by wanding bar code menus located at each data entry station. The data are then transmitted automatically to the PC located on the production floor.

This enables both engineers and operators to generate Paretos and other data queries describing the process on a real time basis. This simple to use "electronic check sheet" has provided focus to the work center's problem solving efforts by highlighting the major process problems in their areas.

SUPPLIER DEVELOPMENT

While the production floor was in the midst of all these improvements the Procurement Department began to focus on supplier relations. Three basic efforts were under way: reducing the supplier base, working for long term relationships and certifying key suppliers for dock-to-stock.

Placing more emphasis on long term purchase agreements has helped reduced the supplier base by 70% within a two-year period. Also, by relying more on dock-to-stock certification instead of mass inspection, the material receiving and handling steps have been minimized. Now, all dock-to-stock material flows from the supplier's truck directly to the production floor where it is used.

Working with fewer, quality certified suppliers has allowed CalComp to work with these suppliers to mutually develop cost saving arrangements such as returnable containers and design improvements. Establishing stronger working relationships with suppliers has allowed CalComp to make substantial advancements toward achieving smaller, higher quality deliveries.

RESULTS TO DATE

The world class manufacturing effort in CalComp's Display Products Division has yielded impressive returns. The major results to date are as follows:

• A 41% increase in yields at first system test
• A decrease in manufacturing cycle time from twelve weeks to four weeks
• A 60% decrease in average inventory
• A 67% decrease in annual scrap and rework
• A 75,000-sq-ft reduction in floor space including the elimination of a 40,000-sq-ft warehouse
• A 53% improvement in supplier on time delivery

Of course, not included in this list are all the intangible improvements, such as better morale, increased company loyalty, and an overall better working environment.

ORGANIZATIONAL STRUCTURE

Continuous improvement has left no area within CalComp untouched. Recently, CalComp management transformed the division's organizational structure from a functional to a product business unit orientation. To use the JIT term, this group technology approach applied to the organizational structure has benefited the company by making it more focused. Business units have been established to give each CalComp product the resources it needs to be designed, manufactured, marketed and sold.

JIT IN THE OFFICE

The latest effort of expanding world class manufacturing within CalComp has been to bring these philosophies into the office environment. Streamlining the production floor has highlighted areas for improvement in supporting areas such as purchasing and material planning. Thus, both buyers and planners have undergone training in Pareto analysis, process flow analysis, cause-and-effect diagrams, run charting and problem solving. By attending weekly problem solving meetings and working on department projects, buyers and planners are being trained to use these simple tools to improve the systems and methods that they use every day.

Also, group technology has been used to make the material acquisition process more effective. Commodity management teams, consisting of buyers, planners, quality assurance engineers and accounts payable personnel, have been established and are responsible for the entire material acquisition process.

Team performance is measured based on supplier quality, supplier on time delivery, supplier base, percent of parts on dock-to-stock, percent of defective invoices and the percent of parts on long term purchase agreements.

CONCLUSION

World class manufacturing is not a program that has a beginning and an end; rather, it is a process of *continuous* improvement. Its philosophies are simple, yet implementation often proves difficult, frustrating and slow. However, the CalComp Display Products Division is proof that the rewards of WCM far outweigh the difficulties. Perhaps the greatest cost in implementing WCM is the cost associated with a bruised ego—after all, it is not easy to accept and operate under philosophies that are in direct conflict with ones that have prevailed for years.

World class manufacturing requires industrial engineers to take a fresh look at manufacturing. Complex manufacturing systems breed complex material handling, material storage, inventory control, data processing and modeling systems.

World class industrial engineers must eliminate the need for complexity by designing simple, highly visible and foolproof manufacturing processes. The IE approach traditionally focuses on automation; however, as this article testifies, automating waste should not be considered a solution. Eliminating waste is the only way this country will be competitive in the world market place. Simplicity is the key.

CalComp's success with WCM can be attributed to the integrated approach that its management used to implement JIT, TQC and employee involvement. Management's belief in the philosophies and vision for the future prevented isolated islands of effort that all too often result in failure. CalComp has learned quickly that manufacturing excellence is truly a competitive weapon.

REFERENCES

Goldratt, M. Eliyahu. *The Goal,* North River Press Inc., 1984.

Schonberger, Richard J. *Japanese Manufacturing Techniques,* Free Press, 1982.

Schonberger, Richard J. *World Class Manufacturing,* Free Press, 1985.

Deming, W. Edwards. *Out of the Crisis.* MIT-CAES, 1986.

Walton, Mary. *The Deming Management Method.* New York: Dodd, Mead & Co., 1986.

Hall, W. Robert. *Zero Inventories,* Dow Jones-Irwin, 1983.

2

HUGHES AIRCRAFT MANAGES
TOTAL QUALITY CONTROL
IN A DoD ENVIRONMENT
HUGH J. HARRINGTON AND JACK B. REVELLE

"**M**ade in Japan" has become synonymous with quality. Thousands of managers have read and listened about the methods and success stories of Japanese companies since World War II. U.S. industry, which had long prided itself on quality, soon discovered it was behind the Total Quality (TQ) power curve. It was not until the 1980s that U. S. industry initiated a concerted effort to cause continuous improvement of the quality of its products and services.

QUALITY EFFORTS IN DEFENSE

The U.S. military has played an important, but often unrecognized, role in the leadership of quality efforts in this country. In fact, many of the now traditional quality control methods attributed to Japanese management were initiated in this country prior to World War II. The use of such practices as Mil Std (military standard) 105-D used for statistical sampling is but one example of their influence.

The Department of Defense (DoD) has an obligation to its "customers," American taxpayers, to provide affordable products. It does so through Federal and Defense Acquisition Regulations (FARs and DARs, respectively). The DoD also has an obligation to its "end-users," U.S. military service personnel, to provide quality products that perform in the field in the way they're designed to do. They meet this commitment by their manner of control over defense contractors, from the conceptual stage, through demonstration and validation, full scale development, and production. Their control is extended beyond specifications and requirements to the manner in which contractors conduct their business, reports and records they submit, and even the charges they are allowed for reimbursement.

Reprinted from *Industrial Engineering,* December 1989; vol. 21 no. 12; Norcross, GA: Institute of Industrial Engineers, 16-21.

Hughes Aircraft Company, a subsidiary of General Motors, is one of the top ten defense contractors in the nation (in terms of DoD contract awards). World-renowned for designing state of the art electronics systems, Hughes has made quality its number one operating priority. This is no easy task, given that the products of today were merely dreams in Hughes' research laboratories only a few short years ago.

TOTAL QUALITY AT HUGHES

Hughes has had two programs available for several decades that encourage individuals at the operating level to recognize a problem and recommend a solution, or to discover ways to do things better, faster, more efficiently, i.e., the Cost Improvement Program (CIP) and the Performance Improvement Program (PIP). Over the years, individual employees have saved the company (and ultimately, the taxpayer) more than one hundred million dollars per year for these contributions. Often these recommendations have, either directly or indirectly, had an impact on the quality of Hughes products or services.

Like many other U.S. companies, the 1970s were characterized by a multitude of quality circles (QC). There were literally thousands of QCs in Hughes with virtually every job category involved. As in other companies, QCs began with great enthusiasm, but often took weeks or months to decide on a problem on which to focus, and after even more time came up with a set of recommendations that were presented to management. Sometimes the problems were critical; sometimes the solutions were valid; and sometimes the recommendations were implemented. Much of this process was accompanied by disillusionment. By the early 1980s, many Hughes managers had come to the conclusion that something additional was needed.

MILESTONES IN TOTAL QUALITY

In the early 1980s, five commitments for the company were established for this decade (see Table 1). Each of these was regarded as critical to Hughes continued success. In 1981 a study was conducted to improve operational quality and productivity. Core reading for executives included works by Deming, Juran, Fiegenbaum, Ishikawa, and Schoenberger. TQ programs were then initiated in diverse organizations on a pilot program basis. In keeping with the Hughes tradition of operational autonomy, each Systems Group (e.g., Ground, Missile, Radar, Space) was permitted to develop TQ in a manner that was most practical within each organization's business objectives. Their results were reviewed by their respective organizational executives.

Table 1. Hughes commitment for the 80s.

• Make Total Quality a way of life.
• Design for low cost production.
• Apply technology to the process of design and manufacturing.
• Release the full capabilities and talents of our people.
• Involve suppliers in reducing costs of Hughes systems.

By 1983 initial planning began (see Table 2) for company-wide direction and leadership. Self-audits were conducted within each organization, in many cases, down to the department level. Cost of quality pilot programs began in an effort to determine, not only the cost of implementation, but the expected return on investment. Outside consultants were also brought in. Basic courses in TQ were undertaken in many organizations, primarily in manufacturing divisions. Presentations were made throughout the company to share success strategies, lessons learned, and accomplishments. TQ councils were formed in different organizations to assume responsibility for project direction.

Table 2. Milestones in Hughes Total Quality.

1981 Internal study performed to improve operational quality and productivity.
1982 Pilot programs for TQ initiated in diverse organizations; results reviewed by executives.
1983 Initial planning began; self audits conducted; costs of quality pilot programs; basic courses offered in TQ; TQ councils formed in each group; Corporate Executive Steering Committee.
1984 Company policy GM-0-1 issued; letter sent to all employees from Company President; each major organization requested to develop a quality improvement plan; supplier certification program initiated.
1985 Corporate quality steering committee and working committee formed; SQC training course developed internally; operated verification programs started; JIT pilot programs initiated.
1986 Company-wide Total Quality Survey conducted, involving all groups of employees.
1987 Industry-wide Total Quality Survey conducted among defense contractors; Supervisor's Guides for team activities distributed; cycle time training began.
1988 Variability Reduction Program (VRP) begun, included Quality Function Deployment (QFD), Design of Experiments (DOE), and Statistical Process Control (SPC); Corporate VRP committee formed; training courses for QFD and DOE (including "train the trainer").

In 1984 Company Policy GM-O-1 was issued for the implementation of TQ (see Table 3) and a letter from the President and the CEO was sent to all employees outlining the company's approach to TQ. Two key points were made: "The ultimate measure of the quality of our products is the degree to which they satisfy the needs of our customers," and "No operating decision will be allowed to impact negatively the quality of our products and operations."

Table 3. Implementation of Hughes Total Quality.

• Assumption by each individual of responsibility for the quality of his/her own effort and output.
• Assumption by management of responsibility to provide systems and training so each individual can perform to his/her highest capability.
• Recognition that each individual has one or more customers, and that the quality of his/her output is measured by the degree to which that output satisfies the needs of those customers.
• Concentration on error and defect *prevention* in all activities through care in work performance and control of equipment and processes, as contrasted with subsequent error and defect *correction*.

Each major organization was requested to develop a quality improvement plan. A supplier certification program was initiated and many suppliers were subsequently trained by Hughes in SQC. SQC applications were refined and quality management reporting tools, e.g., defect reduction charting and process quality indicators (PQIs), were developed. Senior management was deadly serious about quality, as was the customer, the Department of Defense.

1985 saw the formation of a Quality Steering Committee and a Quality Working Committee at the corporate level. An SQC course was developed internally for training personnel. That year, more than 1500 personnel were trained in just one division using this material. Operator verification programs were started. Just-in-time (JIT) pilot programs were initiated and refined. Seminars by Deming, Juran, and Conway were given, as well as several visits made to meet Ishikawa in Japan.

In 1986, a company-wide TQ Survey was conducted— asking frank questions from all groups of employees to evaluate the perceived effectiveness of these efforts and to establish a baseline for a three-year follow up. The following year an external survey on Quality was conducted of major defense contractors. The 100 or so participant companies accounted for approximately half of all DoD contract awards. That same year, Supervisor's Guides which detailed techniques for conducting team activities were distributed. Cycle time management training also began in 1987.

1988 witnessed the greatest efforts to date. The Variability Reduction Program (VRP) was instituted. VRP tools include: Quality Function Deployment (QFD), Design of Experiments (DOE), and Statistical Process Control (SPC).

QFD is an analytical system for use with product (or service) design that assigns customer requirements throughout a contractor's organization and involves all members of the organization. By translating customer requirements into counterpart technical requirements for each stage of product development and production, products can be delivered to the customer sooner with lower costs and improved quality. QFD identifies what tools and techniques to use, the most important product characteristics, what factors need to be controlled, as well as practices, procedures, and instructions for each task.

DOE is a method for selecting critical factors and levels of those factors to determine which levels will optimize the average response level and minimize response (performance characteristics) variability. Because traditional DOE methods sometimes require an inordinate number of "trials" (experimental runs), Taguchi methods, which are fractional factorial designs, rely on orthogonal array tables to organize experimental factors and screen experimental output data. The result is the contractor's ability to control process input so that output is robust, i.e., insensitive, to both the production and operational environments.

SPC is a set of techniques for variously identifying problem areas, facilitating problem-solving, monitoring process characteristics to assess process stability, as well as evaluating process capability and process performance. Hughes has been sufficiently successful in SPC training that they were requested to instruct on SPC and TQ to Navy personnel in 1988 with repeat sessions in 1989.

VRP operations are directed by a VR Committee at the corporate level, responsible for, among other things, issuing company-wide bimonthly VRP progress reports. Four internal VRP training courses have been developed: two for employee training ("The Two-Day Statistician" for SPC and "The New Quality Technology" for QFD and DOE-Taguchi) and two supporting "train the trainer" courses.

The challenge increased dramatically in 1989. It began with the issuance of three documents: 1) a company mission statement that calls for maximum value to customers, employees, business associates, and shareholders; 2) *Hughes Guiding Values* that places customers at the top of the list and reemphasizes the centrality of quality, which requires integrity, teamwork, and an open management style; and 3) a philosophy of continuous measurable improvement through such tools as SPC, DOE, CTM, QFD, simultaneous engineering, and quality indicators. Hughes CEO, Dr. Malcolm R. Currie, set a goal in 1989 for every organization within Hughes—30 percent measurable improvement. Training in quality methods sharply increased and projects flourished—employees took the challenge. A three-year follow-up survey of Hughes employees was conducted to assess their perceptions of progress in quality and a two-year follow-up industry-wide survey was also conducted.

Since the VRP began, over 5,000 persons have been trained in SPC; over 350 trained in DOE; about 35 trained in QFD; and over 100 executives briefed on VRP. A total of 1,200 SPC projects, mainly in manufacturing, but some engineering and administrative applications, have been initiated. There are more than 100 DOE projects, 70 applications of cycle time management, and 10 applications of QFD that are underway this year.

ASSUMPTIONS

There were certain "givens" before the push for TQ began. First, senior management knew that if TQ did not have their full commitment and involvement, it would never succeed. Their role in leadership as well as providing resources, training, and support were understood. Second, they knew that quality is hard work and absolutely necessary if Hughes was to continue to be a leading electronics defense contractor.

LESSONS LEARNED

Many of the lessons learned by experience at Hughes seem obvious and have been written about before. There are countless lessons that others have written about, however, what distinguishes these is that they were learned here firsthand. Sometimes this experience was painful, sometimes costly, sometimes by trial-and-error. But any company that is serious about TQ will, undoubtedly, have a similar learning experience, and the pattern of lessons they learn will be unique.

CHANGING CULTURE

Hughes knows that TQ won't happen overnight, as its brief history indicates. It requires nothing short of a cultural evolution, but cultural change takes a long time to implement. The first lesson was patience. In the industry-wide survey referred to earlier (see References) quality executives at major defense contractors indicated that what they needed in their companies to effect TQ was exactly that—a cultural change. They did not have the opportunity to delineate the nature of that change. The following are some clues from the Hughes experience.

PARTICIPATIVE MANAGEMENT

TQ requires participative management. Participative management, quite literally, resulted in a cultural shock—it was not the traditional management style that successful managers had been accustomed to and it was not easy to adopt. There had to be a conscious shift from managing tasks to leading people, and leadership meant involvement in problem-solving and decision-making of those who were responsible for the day-to-day execution of tasks. TQ management demands a return to recognition of the individual operator's importance and contribution to the product quality effort. Management had to believe that employees are the company's most valuable asset and that people will respond if given a reason and the chance. The second lesson was achieving quality improvement by giving up power.

In addition, management had to discover that they were not in tune with the employees. Clean rooms and security restrictions had isolated employees from management interface—management could not see the old shop floor anymore. New communications capabilities were needed to overcome these restrictions. Top management had to become more involved by visiting work areas and talking to employees. Lesson three was learning to listen.

STARTING PROJECTS

Implementation requires projects. TQ will not be implemented without specific individual projects bringing the change process through organizations. Senior management must influence and guide the projects; they need to establish a goal or direction and stand firm. Then, focus on the basics and use simple measures such as throughput time (cycle time), yield, work-in-process (WIP) reductions, space reductions, labor savings, etc. Measures should relate to organizational goals. Lesson four—keep it simple and smart.

It is best to start with the worst problems. These are the ones with which employees are frustrated and that they are eager to change. Care must be taken not to overregulate. People need room to maneuver and management is too accustomed to giving explicit directions. Also, don't over-plan; this, too, locks people in and prevents discovery of better methods or solutions.

WHICH METHOD IS BEST?

No matter how much one reads, there are no simple solutions or sure-fire methods. Almost everything has been tried and, in fact, somewhere within Hughes every method is being used. But Hughes has not approached TQ with a "mono-method" attack ("I have a hammer, show me a nail!"). Instead, organizations use what works best in their environment. There are organizations that can count on both hands the number of products produced per year (such as satellites) and those that produce hundreds of products per day.

SUCCESS IS CONTAGIOUS

Propagate—other areas will be more willing to listen and act if examples of success can be pointed out. Experts and consultants "out there" are never as convincing as those at home who can demonstrate what works in one's own environment. Most significant is that TQ becomes a rallying point for teamwork. TQ requires the integration of various talents and perspectives; it becomes a focal point and provides a common language for those who represent different functional areas. Facilitating teamwork requires, in addition to a common goal, respect for each participant's abilities and differences. Having a group of people who think alike is less fruitful than a team of diverse talents and viewpoints. Lesson five, quite simply, is that extraordinary things happen when ordinary people work together.

FUTURE STRATEGIES

The Air Force declared 1987 the Year of Quality. They issued a document— R&M (Reliability and Maintainability) 2000, to outline its Variability Reduction Program (VRP). This document describes a process to improve combat capability while reducing development time and costs through defect reductions. The premise is that defect reductions are best achieved by minimizing variance in process output, hence, variability reduction. This is to be accomplished by: more robust designs, greater process capability, and use of the Taguchi "loss function" to reduce costs. Robust design is the primary area of responsibility of engineering; process capability is the responsibility of manufacturing; and management has the primary responsibility of continuous improvement of the systems.

Engineering relies on the use of Quality Function Deployment and simultaneous engineering. In this approach, the "voice of the customer" leads to technical requirements, which, in turn, lead to part characteristics, these to manufacturing operations, which, finally, lead to production requirements. Manufacturing gains control over the process and its capability through the use of Statistical Process Control. Management, engineering, and manufacturing all use Taguchi methods of experimental design.

TRANSLATING GOALS INTO VRP

The Quality Technologies described above can be seen as covering three broad areas: management, analytical methods (QFD), and statistical methods (Taguchi and SPC). Management is responsible for planning, communications, support, commitment and involvement. Table 4 displays how Hughes goals ("commitments for the 80s") are integrated into its Variability Reduction Program.

Table 4.

Involve Suppliers in Reducing Costs	Release Full People Talents	Apply Technology: Mfg. Process	Apply Technology: Design Process	Design for Low Cost Production	Total Quality as a Way of Life	Company Commitments for the 80s			
									THE QUALITY™ TECHNOLOGIES
						Critical areas for improvement	Planning	Seven-M-Tools	Management Methods
						Develop communications	Planning		
						Performance review (periodic)	Planning		
						Document organizational learning	Planning		
						Performance review (annual)	Planning		
						Goals	Communications		
						Objectives	Communications		
						Policies	Communications		
						Resources	Support		
						Discussion	Support		
						Publication	Support		
						Resources	Commitment		
						Consistency	Commitment		
						Participation (meetings)	Involvement		
						Participation (on-line)	Involvement		
						What they say (specs)	Customer Wants	Quality Function Deployment (QFD)	Analytical Methods
						What they don't say (expected quality)	Customer Wants		
						What they don't expect (exciting quality)	Customer Wants		
						Levels of importance	Quality Tables		
						Product functions	Quality Tables		
						Competitive advantage	Quality Tables		
						Bottleneck engineering	Quality Tables		
						Preparation for product development	Manufacturing Deployment		
						Quality tables	Manufacturing Deployment		
						QC planning chart	Manufacturing Deployment		
						QC process chart	Manufacturing Deployment		
						Reliability and maintainability	Total Deployment		
						Technology	Total Deployment		
						Cost	Total Deployment		
						Function variability loss	Loss Function	Design of Experiments (Taguchi)	Statistical Methods
						Harmful side effect loss	Loss Function		
						Parabolic relationship	Loss Function		
						Set concepts	System Design		
						Select technology	System Design		
						Set targets	Parameter Design		
						Statistical design	Parameter Design		
						Sensitivity analysis	Parameter Design		
						Set allowances	Tolerance Design		
						Statistical tolerancing	Tolerance Design		
						Histograms	Defect Prevention (Problem Identification)	Statistical Process Control (SPC)	
						Pareto analysis	Defect Prevention (Problem Identification)		
						Cause and effect analysis	Defect Prevention (Problem Identification)		
						On-line sampling	Defect Prevention (Problem Identification)		
						Scatter analysis	Defect Prevention (Problem Identification)		
						Process capability analysis	Defect Prevention (Problem Identification)		
						Events logs	Defect Prevention (Problem Identification)		
						Control charts	Defect Prevention (Problem Identification)		
						Acceptance sampling	Defect Identification		
						100% inspection	Defect Identification		

Relationships
● Strong = 9 pts.
◇ Medium = 3 pts.
△ Weak = 1 pt.

Now that Hughes has had time for TQ to evolve and the culture to change, it is in a better position to formalize the structure and process. To have set TQ "in concrete" too early in its development could have been disastrous. Hughes has learned the lessons above and few, if any, will say that it has been easy. Although the framework for TQ is now in place, its continued growth will rely on an essence of flexibility and openness. The result of these efforts is that Hughes military customers, their end-users (U.S. service personnel), and their customers (we, the taxpayers), will regard "made at Hughes" as synonymous with the highest standards of quality in the industry.

REFERENCES

Harrington, H. J. and J. B. ReVelle. "Total quality issues and activities in aerospace." *A Quality Revolution in Manufacturing*. Golomski, W. A. and Dingus, V. (eds.). Norcross, GA: Institute of Industrial Engineers, 1988.

3

MANUFACTURING REVITALIZATION AT HARLEY-DAVIDSON MOTOR COMPANY
MEHRAN SEPEHRI, P.E.

York, PA, May 6, 1987 President Ronald Reagan toured the Harley-Davidson Inc. motorcycle manufacturing facility today to see first-hand, in action, the advanced manufacturing techniques that enabled the 84-year-old motorcycle company to regain its competitiveness and return to profitability.

"We invited the President because we believe that Harley-Davidson is an excellent example of a once-troubled American company that aggressively pursued the steps necessary to regain its competitiveness in world markets," said Vaughn L. Beals, chairman and chief executive officer of Harley-Davidson Inc.

In March, Harley-Davidson, the only U.S.-based motorcycle manufacturer, took the unprecedented step of petitioning the International Trade Commission for termination of import relief tariffs on heavyweight motorcycles. The tariffs had been imposed in April 1983 by President Reagan on the grounds that flooding of the U.S. motorcycle market by Japanese competitors, in the face of a sharp market decline, was threatening the American motorcycle industry.

The revitalized company had increased its share of the heavyweight motorcycle market by 50%, from a record low of 12.5% in 1983 to 19.4% at the end of 1986. On the basis of its recovery, the company held a public stock offering in July of 1986 and subsequently acquired Holiday Rambler Corp.

ADVANCED MANUFACTURING

Harley-Davidson was among the first companies in the U.S. to study and implement just-in-time (JIT) inventory principles and statistical process con-

Reprinted from *Industrial Engineering,* August 1987; vol. 8 no. 19; Norcross, GA: Institute of Industrial Engineers, 86-93.

27

trol, among other advanced manufacturing and employee involvement techniques. The company now runs its plants with two-thirds less inventory than in 1981 and has increased productivity by 50%. In addition, manufacturing errors are down by two-thirds and defects per unit are down 70%. The company's annual revenue per employee has doubled since 1981.

Before the turnaround, Harley-Davidson was a prime example of a manufacturing company that, because of layers of quick fixes over the years, was not aimed at improving production and was turning out its product in the face of frequent equipment breakdowns and long lead times. It was a batch processing operation with cumbersome inventories that provided a cushion, hiding the problems and eating up capital.

BACKGROUND

Harley-Davidson was established in 1903 in Milwaukee, WI. The company name eventually became a household term synonymous with motorcycling. In the motorcycle world, Harley-Davidson was associated with quality, durability and value. At one time, Harley controlled the market for large displacement motorcycles worldwide. Unfortunately, like many other American companies, it became complacent about its reputation. Throughout the 1950s, 1960s and 1970s, Harley failed to react to the economic and social changes developing throughout the world.

As late as the early 1970s, consumers were waiting in line to purchase a new Harley. In 1973, the motorcycle assembly and chassis fabrication was moved from Milwaukee to a larger, modernized facility in York, PA. The purpose of this move was to increase production capabilities and decrease the consumer backlog. The engine and transmission manufacture, as well as the corporate offices, remained in Milwaukee.

The move to Pennsylvania allowed Harley to more than double its production rates. Throughout the 1970s, Harley experienced most of the problems typically associated with American industry. Parts shortages were a constant problem, and often line production was based on parts availability. Only a fraction of the employees and assets were used.

Line shutdowns because of parts shortages occurred frequently. Although the company maintained a large warehouse containing millions of dollars worth of raw material, work-in-process (WIP) and finished goods, many vehicles came off the assembly line missing parts. At times, the shop floor was covered with vehicles awaiting rework. High levels of scrap and rework existed, and a large inspection department was given the responsibility, but not the means, to control quality throughout the shop.

Meanwhile, the Japanese had entered the large displacement motorcycle market and were producing state-of-the-art vehicles. The Japanese motorcycles were high in quality and competitive in price, and were gradually taking over portions of Harley's traditional market.

By the early 1980s, Harley found itself producing overpriced, low quality products in direct competition with the Japanese, who were doing just the opposite. In 1981 and 1982, Harley suffered staggering losses, and the survival of the company was questionable.

With a letter of intent in February 1981, a group of Harley-Davidson executives bought the motorcycle business back from AMF—which had bought it from the parent company in 1969. The deal was finalized in June 1981. The executives wanted to turn the 80-year-old motorcycle manufacturing operation into an aggressive, competitive and profitable company again.

JUST-IN-TIME PROGRAM

The condition of the company prompted Harley-Davidson to adopt a JIT approach in 1982. This coincided with the appointment of a new manufacturing vice president, from Ford Manufacturing, who was supportive of productivity programs.

The JIT program was entirely an internal program, not one recommended by consultants or outsiders. The majority of workers were unfamiliar with just-in-time techniques, but they learned JIT concepts from articles, seminars and discussion sessions. Following the basic principles of JIT, the manufacturing employees designed their own version of it.

There were many who felt that JIT was not flexible and that the concept would not work in the Western world. Immediate results showed that the principles could be applied to any manufacturing facility and could work within existing parameters.

Parts of JIT were implemented without changing shop layouts or requiring expensive supporting programs. JIT proved to be extremely flexible and limited only by the organization's ability to be creative, innovative and receptive to change.

At Harley-Davidson, quality was the primary goal and the justification for JIT. Other benefits naturally followed. The most common benefits were reduced carrying costs, increased inventory turns, less scrap and rework, and reduced warehousing requirements. But the most important benefit of any properly implemented JIT program is increased levels of quality.

Several JIT efforts began before setup reduction or preventive maintenance programs started. The original efforts were so successful that they convinced management to devote considerable resources to reducing setups, to implementing statistical control and preventive maintenance programs, and to forming new shop layouts to create dedicated machinery centers.

At Harley-Davidson, the JIT approach is the marriage of three programs: employee involvement, inventory reduction and statistical process control. Each program may stand alone and yield results, but the maximum result comes from simultaneous use of all three programs, which seems to be the only way to become or remain competitive in the market.

MAN PROGRAM

Harley-Davidson christened its JIT manufacturing program "material as needed" (MAN). Company planners also looked hard at the trend in the automotive industry toward JIT delivery of vendor parts to reduce inventory and release capital. MAN encompasses setup reduction, flow processing, lead time reduction, inventory reduction, schedule stability, preventive maintenance, employee involvement, containerization, statistical process control and vendor programs.

To design and implement the MAN system, Harley-Davidson used employee involvement and formed teams of full-time hourly and salaried employees. Working without outside assistance, these teams developed a program that was mostly new from the ground up. It was not easy to implement, and it took dedication to maintain the program, but early rewards were encouraging. The inventory turns alone released some capital for other purposes.

In the beginning, the MAN teams did extensive missionary work. They brought suppliers in monthly to explain the program to them. They even went into supplier plants to hold seminars and make recommendations. Those vendors that were working closely with the company knew what was being accomplished, and they saw potential benefits for their plants. Some came back for assistance in implementing cost-cutting measures within their own plants.

EMPLOYEE INVOLVEMENT

At Harley-Davidson, employee involvement is considered a major component of JIT, and in fact, it is the foundation for the entire philosophy. Genuine employee involvement is a commitment that gives all employees a formal mechanism for exerting an influence on their daily work lives and an environment of trust that will support such commitment.

There are several viable forms of employee involvement at Harley. Preventive maintenance and setup reduction programs are good examples of employee involvement that include those individuals normally responsible for the hands-on aspects of maintenance and setups. Value analysis offers tremendous potential in terms of genuine employee involvement. Statistical process control goes beyond simple charting, and the operators are allowed to take actions based on their charts.

In 1982, Harley implemented a formal quality circle (QC) program, which was the initial means of employee involvement. Although quality circles in America have a tarnished reputation, at Harley-Davidson the program has been successful.

The company used traditional approaches to implementing and maintaining the circles. Volunteers from the same or very similar work areas formed a circle. These volunteers then received training in various aspects of group dynamics and data collection. The training included brainstorming, cause and effect relationships, Pareto analysis, graphing and charting, and curve interpretation. With the training completed, the circles were turned loose to choose a work-related problem perform an analysis, and solve or make a recommendation for solving the problem.

The circles are encouraged to work with other circles, seek outside assistance and use any available avenues to obtain data to support their analyses. In fact, it is not unusual for circle members to make direct contact with Harley-Davidson suppliers to seek information on their products.

Circle efforts have brought about employee training sessions, the design of a new polishing wheel to reduce dust, improved paint quality, recovery of polishing materials and improved plant layout, among other things.

One very successful and significant employee involvement project was carried out during a dealers' convention held in 1983. For the plant tour portion of the convention, rather than present an elaborate program with speeches by company officers, management decided to use QC members to lead the tours and describe their productivity efforts.

Each circle selected a member to guide the dealers through the work area and tell them what workers in that area were doing to make the company more competitive. No one was told what to say by management. Having a welder tell what he was doing to eliminate splatter, a maintenance person describe how he was working to reduce downtime, and so on, made a strong impression on the attendees.

INVENTORY REDUCTION

Before 1982, parts control was Harley-Davidson's most glaring problem. A 40-hour work week on the assembly line was the exception rather than the rule because of part shortages. Fewer than 70% of the motorcycles produced came complete off the assembly line. At the York plant, overtime was a way of life, and the time spent producing missing parts was often at the expense of producing required parts. Motorcycle production was usually based on parts availability rather than the master schedule.

In 1982, complete parts control became the primary objective. The initial thrust was to gain control of in-house manufactured parts. The company needed a system that would place parts control directly on the shop floor and would also help increase part quality.

The relationship between quality and inventory levels may be difficult to understand. Excessive inventories are subject to deterioration and damage from storage and handling. The impacts of obsolescence, engineering change and hidden defects are far greater on excessive inventories. The way to control quality is by first reducing inventories and then implementing statistical controls.

The company used the Toyota Production System as a guide for inventory control and modified it to meet its own requirements. The system used to gain control of raw materials and work-in-process was the kanban or MAN card.

SETUP TIME REDUCTION

Setup time reduction is a fundamental aspect of JIT. In essence, large inventories, with all their associated problems, are encouraged by long setup times. Reductions in setup time can reduce the requirement for large run quantities and can substantially reduce lead times. Setup time reduction also offers a great deal of potential in terms of employee involvement. The workers are best qualified to improve setup times because they are normally responsible for making setups and running production.

One of the company's first moves was aimed at reducing setup times to improve manufacturing and reduce inventories. The company worked first with the fabricated metal operations in the York assembly plant. The setup time reduction programs were continued at the engine and transmission manufacturing operations outside of Milwaukee.

Making setups quickly and simply permitted Harley to make batches smaller and to reduce inventories by implementing better quality control. Further investigations led to the continuous flow process and away from batch manufacturing.

At York, advances in setup time reduction were made in most manufacturing areas. Because machine dedication was required for the continuous flow system, tooling was dedicated to specific machines. This was a major factor in terms of setup time reduction.

In the press department, the area is organized with dies color coded and stored as close as possible to their dedicated machines. Dies have been modified to accept the common shut height and clamping methods of their dedicated press.

In the final assembly area, standard fixturing and air clamping are used. In other areas of the shop, work centers are used with multipiece fixtures and QC-implemented setup and tool kits to reduce setups.

Tool and die modifications to implement setup time reductions required some expenditures. These expenditures were justified not only in terms of reduced labor requirements, but also in terms of reduced inventories.

At Harley-Davidson, setup reduction is a goal with all production equipment. Measurable results can be seen. From 1982 to 1984, setup time was reduced by more than 75% overall on the machines. Many setup operations were combined. Raw materials and WIP inventory turns were increased from 5.9 to 10.8 from June 1982 through December 1983, and to 20 by the end of 1984.

Setup reduction activities involve reviewing the actual setup through the use of video equipment and with the operator. During these reviews, the setup steps are analyzed and classified into off line, main line and unnecessary. Improvements are designed and implemented with close follow-up until these new procedures are accepted by all.

The six basic rules of setup reduction are:

Rule 1—Move main line to off line. Main line items are elements of work that have to be done when the machine is shut off. Searching for fixtures, waiting for equipment and setting of tooling are all elements of setup that can be improved.

Rule 2—Eliminate unnecessary movement. Elimination of walking, reducing manual effort, written setup procedures and having setup teams are ways of reducing this type of movement.

Rule 3—Eliminate fasteners. "C" washers or slotted holes, so that nuts and bolts do not have to be removed from the machine, are a few examples that can be designed into fixturing to reduce setup time.

Rule 4—Eliminate machine base adjustment. This can be accomplished through preset tooling, spacers or guide blocks, to name a few possibilities. What one wants to do is design and build the fixture so that when it is changed, adjustment to the table position is eliminated.

Rule 5—Standardize dies, tooling, fixtures, part design and part specifications. Design engineers must be involved. Before new parts, tooling or fixtures come off the drawing board, the designers must look at what's currently being used to see if the new parts, tooling or fixtures can be made similar to existing parts, tooling or fixtures.

Rule 6—Use block gauges and templates for adjustments. The boring machine is a good example involving the use of a template. Between two jobs, the stops must be moved. A template that is notched out showing proper location can be used to ensure a good setup.

There are three phases in the reduction of setup time. In the first phase, little expenditure is required. These solutions can be achieved in a short period of time and show a 20 to 30% reduction in setup time. It should be noted that this doesn't have to be the "best" solution.

One example of a phase 1 solution was tapering of the splines of a 200 pound drill unit and also those of the drive unit it must be aligned with. This enabled the operator to get the drill unit aligned much more easily, possibly even on the first try.

In the second phase of setup time reduction, minor modifications of dies, tools, fixtures, machines or procedures will be made. Some expenditures will be required. As in phase one, this work can also be achieved in a relatively short period of time. Benefits of 30 to 50% reduction of setup time can be realized.

The third phase of setup time reduction includes design change and standardization of dies, tools and parts. Large capital expenditures may be required and can take years to accomplish. Benefits of 10 to 40% can be expected in the third phase.

EXAMPLES

The objective is to reduce and simplify setup so that the first part after the setup is perfect 100% of the time. The benefits are reduced setup time, scrap, rework and inspection time. Indirectly, as setup time goes down, operator frustrations also go down.

The company found that most setup problems are material, machine or management related. Contrary to popular opinion, labor is a minor factor.

A good example of this is provided by the abrasive sanding machine. The setup involved changing the fixture, but due to the different sizes of fixtures and parts, the operator would arrive at the proper size through a trial and error method.

The Timesaver Co. was asked if anything was available to improve on the trial and error method of adjustment. Timesaver suggested calling a gauge company and having something fabricated. The machine had a digital readout, but the manufacturer's instructions said it had to be reset by the operator after every adjustment.

The electricians investigated how this digital readout worked and suggested that it be made a continuous readout. With some slight modification, the digital readout was changed to a continuous readout.

A log was established for all parts run and the settings were recorded. No guessing is needed to get size anymore during a setup.

In the example below, setup time was reduced from about two hours to about three minutes.

Harley-Davidson manufactures two crankpins that are very similar in shape. The only difference was in the angle of an oil hole. One was at 45°, and the other was at 48°. Due to the angle difference, four fixtures per part were involved in a setup, each with its own hydraulic unit for clamping—a very expensive arrangement.

The design engineering department was given the problem and determined that the angle of the oil holes could be made the same. The problem then went to the tool design department, which came up with a design that used the same four fixtures for both parts. Now when a setup is done, the only thing the operator does is either put on four spacers or take off four spacers that position the part properly.

CONCLUSIONS

Harley-Davidson competes directly with the Japanese, and JIT was adopted so that the company could survive. To become and remain competitive, Harley implemented employee involvement, inventory reduction and statistical process control programs. The suppliers were also involved in these efforts. The company has witnessed substantial results since 1981, including:

• Significant reduction in motorcycle float
• Inventory reduction by 50%
• Reductions in scrap and rework by 50%
• Productivity increase, in terms of vehicles produced per employee, of 32%
• Increase in inventory turns from five in 1981 to 17 in 1984
• Rise of completion rate from 70% to 99%
• Decrease in warranty claims despite increase in warranty period
• Elimination of traditional warehousing of raw materials, WIP and finished goods
• Reduction in supplier base by 30%

Acknowledgment: The author gives special thanks to David Gurka at Harley-Davidson in Milwaukee for information he provided for this article.

SECTION II
SYSTEM DESIGN AND CELLULAR CONCEPTS

The modern discrete parts manufacturing environment must support the dynamic needs of today's customers. Conventional approaches to low-to mid-volume manufacturing of discrete parts using functionally organized job shops have difficulty meeting these needs.

Efficiency in the conventional job/batch shop is driven by the large lot size needed due to high set up time. Complex routing of parts through multiple departments, augmented by a desire for functional independence, results in significant process and move delays. Though potentially very efficient in its use of equipment resources, the conventional job shop is not able to respond quickly to changing customer demands.

Cellular manufacturing offers low- to mid-volume discrete parts manufacturers the ability to take advantage of similarities in the manufacturing of parts, thus achieving efficiency even though small lot sizes are produced. This is done through the implementation of manufacturing cells which are designed to produce a family of parts with similar production requirements.

It is convenient to consider a cell as a small factory within the factory. To as great an extent as possible, the cell should have all of the resources necessary to manufacture its family of parts. Resources are managed by those workers assigned to the cell. Cross training and a team spirit are encouraged through the autonomy afforded those cell employees.

Organizing for cellular manufacturing requires the identification of part families and the assignment of equipment required for production. This problem is solved by a method known as production flow analysis (PFA). PFA can be organized into the following steps:

• *Data collection.* The set of parts to be analyzed must first be defined. For each part that is identified, route sheets are needed, together with such information as anticipated annual production rates and current standards.

• *Analysis of process routing.* Routings are used in PFA to identify the equipment and other resources needed to produce a part. Significant problems may exist with using existing routing sheets due to inconsistencies between planners. For the purposes of PFA, a standard list of processes required to produce each part must be identified. Parts which have identical process requirements are identified as composite parts and do not require further routing.

• *Identification of part families.* Many approaches have been suggested ranging from simple sorting to the use of mathematical programming. Conceptually, one can think of the problem as the reorganization of a matrix. The matrix is organized with each column associated with a composite part and each row corresponding to a special process or machine. For each part, Xs are placed to indicate the processes required. For the purpose of initial cell design, sequencing of operations is not considered.

• *Detailed cell design.* Next, cells are designed to support the identified part families. This requires the allocation of equipment and the organization of the cell to support efficient flow. Significant attention is devoted to the design of specialized fixtures to support the quick changeover from one part in the family to another.

Production flow analysis represents an interesting new problem important to the design of modern discrete manufacturing facilities. For the basics of production flow analysis we recommend the following book by John Burbidge: *Production Flow Analysis for Planning Group Technology* (Clarendon Press, Oxford, 1989).

The first article in this section, "Cellular Manufacturing in the U.S. Industry: A Survey of Users," contains data on companies that have implemented cellular concepts. The article answers questions such as how many cells a typical company has, how large the cells are, and how many parts are produced in the typical cell. The article also includes data on typical savings which companies have realized through the use of cellular concepts.

The next four articles contain descriptions of what actual companies have done in their cellular manufacturing projects. These case studies provide valuable insights into how the concepts have been successfully applied in a variety of environments.

The article titled "Northern Telecom Tackles Successful Implementation of Cellular Manufacturing" by Javad Taheri shows how the concepts were applied to the assembly and testing of circuit boards. Of particular note in the article is how a visual simulation of the operations was used in the design of the cells. Details of worker training, motivation, and other implementation issues are also discussed.

The application of cellular concepts at Deere & Co. is the focus of "Cellular Manufacturing: A Good Technique for Implementing Just-In-Time and Total Quality Control" by Helmut Welke and John Overbeeke. Once again, simulation is used during the initial design and justification phase of the project. The important role of cellular manufacturing in the future of manufacturing at Deere & Co. is stressed in the article.

The organization of information to support decision making in the cellular environment is the main theme of the next article. Donald Knight and Michael Wall in "Using Group Technology for Improving Communication and Coordination Among Teams of Workers in Manufacturing Cells" stresses the importance of supporting the decentralized environment created with the implementation of cells. The authors show the inadequacies of current factory floor information and control systems, and suggest the need for integrated decision support systems that use expert system technology.

The final article in the section describes the implementation of a prototype cell built in a cooperative effort between North Carolina State University and a consortium made up of members of the American Furniture Manufacturers Association, the Wood Machinery Manufacturers of America, the Woodworking Machinery Importers Association, the International Woodworking Fair and the U.S. Department of Commerce. The project described by Thomas Culbreth and David Pollpeter in "A Flexible Manufacturing Cell for Furniture Part Production" shows how cooperative efforts can be valuable. Resource pooling allows significant projects that provide useful data on how best to apply existing technology. Further, these focused projects ensure that research efforts toward the development of new ideas are fitting a need of the consortium.

4

CELLULAR MANUFACTURING IN THE U.S. INDUSTRY: A SURVEY OF USERS

URBAN WEMMERLÖV AND NANCY L. HYER

This paper reports the findings of a survey study of 32 U.S. firms involved with cellular manufacturing. Areas covered include the reasons for establishing cells, benefits achieved, types and sizes of cells, extent of cellularization in the plants, methods used to design the cells, changes to planning and control systems, labour-related issues and important experiences gained by the companies. The data presented here were collected as part of a larger study of various group technology (GT) applications in which 53 companies participated. GT applications other than cellular manufacturing are described in Hyer and Wemmerlöv, 1989, "Group technology in the U.S. manufacturing industry: a survey of current practices," *International Journal of Production Research.*

INTRODUCTION

The increased competition faced by U.S. manufacturers since the late 1970s has made them very receptive to ideas that promise improved competitiveness. Foremost among the ideas that have achieved widespread acceptance is the "just-in-time" (JIT) philosophy. The cornerstones of JIT are elimination of waste and continual improvement of processes (Hall 1983, Schonberger 1982). The implementation of JIT requires more detailed specifications as to what procedures to use. For example, much attention has focused on setup reduction, pull systems and the application of statistical process control. Other building blocks have not received the same attention. We are here referring to the group technology (GT) philosophy and, in particular, its application to manufacturing systems called cellular manufacturing (Burbidge 1975, Hyer and Wemmerlöv 1984).

Reprinted with permission from *International Journal of Production Research,* 1989, vol. 27 no. 9; Taylor & Francis, Ltd., 1511-1530.

41

Cellular manufacturing is an application of GT where a portion of a firm's manufacturing system has been converted to cells. A manufacturing cell is a cluster of dissimilar machines or processes located in close proximity and dedicated to the manufacture of a family of parts (a cell family). The parts are similar in their processing requirements (required operations, tolerances, machine tool capacities, etc.) (Wemmerlöv 1988).

The aim of cellular manufacturing is to reduce setup times (by using part-family tooling and sequencing) and flow times (by reducing setup and move times, wait times for moves, and using small transfer batches) and, therefore, to reduce inventories and market response times. In addition, cells represent sociological units conducive to team work (Fazakerly 1976, Huber and Hyer 1985). This means that motivation for process improvements often arises naturally in manufacturing cells. Cellular manufacturing is closely related to JIT. In fact, it is difficult to conceive of JIT systems that do not employ this idea.

This paper reports the experiences of 32 U.S. firms that operate manufacturing cells. The paper reviews previous research on cellular manufacturing installations and then briefly describes the methodology used in the current study. Following a description of the firms' experiences with machine dedication without rearrangement, an overview of the population of companies included in the study is presented. Subsequent sections discuss how the manufacturing cells were designed, the main characteristics of the cells, impact on production planning and control procedures, and labour issues. We then summarize the benefits achieved by the companies as well as the problems encountered during cell implementation and operation. The paper concludes with a summary of the major findings of the study.

Previous Studies

Most of the knowledge of actual implementations of cellular manufacturing comes from case studies of individual firms. Only a handful of studies have surveyed large groups of companies. Mail survey studies of American and Japanese users have been published in 1977 (Ham and Reed 1977), 1980 (Honda, et al. 1980) and 1984 (Hyer 1984). In 1978, a study of more than 20 U.S. GT users based on unstructured interviews was undertaken (Levulis 1978). Several of these companies were included in the Hyer (1984) study and are represented in the current survey as well. All studies covered GT applications in general and were not focused on cellular manufacturing. In particular, Ham and Reed (1977), Honda, et al. (1980) and Levulis (1978) contain little useful data in this area. Several studies on cellular manufacturing have also been conducted in Britain (see Burbidge (1979) for an overview). The most extensive studies on cell benefits used data from a 35-company sample to determine regression models by which a company's future performance under cellular manufacturing can be predicted (Burbidge and Dale 1984, Dale 1980, Dale and Willey 1977).

Methodology

A mail survey using a 200-item questionnaire which covered a wide variety of areas related to the application of group technology generated the data for this study (see Appendix). Of the 53 companies that returned usable questionnaires, 32 indicated that they had manufacturing cells in place. With the exception of the next section, this paper deals only with the survey responses that are directly related to cellular manufacturing. The remaining data are documented in Hyer and Wemmerlöv (1989).

Equipment Dedication Without Machine Rearrangement

Group technology can be applied to manufacturing systems in three general ways (Hyer and Wemmerlöv 1982). The simplest application, common in batch manufacturing environments, is to rely informally on part similarities to gain setup efficiencies. The second application is to create formal part families, dedicate equipment to these families, but let the equipment remain in its original position (see, for example, Allison and Vapor 1979). The ultimate GT application is to form manufacturing cells.

Before the respondents' experiences with cellular manufacturing are discussed, some data related to equipment dedication *without* rearrangement will be presented. Twenty-three companies out of all 53 surveyed firms (43%) claimed to use dedicated equipment. However, only seven relied entirely on dedication. The remaining 16 companies indicated they used both dedicated equipment and manufacturing cells. Thus, half of the 32 cell users in this study had both cells and dedicated machinery while the remaining half used only cells.

The predominant reason for machine dedication was to reduce setup time. Other reasons were to improve quality and operator utilization and reduce operator skill levels. The most common reason why machine rearrangement had *not* been carried out was cost of relocating the machines. One company suggested lack of knowledge regarding future demand as a reason for not building cells.

Dedicating equipment to part families without changing the factory layout yielded several benefits (see Table 1). Fourteen of the 23 companies (61%) claimed setup and throughput time reductions which averaged 41.1% and 24.3%, respectively. Another benefit, estimated by nine firms, was a reduction in work-in-process inventory (averaging 19.4%). A noteworthy result is the reduction in number of fixtures. Although only claimed by five companies, this reduction averaged 34.0%. For only three measures had the results been assessed through a formal audit (the same company had performed all three audits).

Machine dedication does not bring only benefits, however. About half of the 23 companies had experienced various types of performance degradations. For example, both performance improvements and deteriorations were claimed for machine utilization, number of equipment, WIP inventory, and direct labour costs (Table 1).

The respondents noted several problems that can occur with dedicated systems: low machine utilization, loss of flexibility and increased capital investment to secure dedication. Other problems relate to changes in part mix and product design (e.g., in one case a specialized machine had become obsolete due to design changes). Five companies noted that their PPC departments were reluctant to use GT concepts in scheduling. Respondents also commented on the need for increased preventive maintenance and for relying on alternate processing capabilities in the event of equipment breakdown.

Several firms had realized that machine dedication does not achieve maximum benefits. For these companies, cellular manufacturing was the final goal. This is evident from comments such as "some taste of GT but only minor benefits," "rearrangement would further reduce inventory and material movements," and "does not reach full return; cannot minimize idle time of operator." The remainder of the paper is devoted to the experiences of the 32 companies that had established manufacturing cells.

Population of Surveyed Companies With Cells

The 32 firms involved with cellular manufacturing represented a wide variety of product lines, as indicated by Table 2. The absolute majority were in the metal-working industry. The average company had annual sales revenues of 296 million dollars, a direct and indirect labour force of 577 and 566 employees, respectively, and a plant size of 611,000 sq. ft. The number of product lines ranged from one to six, with an average of 2.8. The range of number of end items produced was very large, spanning from 3 to 80,000 products. The variation in active parts was also large: the number of manufactured parts averaged 33,000 per company, but ranged from 500 to 300,000. Likewise, the average number of active purchased parts was 29,588, with a range from 100 to 260,000. The complexity of the manufactured products was measured by the number of parts per end item. The simplest product had four components and the most complex about 5000. The average product contained 956 parts. (Due to large ranges and highly skewed distributions, the statistics related to averages must be cautiously interpreted.)

Reasons for Establishing Manufacturing Cells

The five most common reasons for establishing cells were to reduce WIP inventory, setup time, throughput time and materials handling, and to improve output quality. These reasons all received average importance scores exceeding 4 when rated on a scale from 1 (marginally important) to 5 (extremely important). With the exception of throughput time reduction, they also had minimum scores of 3. Finally, each of the 15 reasons mentioned by the firms received at least one 5. This indicates great variety in the reasons for establishing cells.

Table 1. Reported benefits and adverse consequences of machine dedication (number of firms with machine dedication = 23).

Benefits	Number of responses	Average improvement (%)	Number of audited results
Setup time reduction	16/14	41.4	1
Throughput time reduction	16/14	24.3	1
Reduction in WIP inventory	10/9	19.4	1
Quality improvement	8/6	15.0	0
Reduction in materials handling	7/5	21.0	0
Direct labour cost reduction	6/5	7.2	0
Reduction in number of fixtures	5/5	34.0	0
Improved machine utilization	5/5	23.4	0
Reduction in space	5/5	16.2	0
Improved job satisfaction	3/3	26.7	0
Reduction in number of pieces of equipment	3/2	25.0	0
Reduction in indirect labour	1/0	--	0

Audited results from machine dedication	Number of responses	Average deterioration (%)	Number of audited results
Reduction in machine utilization	7/5	17.0	0
Increase in equipment used	4/3	10.0	0
Increase in tooling expense	2/2	9.0	0
Increase in direct labour costs	2/1	8.0	0
Increase in WIP inventory	1/1	10.0	0
Reduction in job satisfaction	1/0	--	0
Increase in space requirements	1/0	--	0

Note: Number of responses = A/B, where A is number of companies indicating the result and B is the number of companies also submitting a numerical estimate.

Table 2. Product lines of cellular manufacturing users.

Machinery and machine tools

Mechanical punch presses; power equipment for application of steel and plastic strapping; lamp making equipment; airpower and hydraulic maintenance tools and equipment; mining equipment (overhead cranes and trolleys); mailing machines; collators; postage meters; other business machines

Agricultural and construction equipment

Tractors; loaders/backhoes; rough terrain forklifts; combines; cotton pickers; planters; pipe layers

Hospital and medical equipment

Products for anesthesia; products for infant care; hospital gas and piping systems; hospital sterilizers; operating table components; operating room lights

Defence products

Defence systems and components for navy, marines, army and air force; missile launchers and gun mounts for the navy; navy electrical controls; armoured personnel carriers; light tanks; amphibious assault vehicles; tracked carriers

Engines

Diesel engines

Piece parts and components

Tube and tube fittings; specialty fittings and bearings; fabricated piece parts for hydrostatic power transmission; enclosures for sheet metal and machined parts for electronics industry; fluid power components and systems

Miscellaneous

Automatic control valves; pumps (centrifugal and oil-well submersible); office furniture (wood and steel); transportation signalling systems and controls

The companies also mentioned, but did not assign a numerical score to, other reasons that led them to build cells. Such motivating factors included a desire to reduce the cost of indirect labour and inspection. One company said that cellular manufacturing suited its management philosophy of improving teamwork in the organization. Several firms claimed that their decision was prompted by a need to improve their competitiveness. Thus, cells fitted well into their plant improvement programmes aimed at maintaining state-of-the art manufacturing technology, reducing manufacturing cycle times and increasing output quality.

Procedures Used to Design Cells

Table 3 shows the main approaches to cell formation by 28 responding firms (see Wemmerlöv and Hyer 1986). Nineteen companies (68%) indicated that the cell formation process had begun by grouping similar parts without taking advantage of existing routings. The other three approaches all rely on routings in various ways (one company emphasized that it is frequently necessary to modify existing routings in order to minimize the number of machines in a cell). Eleven firms claimed they had used the key machine approach in which a machine is first established as the core of a cell, and related parts and machines are then successively added (cf. Burbidge's nuclear synthesis method (Burbidge 1975)). Nine companies claimed to have used a part/machine matrix rearrangement method. That approach is probably the most widely known of all cell formation techniques (Burbidge 1975). However, formal algorithms for reordering the machine and part vectors in the matrix (e.g,. King and Nakorchai 1982) are fairly recent and not likely to be widespread in industry. Therefore, it is surprising that over one third of the companies claimed they had used this method. Finally, seven plants had relied on other methods for their cell formation process. These approaches can include simple sorting of routings, creation of from-to diagrams, frequency listings of machine occurrences in the routings, and the use of similarity coefficients based on either part or machine similarity (Carrie 1973, McAuley 1972). Although the respondents did not indicate which specific techniques were used, we expect the first three were the most common owing to their simplicity.

Table 3. Approaches to cell formation.

Method	Number of companies employing this approach
1. A family of similar parts was first identified without consulting existing or planned routings	19
2. A "key" machine (or machines) was selected to serve as the nucleus of a cell. Then, other machines which occurred in the same part routings as the key machine were added to the cell	11
3. A matrix showing the machines required by each part was reordered to simultaneously identify groups of machines which process the same set of parts	9
4. Machine routings were first examined to find parts which are processed on the same set of machines or to find groups of machines which process the same set of parts	7

To determine the value of a GT coding scheme applied solely for the purpose of creating cells, the nine companies that used codes were asked if the costs involved with implementing the classification and coding system, if borne by manufacturing alone, could justify its use in identifying parts for cellular manufacturing. The average score for the companies was 3.56, where "1" means "costs would greatly exceed benefits" and "5" means "benefits would greatly exceed costs." Although the answer indicates that coding systems can be valuable in the cell formation process, it does not reflect a strong endorsement for building a GT database for the sole purpose of establishing cells.

Computer Support in the Cell Design Process

Nineteen firms claimed to have relied on computer support in connection with cell design and evaluation. Conversely, ten of the 29 companies that responded to this question did not. This seems to indicate a low level of sophistication and preplanning before making an often radical change to the factory floor. The types of analyses that were not aided by computers are mostly unknown. However, one firm said it had used a scale model where blocks had been located on a floor plan of the proposed system. Another company had used manual line balancing calculations to design and assess the performance of its cells.

Those that used computer support claimed the following type of analyses had been undertaken: load/utilization calculations, work centre where-used queries, throughput time estimations, and routing analyses. Several respondents had relied on existing data files (such as routings, forecasts, standard data, etc.) and had written programs in-house to access and analyse these files. Load calculations were most frequent. For these analyses, tools such as spreadsheet programs (16 firms) and simulation models (14 firms) were common. (That so many companies would have used computer simulation is not likely. This result can perhaps be ascribed to the often loose use of the term "simulation," interpreted as "projection." Based on comments in the survey forms, however, it is clear that at least four of the firms had, in fact, relied on stochastic simulation modelling). Finally, three companies indicated the use of commercial GT analysis programs.

DESCRIPTIVE STATISTICS OF THE CELL POPULATION

This section describes various characteristics of the manufacturing cells found in the surveyed firms, including types and ages of the cells, extent of cellularization, cell sizes and cell independence, demand and flow characteristics, utilizations and changes over time.

Types and Ages of the Cells

Of the 32 companies surveyed, 25 had only manned cells (low degree of automation; high labour intensity), one had only unmanned cells (high degree of automation; low labour intensity), and six had both types of cells. Seventy-one per cent of the firms with manned cells and 86% of the firms with unmanned cells reported that their cells were devoted only to fabrication. The remaining companies reported cells for both assembly and fabrication/machining operations. The degree of mechanization of materials handling was generally low for the manned cells and about 55% of the respondents said materials handling was totally manual. All companies with unmanned cells and 83% of the firms with manned cells had developed part family tooling.

The number of manned cells per company ranged from 1 to 35, with an average of 5.9 cells. However, twelve companies had three cells or less, while 25 companies (81%) had six or fewer manned cells. Although one firm claimed to have established its first cell in 1950 and eight firms to have done so in the 1960s or 1970s, the majority of the manned cells had been established relatively recently. About three-quarters had been put together during or after 1980. In terms of unmanned cells, five of the firms had only one such cell while two companies had two unmanned cells each. No unmanned cell was established before 1983 and in three of the companies no such cell had been built before 1985.

Nineteen of 28 responding companies (68%) with manned cells indicated that 20% or less of the equipment in the cells was purchased expressly for the cells. Ten of the companies, or 36%, claimed to have purchased no new equipment at all for their manned cells. On the other hand, of the seven companies with unmanned cells, four indicated that 100% of the equipment was new, one that 40% was new, and one that 15% was new. One firm claimed that all equipment in the unmanned cell was old. Thus, creation of manned cells usually takes place with predominantly existing equipment while unmanned cells appear to be accompanied by a higher degree of investment in new equipment.

Extent of Cellularization

The degree of "cellularization" can be measured by the fraction of all annual machine hours in the plant that are expended in cells. For the 27 companies with manned cells that returned estimates, this measure ranged from 0.2% to 88%. For most firms, however, cellular manufacturing is a relatively marginal activity (as can be expected from the low number of implemented cells). For example, 13 of the 27 companies (48%) reported that 5% or less of their annual machine hours were spent in cells. Similarly, 63% of the firms reported that 15% or less, and 74% reported that 25% or less of the annual hours were spent in cells.

The percentage figures for fraction of total machine hours expended in unmanned cells given by five companies were 1%, 2%, 2%, 4% and 11%. Of course, there were fewer cells of this type compared to manned cells.

Cell Sizes and Cell Independence

The smallest typical cell size for manned cells was two machines, while the largest typical cell size reported was 40. Removing the last figure (the next largest average cell size was 15), the average size of the manned cells was 6.2 machine tools. However, two thirds of the companies said they had cells composed of six or fewer machine tools, and about half indicated they had cells in the four-to-six machine tool range. The seven companies with unmanned cells reported cell sizes between one and eight machine tools. The average size of these cells was 4.7 machines.

Creating independent cells, i.e. cells with no linkages to other cells in the factory, is a common goal for cell formation (Burbidge 1975, Wemmerlöv and Hyer 1987). However, it is not always economical or practical to achieve cell independence. Twenty per cent of the companies with manned cells and 14% of those with unmanned cells reported that machines were shared between cells (see Table 4). Another measure of cell independence is the extent to which a part's processing time occurs inside a single cell. The average figure for 29 respondents was 78.3%. Only three companies with manned cells indicated that parts were completely machined in the cells. The data in Table 4 indicate it is rare to find completely independent cells. It also appears that unmanned cells are less independent than manned cells.

Demand Patterns and Material Flows

The demand for the finished products whose parts were manufactured in the cells was not highly predictable. However, since cells frequently are designed to manufacture many parts, often components of different end items, the composite demand pattern for the cell can be steady although requirements

Table 4. Degree of cell independence.

	Question	Manned cells	Unmanned cells
1.	Are machines or processes shared between any of the cells?	Yes: 6 No: 24	Yes: 1 No: 6
2.	Indicate, for the parts processed in the cells, the average percentage of total machining time accomplished in the cells	Mean = 78.3% Min = 10% Max = 100% Median = 90% Number of responses = 29	Mean = 66.7% Min = 10% Max = 100% Median = 75% Number of responses = 6
3.	Indicate, for the parts processed in the cells, the average percentage of the total number of operations required for their production that are completed in the cells	Mean = 74.2% Min = 10% Max = 100% Median = 82.5% Number of responses = 30	Mean = 65.7% Min = 10% Max = 100% Median = 80% Number of responses = 7

for individual parts are not. In fact, 18 of 30 companies with manned cells (60%), and three of the seven companies with unmanned cells (43%), characterized the total aggregate demand for the cells as fairly constant throughout the year.

Ideal manufacturing cells are often thought of as flow lines. When asked to describe the flow pattern in their cells, with a "1" referring to a jumbled flow and a "5" referring to a flow line, the respondents' average score was 3.65 for the manned cells and 4.00 for the unmanned cells. The preponderance of manned cells with dominant flow patterns is evident from the fact that nine companies characterized the flow patterns with a score of 5, and 20 (i.e. two-thirds) gave it a score of either 4 or 5. For unmanned cells, the situation is similar. Only one company indicated its cells had a jumbled flow, while five of the seven companies assigned a flow score of 4 or 5.

Flow patterns and cell sizes are often related. A cell might contain many machines because the processing requirements for the cell parts could not be consolidated (i.e. a large cell is likely to exhibit a lower degree of part similarity than a small cell). The collected data on manned cells show that companies with more jumbled flow patterns also had the largest cells. For example, the average cell size for companies characterizing the flow patterns with 1, 2 or 3 was 11.7 machines, while the average cell for companies reporting flow patterns of 4 or 5 consisted only of 5.1 machines.

Cell Utilizations

The companies estimated the utilizations of machines in cells as well as of machines not allocated to cells. As shown in Table 5, overall average utilization is the highest for the unmanned cells, then for the manned cells, and the lowest average utilization is found for the non-cell machines. That unmanned cells have the largest utilizations might reflect that they require large investments and that preplanning and operation of these cells get more attention than for manned cells. The "Lowest utilizations" statistics in Table 5 reinforce this conjecture. The ranges of the average lowest and the average highest utilizations were 32% to 89% for the manned cells and 55% to 91% for the unmanned cells. Although these are aggregated data, they also indicate the difficulties in achieving load balance in cells. (Note, however, that the load imbalance was even larger for the non-cell machines.)

Changes Over Time

In about half of the companies the manned cells produced parts for which they were not originally designed. The percentage of "new" part numbers averaged 11.3%, with a range from 5% to 25%. These new parts represented an average of 8.1% of total volume produced, with a range from 2% to 20%. Three of the seven companies with unmanned cells had also replaced parts. In one case half of the parts assigned to an unmanned cell were parts the cell was not built to produce.

Table 5. Machine utilizations in cell and non-cell systems.

Utilizations	For machines in manned cells	For machines in unmanned cells	For machines not configured into cells
Average utilizations			
Overall average utilization	64.0%	71.3%	61.8%
Min average utilization	40%	60%	40%
Max average utilization	92%	80%	92%
Number of responses	25	4	26
Lowest utilizations			
Average lowest utilization	31.6%	55.0%	18.1%
Min lowest utilization	5%	40%	1%
Max lowest utilization	80%	70%	70%
Number of responses	25	4	25
Highest utilizations			
Average highest utilization	89.5%	91.3%	90.0%
Min highest utilization	70%	80%	66%
Max highest utilization	100%	100%	100%
Number of responses	26	4	28

Companies that commented upon the impact of these "new" parts in the cells noted two types of changes. Firstly, adding parts to the cells often required additional tooling and fixtures and, secondly, cell utilizations increased. The latter response may indicate that the cells were originally underutilized and that this "free capacity" was later taken advantage of. The potential risk of adding parts to a cell, of course, is that performance is likely to decline as the load increases, more setups are added, and the flow pattern gets more complex.

IMPACT OF PRODUCTION PLANNING AND CONTROL PROCEDURES

With the establishment of cells, the way production planning and control (PPC) is carried out is likely to change (Wemmerlöv 1988). Such changes are discussed in this section.

The following PPC systems were in place at 31 of the responding plants: 28 (90.3%) had material requirements planning (MRP) systems, two had reorder point (ROP) systems (one had ROP and MRP, the other only ROP), three had pull systems (together with MRP), one had an optimized production technology (OPT) system (Jacobs 1984) (and MRP), and two companies had unspecified systems.

Seven companies claimed to have introduced new systems in conjunction with implementation of cells. However, several of these were only at the planning stage. For example, four companies were planning or in the process of implementing pull systems. Two companies were revising their MRP systems to be geared mostly towards purchased material (we interpret this to mean that the MRP shop floor control system would ultimately be replaced by a pull system).

As pointed out earlier, the majority of the companies had a limited number of cells, and three-quarters reported that less than 25% of the annual machine hours were expended in cells. Thus, firms with cells might have to operate two systems simultaneously: one for the cell system and one for the remainder of the factory. For example, pull systems might be appropriate only for the cell system. However, modifications within the bounds of an existing PPC system can also be made to better serve the operation of the cells. These types of changes are shown in Table 6.

Relatively few changes had taken place to the companies' PPC systems. Most noticeably, lot sizes and transfer batches had been reduced, although in two firms lot sizes had been increased (in one case to improve the effective cell utilization). In general, more frequent order releasing took place due to reduced lots (one company pointed out that "PIC had to even the work flow that the MRP system was creating"). In some cases cells, and not machines, had become planning and control points. Quite a few companies were also contemplating, or already using, pull systems to control the material flows.

IDEAL PPC SYSTEMS FOR CELLS

Eighteen firms responded to the question of what type of PPC procedures they *ideally* would like to see for cell systems. One said no additional changes were necessary, another that they did not have enough experience to know what they really needed. A company with an ROP system wanted an MRP II system, and another wanted a system with bar coding and standard containers so that jobs could easily be tracked. Level loading of cells was the concern of one firm that wanted "enhanced capacity planning to make allowances for cells." Another respondent also wanted capacity planning for the cells and, in general, a PPC system with: "the ability to view the cell on two levels. Firstly, as a black box for shop floor control purposes—perform one global operation, such as machining completed up to heat treat. Secondly, to provide a detailed

53

Table 6. Modifications to PPC systems.

Area of modification	Number of responses	Comments, examples
I. Master scheduling	6	Increased build frequencies, reduced planned lead times, developed planning bills in order to migrate to make-to-order.
2.Capacity planning	6	Concentrated on cell bottlenecks alone.
3. MRP lot sizes	17	In most cases reduced. Minimum lot sizes were established for low volume cell parts. Increased lot sizes in two companies.
4. Cell transfer batches (units moved between work stations)	14	In most cases reduced and/or determined by standard container size. A few companies moved parts one-by-one inside cells, and batch-by-batch between cells.
5. Order releasing	10	Undertaken more frequently due to smaller lots.
6. Sequencing/ scheduling	6	Jobs with stated due dates were released to the cells instead of to individual machines. Jobs were scheduled inside cell by foreman (or computer) within due date constraints.
7. Job tracking	4	Completed operations not tracked inside cells (except for last operation). In one case cell operators reported moves in real time.
8. Alternate routings	4	Alternate routings were emphasized less, or not used at all.

level machine loading and specific performance data needed by the cell foreman."

One company noted that the ideal system would be one "that combines the delivery driven MRP system with the cost-driven GT system." The clash between effectiveness and efficiency is most pronounced at the job scheduling level, and one can interpret this statement as a need for scheduling routines which consider not only due dates but setup reductions as well

(Wemmerlöv 1988). In fact, when discussing "ideal systems," nine of the firms focused on the area of scheduling. Of these, four explicitly expressed a need for part family scheduling procedures (Wemmerlöv and Vakharia 1988). Two companies wanted real-time machine scheduling, in one case with a micro-computer in the (manned) cell itself. Another wanted a scheduling system that could accommodate "random production" (again, in manned cells). Only one firm explicitly rejected computer-supported scheduling. Instead, its goal was to rely on pull systems and visual scheduling techniques and place as much control in the hands of the floor personnel as possible.

LABOUR ISSUES

This section discusses operator tasks, degree of mobility, selection procedures, training, payment systems, and resistance to change. A few comments also concerning cell supervisors. Only manned cells are discussed.

Tasks Performed in Cells
Besides "traditional" tasks, operators were in charge of part inspection and materials handling in four-fifths of the companies and for simple maintenance tasks in about half. In one firm the operators were in charge of the tooling and its status, including the acquisition of all perishable tooling. Scheduling and supervision were rare activities, indicating the cells mostly were controlled by supervisors. Only two companies explicitly stated they had autonomous work teams in the cells.

Labour Mobility
The ability of labour to perform a variety of tasks and to move between different work stations is often seen as a prerequisite for the efficient use of both cell labour and equipment (Burbidge 1979). "Intracell mobility" implies the operators are multifunctional and can assist several processes inside the same cell while "intercell mobility" suggests the operators can move between cells (although not necessarily perform different tasks). Of the 31 companies with manned cells, 27 (87%) claimed to have multifunctional operators. The extent of intracell mobility was fairly extensive. Using a 5-point scale, where "1" represents "very little operator movement" and "5" represents "a great deal of operator movement" within a given cell, the average response was 3.6.

Twelve of the companies (39%) claimed to move operators between different cells and the average score for the extent of intercell mobility was 2.5 (on a 5-point scale). These statistics reflect a need for a flexible allocation of capacity (due to volume and product mix changes, operator absenteeism, machine breakdowns, etc.) in dedicated manufacturing systems.

Existence of labour unions (about two-thirds of the companies were unionized) seems to affect how cells are operated (Table 7). Non-unionized

Table 7. The relationship between plant unionization and cell operation.

	Unionized plants (21)	Non-unionized plants (11)
Extent of operator movement	3.37 (19)	4.06 (9)
Extent of operator movement between cells	2.60 (5)	2.43 (7)
Number of activities performed by operators in cells	4.95 (21)	6.30 (10)

Note: The numbers in parentheses indicate number of responses. Extent of operator movement is scored using a scale where 1 = very little movement and 5 = a great deal of movement.

plants had slightly more intracell mobility and more tasks were performed by the cell operators compared to unionized plants. The levels of intercell mobility were about the same, although slightly larger for plants with unions (this could indicate that operators move between similar machines in different cells while resisting the multi-functional operator concept).

Selection of Personnel
In almost half the cases for which responses exist, the operators had volunteered for the cell jobs and were later selected by management while in about one-quarter of the firms a direct selection by management took place. In only four of the 29 responding companies was the union involved in selecting people for the cell jobs. In four companies the operators in the area where the cells were established became the cell workers (in over half of the companies, the cell supervisors were chosen this way). Replacing workers in already established cells apparently took place with little input from the work teams. In one company with autonomous work groups the cell workers chose the replacement when an operator left the cell permanently. Another company had the management select replacements, but on the cell workers' recommendation. For the remaining companies, however, the procedures were split almost evenly between using job bidding systems and direct selection by management or cell supervisors.

Education and Training
The education and training the companies provided ranged from "none" to "extensive." Five of 29 responding firms had not trained their cell workers at all (a few indicated the workers had been selected because of their skills and, therefore, required no additional training). Nineteen companies had provided

mostly on-the-job training on the cell machines, although some firms exposed the operators to formal (classroom) machine education. In only nine cases (31%) had the operators been provided formal education in GT, cell concepts and/or JIT.

The education and training given the cell supervisors also exhibited great variety. At seven of the 24 companies providing answers to this question the supervisors had received no education or training. One company had provided general supervisory skills training, and three had instructed the supervisors in machine operation. In half of the firms the supervisors had been exposed to cellular manufacturing concepts. However, in just seven cases had this been through a formal educational process. In the remaining five companies only informal discussions had been held with the supervisory personnel.

Compensation Systems

Although a large variety of compensation schemes was found among the responding companies, half of them paid the operators a fixed hourly wage (Table 8). While the remaining half had some form of incentive plan in place, only two firms paid on the basis of piece rate.

Apparently, cellular manufacturing's impact on compensation was small: at 84% of the firms cell workers were compensated in the same manner as their functional counterparts. However, cell and non-cell operators do not necessarily receive the same level of pay. Although the pay scales were not explicitly asked for in this survey, a couple of firms indicated that cell

Table 8. Compensation schemes for cell operators.

Type of Compensation	Number of companies	Percentage of 30 responding plants
1. Fixed wage (hourly rate)	15	50.0
2. Individual incentive (piece rate)	2	6.7
3. Fixed wage and individual incentive	2	6.7
4. Group incentive (based on cell output)	4	13.3
5. Fixed wage and group incentive	1	3.3
6. Combined individual and group incentive	2	6.7
7. Fixed wage and merit pay	2	6.7
8. Fixed wage and profit sharing	2	6.7
Total	30	100

operators were paid more. This was based either on higher or more versatile skills or because the machines in the cells had higher pay rates.

Resistance to Change

It is often feared that cellular manufacturing will meet with great resistance from operators and unions. We found little evidence of this. As stated earlier, about two thirds of the surveyed companies were unionized. Asked whether the labour union strongly resisted the introduction of the cell concept, the average response was 2.20 for the unionized firms (1 = strongly disagree, 5 = strongly agree). We interpret this as a low to moderate perceived resistance to change by the unions. In fact, the unions may very well reduce resistance to change. If the scores for perceived resistance by operators and supervisors are separated into responses from unionized and non-unionized firms, the average scores for operators were 1.85 and 1.91, and for supervisors 1.90 and 2.45, respectively. Thus, the resistance to cellular manufacturing was actually perceived by the respondents to be lower in companies with labour unions compared to companies without unions. That the supervisors were perceived to be more opposed to the cell concept than the operators might reflect the increase in required skills and the threat of reduction in direct authority often faced by cell supervisors.

BENEFITS AND COSTS RELATED TO CELLULAR MANUFACTURING

Table 9 shows percentage improvements along a variety of performance variables. Although the results are not as spectacular as those often reported in the literature (for example, a study of ten British firms showed average reductions in WIP and throughput time of 62% and 70%, respectively (Burbidge 1979)), they are still quite impressive. However, there is a very wide range in each category of the benefits received. Also, very few firms actually supplied data from formal audits (Table 9). In most cases, then, the reported results are "guesstimates" by the company personnel.

Most companies reported benefits in the areas of throughput time, WIP inventory, materials handling, setup time and quality improvement. This mirrors the reasons why the cells were set up. The same performance measures also showed some of the largest improvements from cellular manufacturing. A few of the measures, like "job satisfaction" and "quality," are ill-defined. (One company suggested another intangible benefit: "parts do not get lost" in manufacturing cells.) For example, while 16 companies indicated that operator satisfaction was enhanced by cell operations, only eight submitted any numerical estimates. These estimates must be looked upon simply as indicators of perceived direction of change and not as actual measures of change in job satisfaction. Improvement of quality was one of the major

Table 9. Reported benefits from cellular manufacturing.

Type of benefit	Number of responses	Average improvement	Minimum improvement	Maximum improvement	Number of audited results
1. Reduction in throughput time	25/20	45.6	5.0	90.0	5
2. Reduction in WIP inventory	23/19	41.4	8.0	80.0	6
3. Reduction in materials handling	26/23	39.3	10.0	83.0	0
4. Improvement of operator job satisfaction	16/8	34.4	15.0	50.0	0
5. Reduction in number of fixtures for cell parts	9/8	33.1	10.0	85.0	0
6. Reduction in setup time	23/19	32.0	2.0	95.0	2
7. Reduction in space needs	9/7	31.0	1.0	85.0	0
8. Improvement of part quality	26/20	29.6	5.0	90.0	1
9. Reduction in finished goods inventory	14/12	29.2	10.0	75.0	3
10. Reduction in labour cost	15/13	26.2	5.0	75.0	1
11. Increase in utilization of equipment now in the cells	6/6	23.3	10.0	40.0	1
12. Reduction in pieces of equipment required to manufacture cell parts	10/8	19.5	1.0	50.0	0

Note: All improvement figures are percentages. Number of responses = A/B, where A is the number of companies indicating the benefit and B is the number of companies that also supplied a numerical estimate.

reasons for establishing cells and also one of the areas in which most companies had experienced improvements. It is not known whether these results stem from better equipment, faster defect detection from smaller lots, a better trained work force, a higher degree of task repeatability or quality control programmes. Very likely, all these factors combined lie behind the quality improvements.

It might appear peculiar that some companies reported increased machine utilization and fewer machines. Lowered utilization, resulting from duplicated machines, is often mentioned as a potential disadvantage of cells (Wemmerlöv 1988). The probable explanation for responses 11 and 12 in Table 9 is that route consolidation has taken place. That is, the cell parts were previously manufactured using a number of routes involving many different machines. When the cells were established, a limited number of standardized routings were determined involving fewer (and more heavily utilized) pieces of equipment.

Major expense categories associated with cell implementations, suggested by 23 companies, are listed in Table 10. Although these costs are likely to be encountered, the relative size of each cost component obviously depends on the situation at hand. The dominant expenses were for moving equipment in the plant (most cells in this study were manned cells based predominantly on existing equipment).

The overall perception of the balance between achieved benefits and incurred costs was elicited using a 5-point scale. The average response was 4.28, where "1" is "costs greatly exceed benefits" and "5" is "benefits greatly exceed costs." Furthermore, 28 of the 29 firms assigned scores of 4 or 5. These high scores indicate a very strong acceptance of cellular manufacturing and validates it as a highly profitable venture. This is further evidenced by the fact that as many as 22 of the 32 surveyed companies (69%) had plans for more cells in the future.

PROBLEMS ENCOUNTERED DURING IMPLEMENTATION AND OPERATION

The companies were asked to indicate problems during implementation or operation. Because there are many problems that need to be overcome, it can be surmised that respondents listed only the most serious ones. The responses from 18 firms are summarized in Table 11.

Eight companies had experienced resistance to the cell implementation. Also, concern and scepticism towards cells were felt in some plants by work areas that had production transferred into the cells and, thereby, experienced a

Table 10. Major expense categories for cell implementation.

Expense category	Number of times mentioned
1. Equipment reallocation, installation	16
2. Feasibility studies, cell design, planning, meetings	8
3. New equipment, machine duplication	6
4. Training	6
5. New tools and fixtures	5
6. Programmable controllers, software, computers	4
7. Materials handling equipment	2
8. Loss of production during installation	2
9. Higher operator wages	1
Total	50

Table 11. Problems related to implementation and operation of cells.

Type of problem	Number of responses in this category
People-related	
Operator resistance	5
Supervisor resistance	2
Management resistance	1
Lack of team work skills	1
Equipment-related	
Machine breakdowns	3
Need for special tooling	1
Operation-related	
Load and labour balancing	8
Volume/capacity imbalance	3
Cell scheduling	3
Achieving simple flows	2
Total	29

lower level of activity themselves. Initial resistance is natural but likely to subside after people have become involved with the design and/or operation of the cells (as discussed earlier, only moderate operator resistance appeared to be the norm). The problems classified as "operation-related" are more closely tied to the cell concept. Apart from the problem of achieving simple flows through the cells and dealing with out-of-cell operations like heat treat, cleaning, etc., the remaining problems in this category are all related and make up the largest problem group.

"Volume/capacity imbalance" problems (Table 11) refer to situations where either too much or too little work is loaded on to the cells. One company, for example, remarked that product mix changes dried up the cell load, indicating the potential danger of building systems dedicated to a narrow range of part configurations. The problems related to "cell scheduling" were not elaborated on by the respondents. However, the way cells are scheduled can also affect the load balance in the cell. As seen from Table 11, this was the most frequent problem experienced by the firms.

A load imbalance occurs when some cell machines are more utilized than others. Such an imbalance is a function of the way the cell is designed, the current product or part mix, and the way jobs are scheduled and labour assigned. It is not possible, however, to operate manufacturing systems where all machines (and operators) are equally utilized (Burbidge 1979). Thus, load imbalances occur in all systems. In job shops such problems are often "rectified" by releasing jobs early to keep resources busy. The problem might become more noticeable in a cell context where a limited number of resources are confined to one area, dedicated to a limited set of parts, and where visible control of the activities becomes easy (however, the remainder of the factory might have even larger load imbalances). Thus, although design and operation of the cells can affect the load balance to a certain degree, it is likely that a new attitude towards low equipment utilization is required (also see Burbidge 1979).

LESSONS LEARNED

A sample of verbatim responses concerning lessons learned as a consequence of implementing and operating cells are listed in Table 12. Responses 1 to 8, and 18, essentially relate to technical issues (the latter highlights the potential vulnerability of cells due to loss of flexibility), while the remainder of the comments relate to preparing the organization and managing the implementation process. The two most consistent areas deal with involvement and training: the clear message the responses convey is to involve everybody early and to train extensively. Other lessons were: select good people, start with projects with a high probability of success, go slowly, do not underestimate the time requirement, and keep people informed. The experiences gained by the respondent firms are similar to those documented in studies of technology implementations by Ettlie (1984), Meredith (1981) and Rosenthal (1984).

CONCLUSIONS

This paper focuses on the collective experience of cellular manufacturing shared by 32 firms. Some of the more interesting findings are summarized here.

Machine dedication in job shops was very common: 43% of the 53 companies in our complete study and half of the 32 firms with manufacturing cells had dedicated equipment. Overall, the companies had experienced good results. However, several had also found dedication to be dysfunctional and concluded that cellular manufacturing was necessary to reap full benefits.

Table 12. Lessons learned (a sample of verbatim comments).

Cell design
1. Group technology analysis is essential in planning manufacturing cells
2. Consider the life cycle of the product
3. Avoid jumbled cross flow within the cell
4. Do not ignore gauging
5. Do not short change tooling cost allocation
6. Aggressively update equipment and methods within the cell
7. It [i.e. cellular manufacturing] is easier to accomplish in new facility design
8. Expect and plan for several iterations of cell redesign: consider cell development is evolutionary and therefore always in a state of flux

People involvement
9. Let operators be involved (our assembly cells were developed by operators supported by management)
10. Get supervisors and production workers involved early: some have never heard words like throughput before
11. Include all production areas in the planning phase of the cells
12. Do not underestimate workers' acceptance once the concept is understood

Training
13. Provide training for operators so they can run any machine in the cell
14. Assure that cell foreman is trained in cell techniques before assigned to a cell
15. Train, train, train

The implementation process
16. Start with a pilot cell
17. Select the first cell that is simple and has a high potential for success
18. Do not depend on the cell as the only source of supply during implementation: stockpile parts to have an alternate source
19. Be sure to orient personnel fully on reasons for changes and objectives of programmes
20. For unmanned cells, select your best people
21. Do put cells in, regardless of doubts

Cellularization was a modest and relatively new undertaking in most companies. The majority of the firms had manned cells with a low degree of automation. The cell workload in about half the firms represented only 5% or less of the total plant load. Also, over 80% of the companies had six or fewer cells, and three-quarters of all cells had been established after 1980. Over 90% of the firms had MRP systems in place and about 25% had, or were planning to install, pull systems.

The concept of multifunctional operators was well-practised: 87% of the companies claimed to have mobile operators in the cells and 39% had operators who moved between cells (although with less frequency). The latter statistic in particular supports the notion that some degree of flexibility must be available in systems with dedicated resources. Half of the firms paid their cell operators fixed hourly wages and in only two instances were piece rate systems in effect.

The two most frequent problems were load balancing of the cells and resistance to change. The severity of the latter problem is probably only moderate. Interestingly, while resistance to change generally was perceived to be fairly low by the respondents, it was higher for union officials than for operators and supervisors, higher for supervisors than for operators, and higher for both operators and supervisors in non-unionized firms compared to their counterparts in unionized firms. The problem with load balancing is inherent in discrete part manufacturing systems. A new managerial attitude (already emerging) that favours fast material flows rather than high utilizations will probably lessen the perceived importance of this problem.

The most common cost category in conjunction with cell establishment was machine relocation expenditures (most cells were based on existing plant equipment). The cost of moving equipment was also the most common reason given by the firms that practised machine dedication rather than building cells.

Large benefits were achieved in many areas, for example: reductions in throughput time by 45.6%, in WIP inventory by 41.4%, in materials handling by 39.3%, in setup time by 32.0%, and improvement in quality by 29.6%. These figures are averages and the benefits achieved by individual firms varied substantially. Furthermore, very few results had been derived from formal audits. These circumstances should make companies somewhat wary of uncritically adopting published results for their own cost/benefit assessments. However, the surveyed companies gave enthusiastic support for the cellular manufacturing concept, indicating that benefits exceeded, or greatly exceeded, costs. Close to 70% also stated that more cells will be built at their plants in the future.

The most valuable lessons learned by the companies from their experience with cellular manufacturing were people- and not technology-oriented. In summary, the users stressed the importance of training and involving people early in the process of change. The recommendations to train refer mostly to the cross-training of operators on multiple machines. Only in one-third of the companies did the operators receive education in the concepts underlying the cellular manufacturing approach. Supervisors were exposed to these ideas in half of the firms but often only through informal discussions. These findings are somewhat surprising, given the fact that cellular manufacturing requires a very different outlook on manufacturing practices compared to traditional batch manufacturing. It could be that the majority of the firms combined informal education with the involvement process with the employees gradually developing an understanding of cellular manufacturing during the planning and conversion phases.

Research into cellular manufacturing practices must continue (Wemmerlöv and Hyer 1987). For example, several companies expressed a need for scheduling routines oriented towards part families. Another critical area was the need to provide flexibility in dedicated systems. How to achieve flexibility, and at what level it should be established, are important questions. A final area of great interest relates to performance measurements and achievements. Why do some companies achieve spectacular results while others do not, and how believable are published results in this area?

APPENDIX

Methodology

The methodology for this survey study is detailed in Hyer and Wemmerlöv (1989). Thirty-two of the 53 facilities in the study employed one or more manufacturing cells. These represent 11% of the entire sample of 285 firms and 60% of the final, usable sample of GT users. Because study participants do not represent a random sample, the results obtained are not necessarily statistically representative of the broader population of CM users.

REFERENCES

Allison, J., and J. Vapor. "GT proves out." *American Machinist.* 123 (1979): 86-89.

Burbidge, J. L. *The Introduction of Group Technology.* New York: John Wiley and Sons. 1975.

Burbidge, J. L. *Group Technology in the Engineering Industry.* London: Mechanical Engineering Publications, 1979.

Burbidge, J. L., and Dale, B. G. "Planning the introduction and predicting the benefits of group technology." *Engineering Costs and Production Economics.* 8 (1984): 117-128.

Carrie, A. "Numerical taxonomy applied to group technology and plant layout." *International Journal of Production Research.* 11 (1973): 399-416.

Dale, B. "Digging deeper into GT's potential." *Machinery and Production Engineering.* 5 (1980): 39-41.

Dale, B., and P. Willey. "The need to predict the potential for GT in manufacturing." *Machinery and Production Engineering.* 130 (3342): 9-15. 1977.

Ettlie, J. "Facing the factory of the future." Working paper. Michigan: Industrial Technology Institute, 1984.

Fazakerly, G. "Research report on the human aspects of group technology and cellular manufacturing." *International Journal of Production Research.* 14 (1976): 123-135.

Hall, R. W. *Zero Inventories.* Homewood, IL: Dow Jones-lrwin, 1983.

Ham, I., and W. Reed. "First group technology survey." *Machine and Tool Blue Book.* 72 (1977): 100-108.

Honda, F., et al. *Group Technology.* Tokyo: Japan Society for the Promotion of Machine Industry, 1980.

Huber, V., and N. L. Hyer. "The human impact of cellular manufacturing." *Journal of Operations Management.* 5 (1985): 213-228.

Hyer, N. "The potential of group technology for U.S. manufacturing." *Journal of Operations Management.* 4 (1984): 183-202.

Hyer, N. L. and U. Wemmerlöv. "MRP/GT: a framework for production planning and control of cellular manufacturing." *Decision Sciences.* 13 (1982): 681-701.

Hyer, N. L. and U. Wemmerlöv. "Group technology and productivity." *Harvard Business Review.* 62 (1984): 140-149.

Hyer, N. L., and U. Wemmerlöv. "Group technology in the U.S. manufacturing industry: a survey of current practices." *International Journal of Production Research.* 27 (1989): 1287-1304.

Jacobs, F. R. "OPT uncovered." *Industrial Engineering.* 16 (1984): 32 41.

King, J. R., and V. Nakornchai. "Machine-component group formation in group technology: review and extension." *International Journal of Production Research.* 20 (1982): 117-133.

Levulis, R. *Group Technology 1978: The State-of-the-Art.* Chicago: K. W. Tunnell Company, 1978.

McAuley, J. "Machine grouping for efficient production." *Production Engineer.* 51(2): 53-57. 1972.

Meredith, J. R. "The implementation of computer based systems." *Journal of Operations Management.* 2 (1981): 11-21.

Rosenthal, S. R. "Progress toward the factory of the future." *Journal of Operations Management.* 4 (1984): 203-230.

Schonberger, R. J. *Japanese Manufacturing Techniques: Nine Hidden Lessons in Simplicity.* New York: The Free Press, 1982.

Wemmerlöv, U. *Production Planning and Control Procedures for Cellular Manufacturing Systems: Concepts and Practice.* Falls Church, Virginia: American Production and Inventory Control Society, 1988.

Wemmerlöv, U., and Hyer, N. L. "Procedures for the part family/machine group identification problem in cellular manufacture." *Journal of Operations Management.* 6 (1986): 125.

Wemmerlöv, U., and Hyer, N. L. "Research issues in cellular manufacturing." *International Journal of Production Research.* 25 (1987): 413-431.

Wemmerlöv, U., and A. J. Vakharia. "Job and family scheduling of a flow-line manufacturing cell: a simulation study." Working paper. School of Business, University of Wisconsin—Madison, 1988.

5

NORTHERN TELECOM TACKLES SUCCESSFUL IMPLEMENTATION OF CELLULAR MANUFACTURING

JAVAD TAHERI

Numerous success stories on the application of the world class manufacturing concept, such as "just in time," "total quality control," and "total preventive maintenance" are reported in literature. These stories not only fuel the interest in the application of these principals, but they also demonstrate that the concept is a never ending dynamic phenomenon.

The DMS-100 Switching Division of Northern Telecom undertook a major step in its continuous effort toward reaching world class manufacturing goals in the implementation of the cellular manufacturing concept for the circuit pack assembly and test portions of the operations.

Implementation of the project resulted in more than $2 million in annual cost savings from the reduction of overhead and work in process inventory, as well as improvement in throughput and quality. The project affected more than 500 people and involved the rearrangement of 60,000 square feet of factory floor with a modest capital cost requirement for material handling equipment.

Northern Telecom is a leading supplier of digital telecommunications systems. The DMS-100 Switching Division, with 2,750 employees in Research Triangle Park, North Carolina, is prime for building families of DMS-100/200 central office switches. A central office switch consists of a network of cabinetized modules (frames), each with several shelves of circuit packs. These switches are utilized by the Bell system as well as independent operating companies to provide communications services, such as telephone call routing to their customers.

Reprinted from *Industrial Engineering,* October 1990, vol. 22, no. 10; Norcross, GA: Institute of Industrial Engineers, 38-43.

MANAGEMENT COMMITMENT

To launch a project of this magnitude, with costs running in the hundreds of thousands of dollars and involving hundreds of people, requires the commitment of top management. Prior to investing significant amounts of time to develop a detailed proposal, a high-level management conceptual understanding and approval must be obtained. This will lead to creating a clear direction, policy statement, and framework for the project and eliminate any organizational barriers. This can only be achieved if management can see the "big picture" and understand the potential risk. A visual simulation is an invaluable tool to do just this.

For this purpose, a high level simulation model of the 1988 and 1989 layouts was developed, using SIMAN/CINEMA of Systems Modeling, that demonstrated the material flow throughout the plant and showed how everything was going to work together. To develop this model, we used some of the expected post re-arrangement results such as test yield and set-up times, estimated from the results of implementing a prototype cell earlier in the beginning of 1988. The animation of the simulation was used to demonstrate the proposed concept and expected results, such as the WIP inventory levels, throughput, and flow times.

DESIGN AND CELL CONFIGURATION

The process for assembly and test operations for building circuit packs lends itself to the cellular manufacturing concept. Some of the key factors that make cellular manufacturing sensible at DMS-100 Switching Division were:

- Packs can be partitioned into distinct product families, as explained below, based on volume, size, and technology.
- Certain pack types are required daily in large volumes.
- Work stations are standard, modular, and are fairly easy to move. A standard utility distribution panel installed on each work station has added to this flexibility.
- Most equipment types are standard, such as test equipment, conveyors, wave solders and cleaners.
- Typically, several of the same equipment types are available so capacity can be divided.
- The equipment is heavy but can be easily moved, installed, and running within a few hours.
- DMS-100 Switching Division is an "open factory"; no walls exist in the pack assembly and test areas.
- Northern Telecom culture is accustom to change.

GROUP TECHNOLOGY

To develop the cells, using the group technology concept, the packs were partitioned into three hierarchical aggregation levels based on size, technology, and volume:

1. Small (Line cards)
   1.1 High Volume Line Cards (Cell 1)
   1.2 Low Volume Line Cards (Cell 2)

2. Large Packs
   2.1 Multi-Layer (Cell 3)
   2.2 Double Sided
      2.2.1 Low Volume 10 x 12-in. (Cell 4)
      2.2.2 High Volume 10 x 12-in. (Cells 5, 6, and 7)

In addition to the above criteria, consideration had to be given to the test process requirements in order to provide maximum flexibility with no additional capital investment in test equipment. More specifically, the Double Sided Low Volume 10 x 12-in cell, referred to as the Specialty cell, can accommodate any of the packs from the Double Sided High Volume 10 x 12-in. cell (High Volume Cells for short). Furthermore, each High Volume cell can also accommodate several of the other packs. This provides a flexibility for absorbing some of the fluctuations in the production schedule by reassigning the packs to different cells.

U-SHAPED LAYOUT

The physical layout for the cells is U-shaped. One well known advantage of the U-shaped layout is that it provides manpower flexibility—it is simpler to move people around to balance the operations. In our case, however, the most benefit was gained from enhancement of the feedback mechanism between post wave test operations and pre-wave insertion operations, that are now back to back in the U-shaped layout.

APPLICATION OF SIMULATION

To analyze the proposed layout designs and the associated operational policies, a detailed simulation model for each cell was developed. The animation of the simulation models was demonstrated to the supervisors and some of the operators of the lines to incorporate their input in the design of the lines. This was very helpful, not only in developing more effective layouts, but also including supervisors, and in some degree operators, in the design phase contributed to the acceptability and thus the success of the project.

The models were specifically used for
- line balancing, determining the required number of manual assembly work stations,
- sizing the WIP buffer for each equipment type and work station,
- distributing the pack types to different cells,
- determining capacity levels,
- developing cell performance measures such as flow time, expected work in process inventory levels, and throughput.

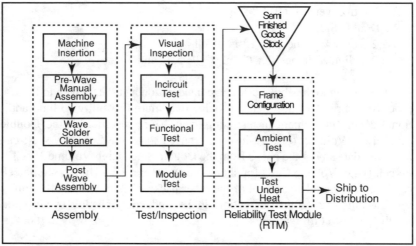

Figure 1. Overall process flow at Northern Telecom.

REORGANIZATION

One of the key factors contributing to the success of the cellular manufacturing concept is the fact that with the cells comes single point of accountability along with an emphasis on team performance.

Prior to the implementation of cellular manufacturing in the DMS-100 Switching Division, the linear process of pack assembly and test operation was segmented into resource centers which were also cost centers. Organizationally, they were considered as separate departments; transactions were required to transfer materials from one department to another, and they were also managed by different supervisors. With the implementation of the cells, one supervisor is responsible for the entire cell. Furthermore, the support groups, such as manufacturing engineering, were also moderately restructured to provide the necessary skills to operate the autonomous cells more effectively.

The emphasis on teamwork spirit and group harmony was one of the essential elements in post rearrangement problem solving activities. Furthermore, the flattening of the organization resulted in significant overhead reduction.

TRAINING PRIOR TO REARRANGEMENT

Training the shop floor operators prior to the implementation of the cells was another important contributing factor in the success of the project. In addition to introducing the concept of cellular manufacturing to the operators, several other objectives had been set for our training program.

- *Rumor control*—During the last quarter of 1988, Northern Telecom had announced several plant closings nationwide as a result of a simplification and cost reduction program. It was very important to control the various false rumors which could adversely affect morale.
- *Team Building*—As mentioned, decomposition of the factory and building cells necessitates a reorganization. In many cases the reorganization meant the breakage of relationships between supervisors and operators, some who had been working together for a long time. New teams had to be built and opportunities for new relationships and friendships had to be created.
- *Employee Morale*—Once the operators understood the concept of cellular manufacturing and developed a bond among each other, their excitement and enthusiasm generated the necessary post-implementation momentum that was essential in working on the uncovered problems.

To meet the above objectives, several factory-level reorganization gatherings were held by managers. In these meetings, the overall manufacturing strategy and the reasons behind the changes were explained. In addition, a two-hour formal orientation course was provided for all the operators, with operators who would be working together in the same cell attending together. The primary objective of this course was to introduce the people to the new organization and their new jobs and work place. The course also included an introduction to the concept of cellular manufacturing and continuous flow, where simulation and animation were used to show how the cells were expected to work and what benefits were anticipated.

FACTORY REARRANGEMENT

It is important to distinguish between implementing cellular manufacturing and implementing the rearrangement. Implementing cellular manufacturing

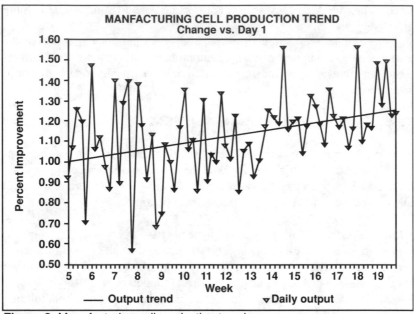

Figure 2. Manufacturing cell production trend.

is a continuous and evolutionary process while rearrangement of the factory is the step in which the stage is set up.

At the DMS-100 Switching Division, the circuit pack assembly and test operation portion of the factory is an open area. There are no permanent barriers or walls in the manufacturing area. The machines are heavy but relatively easy to move. The majority of the rearrangement took place during the Christmas holidays so that impact on production would be minimal. At midnight January 2, operations re-started very smoothly with only a handful of non-vital computer terminals and test equipment requiring additional attention. In addition, only a few minor deviations from the designed layout needed to be made. The smooth implementation was the result of excellent planning and coordination as well as daily visits by management to demonstrate their commitment.

POST REARRANGEMENT ACTIVITIES

The rearrangement of the factory was only the beginning. As was expected, coupling the processes and limiting the WIP buffers caused many manufacturing and quality problems to surface. The challenge was now to organize appropriate task forces with the right people and right skills to work on solving these problems, and to establish methods for exchanging information and communicating the current issues.

As one might expect, we did experience some confusion right after the rearrangement. This confusion was clearly evident from the feedback we received verbally, during daily cell meetings in the "communication centers" on the floor, and also through pages of written comments on the easels placed near each cell for capturing comments and suggestions. In the high volume cells, the difficulties were further compounded by a 20% increase in production requirements over the planned capacity.

Consequently, to bring the process under control and most of all to meet the business requirements several tactical and short-term decisions were made:

- To resolve the volume increase in the high-volume cells, two packs were reassigned to other cells.

- For a few pieces of equipment, the WIP buffers were enlarged to deal with equipment downtime and longer than anticipated set-up times.

- To control the degree of interruption in production, the implementation of the preventive maintenance program was slowed. (The combination of the size of the WIP buffers and the distribution of the downtimes was used to limit the impact of downtime and preventive maintenance to 2% - 3% of the throughput).

- Cross training that had started too aggressively was limited to a few skills to preserve the accountability for quality as well as capitalizing on the learning process.

PROBLEM SOLVING

The type of problems encountered varied in nature. Typically, problems were assigned to one of several Employee Involvement Teams (EIT). In addition to the cell operators, the teams included representatives from manufacturing engineering, quality, and maintenance. The meetings were normally held in the "communication centers" on the floor, and were facilitated by cell supervisors. A daily management review meeting was also held to provide guidance and to solve any "turf" issues.

Many of these problems were resolved by simply establishing proper communications. For example, the supervisors in the third shift were under the impression that the WIP buffers should be at the minimum level when the shift was over. With this in mind, at the end of the shift, the pre-wave operators were moved to post wave to flush out the WIP. The results being that at the beginning of the first shift, the post-wave stations were at a state of starvation.

This particular class of problem, although easily remedied, might have been avoided by more pre-rearrangement training.

The engineers were also responsible to review the comments on the easels and provide a written response. One of the reasons for documenting these activities on the easels was to capture input from all three shifts operators and also to inform everybody in all three shifts of any problems, thus eliminating any duplicated effort.

It is extremely important that every comment and issue be taken seriously and a response provided immediately no matter how trivial the question may appear to be.

CELL PERFORMANCE INDICATORS

To provide immediate feedback to each team, a set of performance indicators for the cells, such as WIP inventory level, equipment downtime, quality related figures and throughput, were posted at several locations in the cell. Considering that all of these indicators directly effect throughput, we used throughput as the key indicator to measure cell productivity representing the overall team performance measure. In the early days after rearrangement, the cells were performing only in a 50-60% range of the expected results derived from the simulation models.

PROCESS SIMPLIFICATION

One of the significant benefits of cellularization was to facilitate process simplification which was the key factor in reducing the WIP levels within the cells. The overwhelming portion of the process simplification was the result of the efforts of test engineering.

Within the first three months, test engineering consolidated the module test into functional test by increasing the test coverage of the automated test equipment. This eliminated one step out of the process. They also reduced test time by 50% by the elimination of some of the duplication between in-circuit test and functional test. On certain packs the in-circuit and functional tests are consolidated onto one piece of test equipment, resulting in only one set-up.

The results of the efforts of the DMS-100 cellular manufacturing team is shown in Figure 2 and shows the trend and rate of improvement for the first 20 production weeks of 1989 for the High Volume cells. Another interesting indicator that is not shown in this figure is the reduction of WIP inventory by 82% during this period.

CHALLENGES AND OPPORTUNITIES

At the DMS-100 Switching Division, there is a common understanding within operations that the DMS-100 world class manufacturing goal is to organize the plant into a set of hierarchical cells in which the packs are assembled, tested, and configured into frames as final products, and then tested and shipped to customers; eliminating the semi-finished goods inventory (Figure 3).

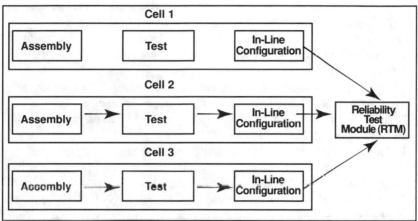

Figure 3. In-line configuration at Northern Telecom.

The 1988-1989 cellularization of the circuit pack assembly and test operations can be considered the beginning of implementing this strategy. As 1988 was the year for planning and developing the cells at the pack level, 1989 has been the year for implementation of this phase, as well as developing and implementing the second phase of the project, namely, the "in line configuration," which will be extended to 1990.

Several significant opportunities are expected.

• The most obvious benefit is the savings associated with the reduction of semi-finished goods inventory.

• As in the case of pack level test, it is expected that linking the RTM process and the pack assembly operation provides an opportunity to simplify the test process, resulting in significant savings in associated overhead and WIP; 75% of the work-in-process inventory in the plant is in this area.

• Since a significant percentage of the final products are configured for specific customer orders, any reduction in flow time through the RTM area will directly impact customer service.

The success of the cellular manufacturing strategy depends on the degree of flexibility that is placed on the planning and development of the operations system. Emphasis on flexibility produces a new set of criteria that must be incorporated in all levels of the decision making process. The majority of the challenge falls in this category. A few examples are:

• Organization structures need to be visited to eliminate departmental barriers and develop opportunities for team building.
• Human Resources and Operations Training need to work toward developing a flexible work force with an emphasis on job enrichment.
• In developing the test process for new products, the strategy should be working toward common processes, similar test equipment, and flexible fixtures.
• In selecting manufacturing equipment, considerations should be given to avoiding too many variations; thus simplifying maintenance.
• In selecting manufacturing and test equipment and fixtures, considerations should be given to set-up reduction.
• Rather than concentrating on reducing the re-arrangement activities, the emphasis should be placed on making the re-arrangement easier and less costly. This must be considered when selecting new equipment.
• Similarly, modularization and commonalty of material handling equipment should be considered. Avoiding any permanent and bulky storage medium in the factory.
• In developing the factory network, consideration must be given to the ease of adding or eliminating equipment or programs within the cells.

SUCCESS IS EVIDENT

The results have been outstanding: more than $2M in annual cost savings from the reduction of overhead and WIP inventory (by 82%), as well as improvement in throughput (by more than 50%) and quality (visual inspection by 70% and composite yield by 7%).

We feel that the results are proof of a success story for application of the world class manufacturing concept and philosophy at the DMS-100 Switching Division of Northern Telecom.

6

Cellular Manufacturing: A Good Technique for Implementing Just-in-Time and Total Quality Control

Helmut A. Welke and John Overbeeke

Cellular manufacturing is one of the best vehicles used to implement Just-In-Time manufacturing and total quality control. It allows for a total plan and acts as a way of tying all the strings together.

CIM technology can greatly enhance the effectiveness of cellular manufacturing, and it most certainly should be the long range goal for all manufacturing companies. The benefits that are derived from cellular manufacturing are becoming more evident as we gain greater knowledge and understanding of their behavior in the manufacturing environment.

Despite these benefits, there are many small businesses that cannot move as quickly toward CIM and group technologies as easily as the larger firms, due to the large capital investments required.

Yet the many advantages, tangible and intangible, of cellular manufacturing can be realized by firms of all sizes, no matter what their capital budget may be. Cellular manufacturing is the best technique available to achieve Just-In-Time manufacturing philosophies.

Manufacturing cells can be created in all areas of manufacturing. They have been very successful in the machining of primary parts and also with sheet metal and welding primary parts. Figures 1 through 3 are provided as examples of cellular manufacturing in various degrees of application. Some of the documented advantages of cells are as follows:

- Reduction in material handling
- Less scrap/improved quality
- More stimulating work environment
- Reduction/elimination of WIP storage areas
- Improve scheduling

Reprinted from *Industrial Engineering*, November 1988, vol. 20, no. 11; Norcross, GA: Institute of Industrial Engineers, 36-41.

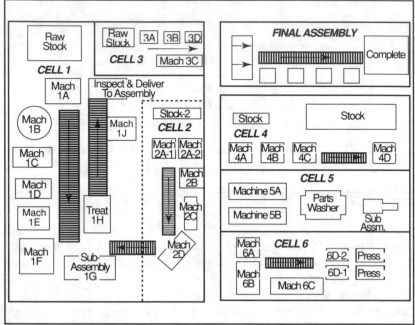

Figure 1. "Cells With a Cell" consisting of six cells plus adjacent assembly area.

- Greater flexibility
- Reduced lot sizes
- Reduced overall throughput time

DEVELOPING CELLS

Getting started in cellular manufacturing requires a long term commitment on the part of management, engineering and, most importantly, the shop floor. Some of the most successful efforts in implementing manufacturing cell required little or no investment in equipment. In the past, manufacturing engineers were always concerned with gaining the maximum utilization from a machine, particularly if the machine were new. This led to the effort of optimizing the machine load by obtaining as many parts that could be manufactured by the machine, regardless of how far away these parts had to travel or how far away their final point of use was.

At Deere & Co., the use of group technology (GT) has allowed engineers to group parts into similar part families by geometric similarities or part/product likeness. Once the families are established, machine requirements are then determined. The main goal is to identify and dedicate existing machines to the specific groups of parts or product.

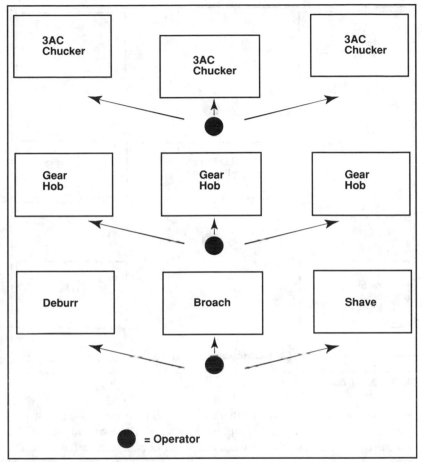

Figure 2. Typical gear manufacturing cell.

When a group of machines has been determined, they are then located physically next to each other, preferably right next to where the parts or sub-assemblies will be finally used. Setups are thus greatly reduced or eliminated. Careful emphasis must be given to the core business strategy of the company to help identify what products and components should be manufactured in house and what should be outsourced.

While smaller firms may find it easier to focus on their core business, many larger companies will need to perform a computerized analysis of all part schedules and routings. Generally, such an analysis will reveal that 20% to 30% of the total routed part numbers make up 90% of the total machine loads. This means that roughly 75% of the routed part numbers contribute 10% or less of machine load.

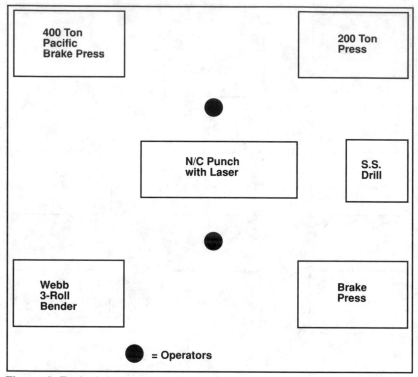

Figure 3. Typical sheet metal cell.

It is important to realize that these 75% of all parts can cause production interruptions and special expediting requirements. These are the ones to be considered for outsourcing. In most cases, an outside supplier will be the lower cost producer. These low value added parts are normally made up of service parts and special low volume options. If outsourcing is not a good option, a separate low value added cell is another method of removing them from the core business cells.

The parts and their necessary machines are "tied" together by conveyors or skids on wheels in order to minimize handling times between them. Instead of being organized by process, the machinery and necessary processes are organized by product or part family. Assembly line balancing techniques are used to stabilize product flows and reduce queues. Set-up reduction methods and locating tooling at the machine will also help. Some cells may appear crowded, but then the objective is not appearance, but rather reduced cost of manufacture.

The most successful efforts at implementing manufacturing cells included unified and well-defined objectives. At Deere, these were communicated and became goals for all members of the manufacturing team. From the very beginning, shop floor people need to be involved as equal team members. Cellular manufacturing puts new and sometimes different demands on the machine operators.

TAKING RESPONSIBILITY

Under this new environment, shop floor employees may be required to take on greater responsibility. In addition to running different types of machines in the cell, operators will need to do their own machine set-ups (if any is left) and material handling. Often, job scheduling within the cell is also left up to the operator(s) if there is a choice in parallel processes.

Since there is less inventory to act as a cushion, downtime can become much more critical. Preventive maintenance procedures must be carried out as part of the daily routine.

Once the objectives are defined, it is important that the team have full authority for implementation and authority for making decisions concerning the cell design and operation. It must be clearly visible that all levels of management—not just production and engineering—support the cellular concepts and the implementation teams.

Cellular manufacturing will impact the way in which all departments will function including purchasing, accounting, maintenance and materials management. (Steering committees made up of these various disciplines will enhance the effectiveness of the implementation teams.)

SIMULATION

Computer simulation has become especially popular in the last few years. Powerful hardware and the availability of numerous packages designed for PCs and workstations have accelerated the growth in simulation interest.

At Deere, simulation has long played a significant role in the planning of new manufacturing systems, especially of large systems involving conveyor systems and the interaction of many departments. Decisions concerning queue sizes (ex: overhead conveyor load bar accumulators), lot sizes and the number of transporters (ex: AGVs) all benefited from the analysis.

Today, we still rely on in-house experts that provide sophisticated models usually in the GPSS language. Animation add-ons have provided a method to "see" the proposed system in action. The animation allows the planning group to understand more of the interactions of machines or different product mixes and how they impact an individual cell or groups of cells.

INTERRUPTIONS' EFFECTS

When interruptions are introduced into the simulated system (as they invariably occur in the real world), the animation allows an understanding of up stream and downstream implications that often cannot be easily gleaned from columns of numbers in the simulation output. Strategies and specific procedures can then be suggested in advance that minimize the overall negative impact on the manufacturing system.

Another advantage of simulation with animation is during advance training. An animated picture on a CRT of a focused factory under construction was recently used by Deere to train operators, supervisors and maintenance crews. Since a large number of people were involved, numerous sessions were held to allow everyone a chance to "see" how the new manufacturing system would operate, how the "triggers" (kanbans) would regulate the product flow and what the impact of various disruptions would be.

Sophisticated simulations on large computers and the availability of programming experts can be justified on large projects. At the other end of the spectrum are the smaller, individual cells. In the past it was not cost effective to simulate small or even medium sized cells. Today, a number of PC-based, simulation "shells" are available that allow almost any engineer to bring the advantages of simulation to his own project no matter its scope.

STARCELL is a new software package for simulating a variety of manufacturing applications. A feature that makes STARCELL or any software especially attractive in cell design and operation is its ability to assign a variable number of operators to various portions of the cell being modeled. This is an important feature because keeping operator assignments balanced within changing schedules is considerably more difficult within the cellular manufacturing environment.

Queue sizes and transfer batches can also be easily limited to determine their effect on the cell; which, in addition to the usual cycle times, set-up times, and lot sizes, provide numerous combinations to be tested for the desired production levels and throughput times.

Figure 4 is an example of simulation output showing both the work station and operator performance reports. The cell modeled in this case produces high volumes of a single small part.

Fine tuning of the operation, with varying manpower requirements is facilitated with reports such as these because the engineer can see in advance where the opportunities are. The items to look for may include too much equipment capacity lost due to handling times and machine interference or poor work balances due to inappropriate manning of the cell.

As we increased our application of cellular manufacturing techniques, we recognized the need to involve employees at all stages of the project because it was *their* workplace that was going to change drastically. As the technological systems go through these changes, modifications to the human

WORK STATION PERFORMANCE REPORT -- Period #2										
	Queue Length			Station Utilization (Hrs.) in Period						
W/S No. # Mach	End	Avg.	Max.	Setup	Process	Hdlg	Intfer.	Idle	Break	Pieces Completed
1 - 1	93	63.82	126	0.0	5.4	7.0	3.6	0.0	0.0	4011
2 - 2	144	53.18	144	0.0	17.1	9.7	0.1	3.9	1.2	969
3 - 2	8	70.54	165	0.0	18.1	10.4	0.0	1.2	2.2	1031
4 - 2	58	53.85	124	0.0	17.4	9.9	0.1	4.4	0.2	988
5 - 2	86	61.61	141	0.0	17.7	10.1	0.1	2.1	2.0	1007
6 - 1	0	44.63	232	0.0	1.4	5.8	1.6	7.2	0.0	3906
7 - 1	0	35.18	121	0.0	0.1	8.9	1.0	6.9	0.0	3798

OPERATOR PERFORMANCE REPORT -- Period #2				
Operator Utilization (Percent of Time)				
Operator Number	Shift 1 (8.0 hours)		Shift 2 (8.0 hours)	
	Busy	Idle	Busy	Idle
1	75.30%	24.70%	74.75%	25.25%
2	62.44%	37.56%	59.46%	40.54%
3	63.17%	36.83%	66.51%	33.49%
4	62.66%	37.34%	61.60%	38.40%
5	61.78%	38.22%	64.86%	35.14%
6	62.96%	37.04%	58.53%	41.47%

Figure 4. Simulation output example showing work station and operator performance.

(or social) systems are often required if the new system is to reach its full potential.

Most of the technical changes have been mentioned already. Moving different processes close together will require employees who previously were in different departments to work more closely together. As they become teamworkers, their flexibility will also have to increase in order to maintain an assembly-line like balance when disruptions occur such as set-ups or a down machine.

Quality will also become more critical because parts that used to sit in WIP inventories will now go directly to the next process. The contribution of each employee assigned to the cell will become more apparent to all.

Regular team meetings of all employees involved should be considered both before and after implementation. Because teamwork is so critical, a group incentive of some type could be considered in order to reward employees for working together to achieve maximum throughput of quality products through the cell.

For smaller cells, with five or fewer operators, a bonus based on the total uptime of the cell could be considered. In a variety of cases, focusing the team's rewards on realizing the objectives of the cell is becoming an increasingly popular approach.

The role of the supervisor in a large cell or group of cells is also undergoing change. In large batch manufacturing, the supervisor of a welding or machining department often became overly concerned with running after parts from the previous department or looking for a particular load of parts somewhere in WIP inventory. Since cells will greatly reduce this need, the role of the supervisor becomes more of a product or component manager. He will have more time to be involved in helping to orchestrate continuous improvements in not just the operation of the cell but also the design of the product.

FUTURE CONSIDERATIONS

When a move is made to implement a manufacturing cell of a specific type and purpose within a company, normally the cell is constructed and based on products that are currently being manufactured. In order to maintain the health of these manufacturing cells, certain plans must be made as to how products can be designed to fully conform to the existing manufacturing cells and core processes (design for manufacturing).

A successful future of cellular manufacturing concepts is based on manufacturing becoming fully integrated with the design engineering function. New product designs in the future must be done in a manner that is aware of what "cellurized" processes exist to manufacture the new products. The use of computer aided design on engineering work stations linked to a group technology data base will be the basis for development of the manufacturing environment of the future. This will allow for information relative to part geometries and manufacturing processes within the group technology data base to be the influencing factors as to how the new parts will be designed and routed within a focused factory.

SUMMARY

Based on what we have learned so far about the changing factory floor, cellular manufacturing is the *key* tactic in achieving the twin strategies of Just-In-Time and Total Quality Control. A compact cellular environment with employees who feel ownership over the operation will drastically reduce lead times and inventories and almost certainly increase quality. Cells are increasing the opportunity for achieving flexibility in product scheduling as well as creating more interesting and variable work for all employees.

Cells' advantages can be achieved in all manufacturing situations—from small parts suppliers to the large integrated corporations. They can be applied in not just machining operations, but also in metal forming, welding, assembly and especially in various combinations.

The following points will be helpful whenever cells are considered:

- A well-defined objective and overall goal of the cell(s) should be identified.
- Management must make it clear to all employees that manufacturing cells receive their full support.
- Early involvement of all employees is critical. A proposed layout should be made available for study and critique. If one or more new machines are involved, take the future operator of the machine with on the run-off.
- Use simulation to fine tune the cell design early—and discuss the results.
- Keep lines of communication open. Include topics such as preventive maintenance, supplier information, statistical quality control requirements and inventory and sales information.
- If the work culture is appropriate, install a gainsharing plan or group incentive that rewards the employees for helping to meet the cell's objectives.
- Don't stop with individual cells. Focus the entire factory floor so that it becomes a cohesive collection of cells within cells.
- Strive to design future products with manufacturability in mind, utilizing as many benefits of your cells as they become available.

When the above items, and all other tools available to industrial and manufacturing engineers are utilized in a team atmosphere, we are confident that American manufacturing will continue to prosper and provide quality products to the world.

7

USING GROUP TECHNOLOGY FOR IMPROVING COMMUNICATION AND COORDINATION AMONG TEAMS OF WORKERS IN MANUFACTURING CELLS
DONALD O. KNIGHT AND MICHAEL L. WALL

G roup technology (GT) is often used to identify families of parts that can be manufactured by similar operations. A manufacturing cell of workstations and machines can then be organized for these operations, resulting in a much simpler flow of parts through the cell than with functionally-oriented layouts.

The group technology principle may also be considered to organize planning and control functions for the team of workers who operate such a cell.

GT BENEFITS

The benefits of applying GT to the organization of vertical manufacturing tasks can be compared to the simplifying effects of its current use for grouping horizontal production processes.

Often, manufacturing support functions such as manufacturing engineering, quality planning, materials management and production control are in separate organizations, resulting in difficult communications, coordination and help for the factory people. This inefficiency can be streamlined by decentralizing some of these functions to the individual cells.

Benefits of more autonomous operation can be greater acceptance of change, increased productivity and a more fulfilling work environment. But, as shown in Figure 1, responsibilities and goals must be allocated and knowledge must be available to the cell team. This article will explore some of the organizational, systems interface and decision support requirements for this autonomous operation.

Reprinted from *Industrial Engineering*, January 1989, vol. 21, no. 1; Norcross, GA: Institute of Industrial Engineers, 28-34.

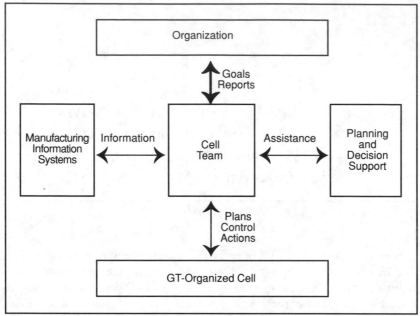

Figure 1. Allocation of responsibilities and goals.

ORGANIZATION NEEDS

Group technology work cells have already affected manufacturing organizations. Production supervision is often reorganized by GT product families rather than by functional process areas. The cell team workers may have more variety in their work by operating many different types of equipment in the cell.

The shop people also can feel a higher sense of participation and teamwork by seeing and being involved in a production process from start to finish. Finally, there is the potential for allowing the team to have more decision-making authority and management of the cell.

Indeed, manufacturing planning and control tasks are already being decentralized in automated factories as cost and time pressures force industries to streamline production support groups, train workers for a variety of tasks and act quickly when change is necessary.

Traditional scientific management theories of rigid organization structures, responsibilities and reporting procedures are being questioned and altered for these changes.

We assert that regimented, centralized decision functions and bureaucratic organizations will be extinct in automated factories long before the people disappear. Even when the numbers of people in automated factories shrink, those remaining become more important as their individual responsibilities grow.

The operators of a GT cell can most efficiently manage their area, plan their activities, control their processes, recognize problems and find solutions. However, organizational barriers must be overcome and information and support must be provided to execute these tasks.

ORGANIZATIONAL STRATEGY

An organizational strategy of increasing cell autonomy should decentralize all appropriate operational and tactical functions to the point of execution.

The strategy must also encourage, prepare and support workers to assume the planning, control and decision tasks. The tasks referenced in Table 1 are candidates to be allocated to workers as manufacturing organization becomes more simplified and focused.

Cell members with greater responsibilities must be able to interact with computerized systems to obtain information, solve problems and make decisions. Unfortunately, the current generation of factory floor information and control systems does not facilitate flexible information exchange during operator transactions. These systems may have excellent resource tracking, data collection and reporting capabilities, but are usually not designed to guide the users to decision support applications or to information in manufacturing databases.

The desirable computer interface to the workers is easy to learn, simple to understand and able to share the types of information needed during a session with a user. Improved graphics capabilities, input/output devices and object-oriented programming techniques provide capabilities to improve the usability of computer systems for workers.

Table 1. Tasks for the autonomous cell team.

- Cell layout consultation
- Production planning over the operational horizon
- Controlling resources, costs and performance
- Process planning and prove-in
- Quality planning and process control
- Methods development and workplace layout
- Time standards development
- Device programming
- Equipment set-up, operation and preventative maintenance
- Managing WIP inventory, handling and flow
- Determining work schedules
- Reporting problems and assigning corrective action
- Training and orienting new members

EXPERT SYSTEMS

Expert system (ES), or knowledge-based, capabilities can also help the factory floor system communicate with people and manage information needs, due to the ES ability to capture and reason with knowledge.

An expert system can improve the worker-computer interaction by maintaining customized worker interfaces, or user models, that characterize skills and typical needs.

Such capability allows the system to adapt the interaction to suit individual needs and proficiency, which can range from a worker who has very little computer exposure to an experienced operator who needs to quickly obtain information.

A dialog management ES module can interactively adjust the media and structure of an exchange based on dialog knowledge and the user model's assessment of ability. The dialog strategy can be structured to allow the user to experiment without advisement until receiving a specific query, or could provide unobtrusive advice, request for confirmation or an automatic correction.

Advice might be presented as an on-screen message, or the system might go directly into a tutorial or simulation mode to let the user learn the proper method. The dialog manager of a shop floor management and decision support system might also include some language parsing, speech recognition and speech generation ability due to the limited computer background of many factory people.

Utilization of many of these technologies can improve the knowledge exchange between factory people and information and control systems. However, the problem solvers and decision makers of the GT cell will also need some additional decision support and expert system capabilities to properly manage their operations.

DECISION SUPPORT SYSTEMS

As more logical tasks are allocated to the members of a GT cell, they must also be provided assistance for the increased responsibilities. A decision support systems (DSS) may be useful to help the factory-floor decision makers analyze complex situations.

Current systems are often computer-based and try to organize information, attributes and proposed solutions of a problem by using visual aids such as graphs, tables, algorithms and decision trees. A capable DSS would operate as an assistant in a typical decision-making process as shown in Figure 2. Now, we know of no available systems with all these capabilities for realistic problems, but there are available tools and techniques that can provide at least some of these functions. We will examine these tools after specifying some decision support requirements for the factory floor.

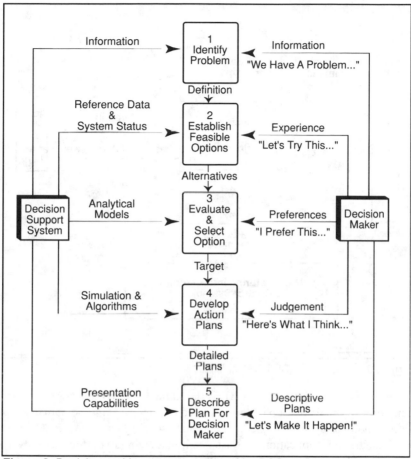

Figure 2. Decision-making process assisted by DSS.

DSS IN THE GT CELL

An effective set of tools for cell team autonomy must not only assist in making plans for the cell, but must also help alter plans based on the latest feedback. Interactive response, reports and analysis should be available for problem notification, structuring and input by the members of the cell.

The decision tools would preferably be accessed through work stations that are integrated with existing manufacturing information and control systems. Figure 3 provides a concept of such a DSS.

Expert systems can assist the decision-making process, especially for less-structured problems. A shop floor expert system can be used for consul-

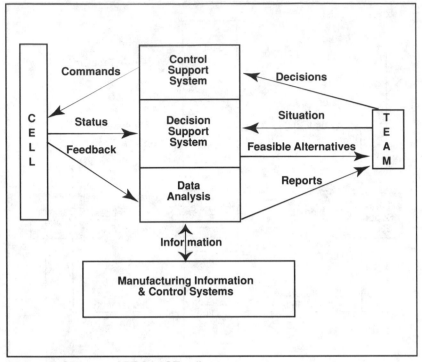

Figure 3. Concept of DSS in GT cell.

tation on non-routine problems when the human experts are not available. This ES can obtain and update its knowledge directly from the human shop floor experts or by accessing computer databases for facts.

Another ES application is assistance in managing the information overload that often occurs in dynamic factories from computerized planning systems, CAD/CAM data and data gathering systems using automatic identification devices. The ES would use rules to determine who gets what data and how it should be presented.

The following information and decision support might be distributed to shop people to maximize real-time control and decision making abilities:

• Attractive, easy-to-understand decision aids for planning, scheduling and materials management for the factory people.
• Ability to program, monitor and control processes from intelligent workstations with easy-to-understand output interfaces.
• Assistance for problem analysis and corrective action through DSS, ES and communication facilities.
• Status and feedback on work area performance compared with the overall goals from the higher-level systems.

Implementing these decision support systems to the cell people requires analyzing their tasks and getting them involved.

DSS IMPLEMENTATION

In a sense, decision support system installation is easier than other information systems because the system is usually built up from modules than can be changed in a less disruptive manner than large MIS programs.

The key implementation strategy is to involve the users throughout the design and implementation, since the system absolutely must be useful to the decision makers who are to use it.

The design of a manufacturing DSS should address these major development issues:

- *Type of decision maker*—expertise, ability, situation, personality, understanding of task, goals.
- *Type of problem*—frequency, urgency, causes, symptoms, outcomes, system context, organization issues, degree of uncertainty, solution criteria.
- *Support needs*—train, aid, solve, predict, data management, model representation, quantitative analysis, graphics analysis.
- *Evaluation criteria*—analytical evaluation, empirical results, effectiveness, productivity, speed of response.

A task analysis should be one of the first jointly conducted activities to define the problems and determine the types of support that are most cost effective and feasible.

These requirements from the task analysis can then be used to develop prototype models and interfaces which allow subsequent testing and refinement of the system to best support the user requirements. Concentration on prototype design provides a realistic and iterative approach to decision support system design.

SOFTWARE TOOLS

A DSS designer must take the requirements, design a prototype, evaluate the prototype with the users, modify the design and repeat this process until the design is acceptable. This approach allows the cell team to participate early and often in design of their system.

Fortunately, there are software tools available "off-the-shelf" that can be used to facilitate prototype implementation. Some packages have capabilities that might even be appropriate for the final system.

Many of these aids have data communications facilities and can be linked to the existing factory information systems. An integrated set of decision support modules can be applied at different levels of the decision-making process to provide specific, customized help while maintaining communications.

For example, DSS modules could develop effective operational schedules by interfacing with the plans and decisions of the tactical and strategic planning levels.

SUMMARY

Group technology provides the organization and simplification of parts and processes to allow product oriented manufacturing cells to be established. Use of this organization and the increased familiarity of the cell workers with the processes of the cell presents an excellent opportunity to distribute more control and management of cell operation to the cell team.

There are many organizational issues, computer-human interface improvements and decision support needs to be addressed, but the resulting work cell autonomy promises a much simpler, faster manufacturing system response.

REFERENCES

Bullinger, H. J., H. J. Warnecke, and H. P. Lentes. "Toward the factory of the future." *International Journal of Production Research*. 4(1986): 697-741.

Carroll, John M., and Jean McKendree. "Interface design issues for advice-giving expert systems." *Communications of the ACM*. January 1987, 30(1): 14-31.

Chen, P.H., and J. Talvage. "Production decision support systems for computerized manufacturing systems." *Journal of Manufacturing Systems* (2)1982: 157-167.

Hersh, Harry, and Richard Rubinstein. *The Human Factor*. Burlington, MA: Digital Press, 1984.

Nickerson, Raymond S. *Using Computers: The Human Factors of Information Systems*. Cambridge, MA: The MIT Press, 1986.

Parks, Michael W. "Expert systems: fill in the missing link in paperless aircraft assembly." *Industrial Engineering*. January 1987, 19(1): 37-45.

Sage, Andrew P., and William B. Rouse. "Aiding the human decision maker through the knowledge-based sciences." *IEEE Transactions on Systems, Man, and Cybernetics*. July/August 1986, 16(4): 511-520.

Shunk, Dan L. "Group technology provides organized approach to realizing benefits of CIM." *Industrial Engineering*. April 1985, 17(4): 37-45.

Turbin, Efraim, and Mehran Sepehri. "Applications of decision support and expert systems in flexible manufacturing systems." *Journal of Operations Management*. August 1986, 6(4): 434-447.

8

A FLEXIBLE MANUFACTURING CELL
FOR FURNITURE PART PRODUCTION
C. THOMAS CULBRETH AND DAVID L. POLLPETER

Since 1980 a dramatic increase in the use of computer numerical control (CNC) woodworking machinery has taken place. Almost all major furniture manufacturers utilize intelligent machines to produce furniture parts. These machines have been used as replacement for their more labor intensive counterparts. Limited work has been done to integrate CNC woodworking machinery and robotics into production systems, particularly in the form of automated systems such as flexible cells.

A research effort to establish a prototype flexible cell is now underway at North Carolina State University through the furniture manufacturing and management curriculum, a program within the department of industrial engineering.

THE FURNITURE INDUSTRY

The domestic household furniture industry has traditionally been a very fragmented one comprised of hundreds of small manufacturers. Through recent mergers and acquisitions, considerable ownership consolidation has occurred but the number and size of manufacturing facilities remain relatively unchanged. Factories tend to be very labor intensive and are set up to produce a wide range of products.

Furniture, like clothing, is a fashion industry that experiences short product life cycles. This causes the large part populations to be very dynamic, making automation difficult for most companies to justify.

Manufacturing efficiency is often traded for increased flexibility so that the broadest range of furniture styles and types can be produced. This flexibility is obtained by organizing the factory into a process oriented layout with

Reprinted from *Industrial Engineering,* November 1988, vol. 20, no. 11; Norcross, GA: Institute of Industrial Engineers, 28-34.

machine centers formed by grouping similar types of woodworking machines. Parts are then batched through selected machine centers until processing is complete.

Typically, each type of machine performs a single operation and parts with complex machining sequences travel the shop floor extensively. This results in long make spans, high setup costs and high levels of work-in-process inventory. The economics of this type of system become unfavorable as lot sizes diminish. Most furniture companies are actively searching for manufacturing systems that will reduce lead times and allow the economical manufacture of very small lots.

The development of flexible manufacturing systems offers the furniture industry a promising approach to automation. Since CNC versions of most woodworking machines are available and in use, the next step is to incorporate these machines into flexible cells. Such systems can economically produce furniture components in moderate-to-small lot sizes, while preserving the design freedom the industry requires. This capability will be necessary as the industry continues to face competition from off-shore producers.

PROJECT SUPPORT AND OBJECTIVES

The furniture cell project is sponsored by a consortium made up of the American Furniture Manufacturers Association, the Wood Machinery Manufacturers of America, the Woodworking Machinery Importers Association, the International Woodworking Fair and the U.S. Department of Commerce. In total, project funding exceeds one-half million dollars.

The research has two primary objectives. First, the automated cell is to be a fully functional prototype to demonstrate the feasibility of flexible manufacturing systems in furniture production. A number of related manufacturing technologies, e.g., CNC machining, robotics, machine vision and other sensory mechanisms, will be applied specifically to woodworking operations. The resulting production system will be just one of several possible types of flexible cells that could be created using woodworking machinery.

The second objective of the cell is to serve as an educational resource for students and as a technology transfer vehicle for industrial audiences. Workshops and seminars will provide an opportunity for furniture industry representatives to interact with and evaluate this technology.

Figure 1 shows the planned configuration for the cell, which includes:

1. CNC router
2. CNC boring and grooving machine
3. Six-axis, pedestal-base robot
4. End-effector system with quickchange interfacing
5. Machine vision system
6. Cell control computer

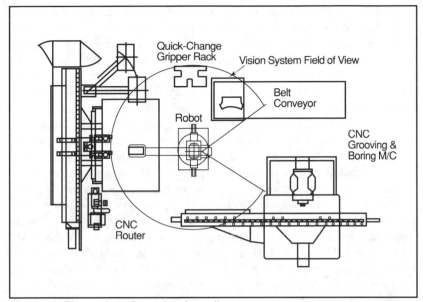

Figure 1. Planned configuration for cell.

Currently, the cell includes all the items listed above except for the CNC boring and grooving machine, which is planned as a later addition. The combination of these two machines will provide the processing capability to completely machine a substantial family of furniture components. Both of these woodworking machines have automatic tool changing mechanisms that increase the range of work they can perform without manual intervention.

The pedestal-base robot being used in this project has a maximum payload of 132 lbs. and a work envelope radius of seven feet. A large capacity unit was selected because many furniture components, such as tops and end panels, can be large and heavy. (Available space was a limitation in this project but it is likely that in an industrial installation, a gantry robot would be required to move large parts among several machines.) The unit has a repeatability of +.02 in. at maximum extension, which is more than adequate to perform parts transfer.

A primary reason for selecting this unit was the availability of a two-dimensional grey scale vision system already integrated into the robot controller. The integrated vision system consists of a three-board set included on the backplane of the robot controller and programmed via the same language used for robot programming. Thus, the effort required to integrate the vision system into the cell was limited to the installation of the lighting and camera systems and the calibration of the vision system viewing area to the robot coordinate system.

Machine vision was selected as the primary sensory mechanism for the cell since it offers the greatest flexibility for identifying and locating parts. The fashion nature of the industry results in a large, constantly changing part population with many shapes and sizes. It would be difficult to design hard (non-flexible) fixtures to achieve effective parts presentation for the robot. The vision system provides a workable method for dealing with the part diversity that any cell might be called upon to process.

The cell control computer selected for this project is a 32-bit workstation with 16 megabytes of RAM and 280 megabytes of off-line storage. All cell control software will be developed in C language, running under a multi-tasking operating system on the workstation. Real-time processes will be monitored through a digital I/O board with a two ms. response time.

Versatility was a major reason for selecting this type of computer as the cell supervisor. It can effectively function as a cell controller and also serve as a high-performance graphics platform. Prior to operating the cell, a CAD drawing file will be created for each part, and the numerical control programs will be generated directly from the drawing files using specialized software. In a factory, one computer would never perform both functions, but in an educational setting, this arrangement is quite appropriate.

PART POPULATION ANALYSIS

To effectively organize a shop floor into manufacturing cells, flexible or otherwise, the part population must first be analyzed. Part processing requirements and production quantities must be evaluated to identify potential machine groups and to map individual parts to the proper cells. Industrial classification and coding systems and certain clustering algorithms can assist in this process.

A sample part population containing rails, panels and open frames is being used in the project. An extreme variety of part types has been chosen since one of the challenges in this project is to design the proper gripping and fixturing mechanisms for the broadest range of parts. Figure 2 illustrates the sample part population.

By virtue of automatic tool changing, the two machines shown in Figure 1 can produce all the sample parts. In an actual factory-based cell, other machines might be added to the cell to improve machining efficiency. Space limits the current project to a two-machine cell, but conceptually it is no different than a larger cell.

The two machines included in the cell presented only one major fixturing problem. The boring and grooving machine processes parts in a way that requires no additional fixturing. The CNC router, however, needed an effective flexible part-holding system for its work surface.

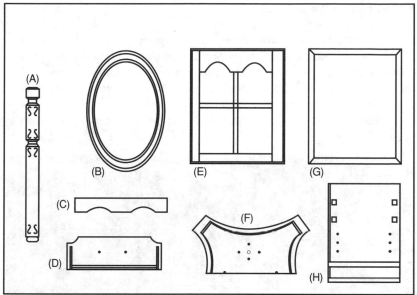

Figure 2. Sample part population.

Usually, these machines are equipped with a vacuum table on which a plywood or medium-density fiberboard fixture, called a waste sheet or spoil board, is placed. On the top surface of this sheet, a rubber gasket outlines the completed shape of the part and holes are bored through the waste sheet inside the perimeter of the gaskets. When the part blank is placed over the gasket, a seal is formed and the vacuum holds it securely during machining. These fixtures are not very flexible since they are normally constructed to accommodate only one type of part and must be changed manually.

The flexible router fixture developed for this project is a programmable version of the fixture just described. Each part has a dedicated location on the sheet. Thus, there are eight zones on the waste sheet where vacuum must be controlled. If a part is not located over its gasket, vacuum must be turned off to that zone or suction will be lost everywhere, causing the machine to enter a feed-hold condition.

Eight solenoid valves are located in the vacuum table under the waste sheet and flexible tubing connects each one to a zone on the waste sheet. A discrete input/output board in the cell control computer activates vacuum by turning on the solenoid valves in any pattern arrangement that is called for by the cell management software. Thus, parts can arrive and be processed in any sequence without the need to change the fixture.

END-EFFECTOR SYSTEM

If parts transfer is to be performed by a robot, a gripper or set of grippers must be designed to accommodate each part. It was decided to use multiple end-effectors and a quickchange device instead of a single multipurpose unit. The multiple end-effector system provides more flexibility in gripping parts and is less bulky. Three different end-effectors are necessary to effectively handle all of the parts. These units and the quick-change storage rack are shown in Figure 3.

Figure 3. End-effectors and quick change storage racks.

A multiple-cup vacuum device is used for handling panel stock. It has an array of 20 vacuum cups positioned on a frame made of aluminum tubing. The size of the frame is adjustable, as is the location of the vacuum cups on the frame. This type of construction allows the vacuum gripper to be reconfigured as new part shapes are encountered.

The cups are activated by solenoid valves controlled through discrete I/O lines from the robot controller. Different suction patterns can be turned on depending on the part that is to be gripped. Figure 4 shows the positioning of the vacuum cups overlaid on the outlines of each sample part it will handle.

The second gripper is a standard parallel jaw mechanism that will be used to handle short, narrow rail stock. Even this off-the-shelf gripper has a custom finger mounting platform that allows the manual relocation of the fingers. The gripper has a maximum travel of 4 in. and depending upon finger placement can handle part widths that range from .5 in. to 4 in., 3 in. to 6.5 in., or 4.75 in. to 8.25 in.

100

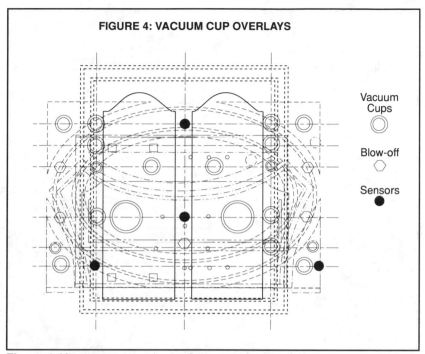

FIGURE 4: VACUUM CUP OVERLAYS

Vacuum Cups

Blow-off

Sensors

Figure 4. Vacuum cups and sample parts to be handled.

The other custom-engineered end-effector is a dual parallel jaw gripper unit with the grippers placed on a spreader bar. This unit is used to handle rails that are too long for the single unit gripper. It can also grip open frames by rotating the jaws 90° relative to the axis of the spreader bar. The gripper then picks up the frame by grasping two opposing rails.

The location of the jaws on the spreader bar is also adjustable so that open frames of different sizes may be accommodated. This particular unit requires manual rotation of the jaws or relocation along the length of the spreader bar. Both of these functions could be made automatic by adding linear and rotary actuators to the gripper. Each of the three grippers is equipped with one or more fiber optic proximity sensors that serve as part-presence detectors.

CELL CONTROL

The distributor control structure for the cell is shown in Figure 5. Although there is a hierarchy, much of the control is centralized in the cell supervisory computer which manages all scheduling, resource allocation and traffic coordination.

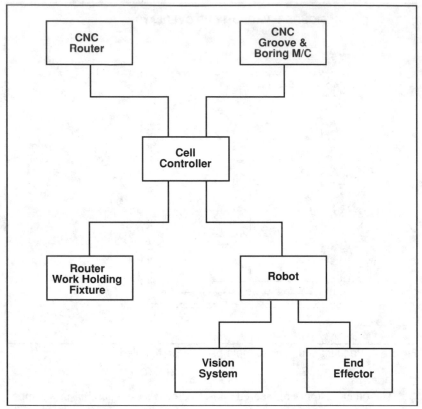

Figure 5. Distributor control structure.

A star network is formed via serial communication lines linked through RS-232C ports on the cell controller, the robot controller and the machine tool controllers.

Each of the machine tool controllers supervises its own machining activities once the host downloads a CNC program and initiates it. The robot controller supervises its own motions, although all robot activities can be initiated, suspended or terminated by the host. The vision system function of part identification and location is initiated by the host but all image processing is performed by the robot controller. All gripper control functions are handled through digital I/O lines from the robot controller. The cell supervisor is directly in control of the flexible fixture on the router table using digital inputs and outputs.

CELL OPERATION

The simplest possible operation sequence of the cell is shown in Figure 6. The cell would not normally operate in this fashion, but a simplified process allows for a brief discussion of the interaction of system components.

A part arrives at the cell on the conveyor. A limit switch stops the part in the field of view of the vision system. The vision system identifies the part and its exact location and orientation. Depending upon the preceding part, the end-effector may need to be changed, necessitating a robot motion to the quick-change gripper rack. The robot then loads the part onto the router bed and machining is performed. If the shape of the part is sufficiently altered by machining, a second gripper change may be required before the part can be offloaded.

Depending upon processing requirements, the part is either moved to the grooving and boring machine for more machining or is placed on the outfeed conveyor. Parts processed by the grooving and boring machine are loaded and unloaded at the same point, allowing the robot to remove each part and place

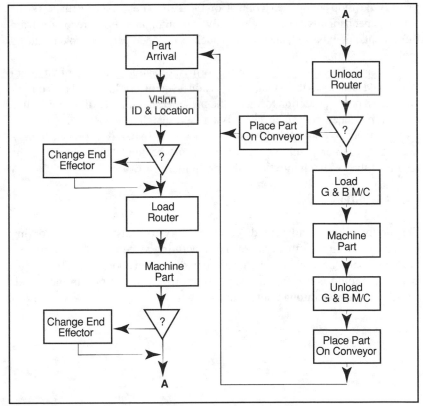

Figure 6. Simplest possible operation sequence of cell.

103

it on the outfeed conveyor. Space limitations dictate that a single conveyor be used for both infeed and outfeed of parts, but the material delivery system could easily be the deck of an AGV or some other device.

The simple sequence just described has only one part in the cell at any point in time. In normal operation, a number of concurrent processes would be active. Control of the robot then becomes more complicated as it tries to serve both machines so as to maximize overall cell productivity. At this stage of the project, it is premature to speculate about how sophisticated the cell management software will become in terms of overall process optimization.

RESEARCH OPPORTUNITIES

The cell configuration chosen for this project is but one of many that could be developed using CNC woodworking equipment. It is hoped that as the capabilities of CNC woodworking machines are expanded, the cell can evolve and incorporate the most advanced machine tool technology.

Considerable work beyond the scope of the initial project will be needed to fully develop automated control of the cell. The present cell lacks the sensory mechanisms necessary to allow for automated error recovery from infrequent, but expected, occurrences such as dropped parts or broken cutting tools.

Expanded vision capability in the form of dynamic guidance of the robot arm could assist in this area. The vision system could also be used for automated parts inspection to verify the presence and quality of the machined features produced in the cell. There is active research at NCSU and elsewhere on techniques to control the dynamic allocation of shared resources such as the robot/ gripper combination. Efforts must be made to incorporate the results of this research into the cell management software.

CONCLUSION

The prototype cell will provide a test facility to assist the woodworking industry in evaluating this type of manufacturing system. North Carolina is the leading producer of wooden furniture in the nation and having this facility at NCSU should aid in finding ways to improve productivity in the wood-working industries through automation.

SECTION III
JUSTIFYING INTEGRATED SYSTEMS

The articles in this section describe approaches to justifying the cost associated with new computer integrated manufacturing systems. Significant problems currently exist with traditional approaches to capital expenditure justification when applied to automated systems. Many of these problems center on the methods used for allocating overhead expenses together with the consideration of long-term strategic benefits from automation.

It is critical that companies recognize the importance of ongoing investment to ensure long-term competitiveness. Companies must recognize that reinvestment is required simply to maintain existing earnings capability. This is due to the rapid rate of deterioration of their current competitive position from technological obsolescence. The relative size of the investment in high technology equipment, together with the discrete nature of the investment, make these decisions difficult.

These decisions require a long-term view of the strategic needs of the manufacturing operation. Short-term pressure together with uncertainty of future business, make positive decisions difficult. From the selected articles, we see that the analysis required involves more that just populating a simple spreadsheet.

The key concerns today's managers have in making these technology-oriented investment decisions are the following:

• How long will it take to obtain a return on the investment?
• How profitable is the investment?
• How smooth is cash flow? Are sufficient funds available to cover expenses?
• How accurate is the analysis?

These concerns are addressed by many of the conventional approaches to justification analysis. Such techniques as payback period, break even analysis, present value analysis, internal rate of return, and cash flow analysis are all available.

These conventional approaches, though important, do not address the strategic issues which are vital to the long-term success of the company. Examples of some of the strategic questions which must be answered include:

• What are the features missing from existing products which are desired by our customers? How will adding these features impact our production process?
• How can new technologies impact the internal and external quality of our products?
• What is the nature of the advantages our competition is gaining through the use of technologies which we have neglected to implement?
• How can the use of new technologies change the way we do business with our customers?

Proper answers to these strategic questions ensure the long-term viability of a company. Further, they must be included in the justification of new technologically advanced equipment.

The articles that follow provide a review of the conventional techniques together with descriptions of how strategic issues can be brought to the analysis. The first paper written by Joel Polakoff, "Computer Integrated Manufacturing: A New Look at Cost Justifications," reviews all of the conventional models with an introduction to the more subjective and intangible strategic issues.

Two articles from the July 1988 issue of *Industrial Engineering* provide insight into the problems one must address due to current accounting practice. Ideas for how these problems can be solved are contained in "Corporate Accounting Practice Is Often Barrier to Implementation of Computer Integrated Manufacturing" (by Eric Bolland and Sally Goodwin) and "Indirect Costs Take on Greater Importance, Require New Accounting Methods with CIM" (by Dileep Dhavale).

The final article by Mariann Jelinek and Joel Goldhar, titled "Economics in the Factory of the Future," directly compares the assumptions made in justifying the technologies of the past with assumptions appropriate for new technologies. The article provides numerous examples of how new technologies have impacted not only cost, but also the strategic position of the company. Examples of how the strategic benefits can be evaluated are included in the article.

9

COMPUTER INTEGRATED MANUFACTURING: A NEW LOOK AT COST JUSTIFICATIONS
JOEL C. POLAKOFF

Have you ever attended a manufacturing trade show and watched a numerically controlled machine that could reduce direct labor and associated overhead costs by 20% to 25%? How about a live demonstration of computer-aided manufacturing/computer-aided design (CAD/CAM) illustrating its flexibility and potential cost savings due to reduced manufacturing cycle times and increased use of standardized parts? Have you attempted to convince top management of the virtues of implementing advanced manufacturing technology? Have your clients asked for advice on the subject?

This article details the importance of computer integrated manufacturing (CIM) for today's manufacturer and describes the traditional cost justification techniques used by CPAs in industry and their advisers in public practice. It also explains how to handle the strategic issues in manufacturing that are subjective and intangible.

WHAT'S CIM?

CIM generally refers to a network of computers and machines run by people to achieve optimal manufacturing productivity. CIM's complexity tends to increase the closer you get to a traditional, complex factory. Conversely, it becomes more simplistic as you move to a continuous factory or just-in-time (JIT) operation.

Exhibit 1 lists the pieces of CIM that are waiting to be installed and implemented in a manufacturing operation. According to the National Resource Council, the following potential savings are available from implementing CIM:

Reprinted with permission from the *Journal of Accountancy*, March 1990. Copyright © 1990 by American Institute of Certified Public Accountants Inc. Opinions of the authors are their own and do not necessarily reflect policies of the AICPA.

107

Savings	Function
5%-15%	Reduction in personnel costs
15%-30%	Reduction in engineering design costs
30%-60%	Reduction in overall lead time
30%-60%	Reduction in work-in-process
40%-70%	Gain in overall production
200%-300%	Gain in capital equipment uptime
200%-300%	Product quality gain
300%-3,500%	Gain in engineering productivity

Sound intriguing? If these are the benefits your company or your clients want from CIM, the first step is to explore the traditional cost accounting justifications to make that CIM machine a profitable reality rather than an unwarranted expense.

TRADITIONAL JUSTIFICATION METHODS

All approaches used to justify an expenditure of capital for new manufacturing equipment require a quantitative appraisal to determine the financial consequences. In essence, the idea is to discover if cash flow equals benefits less costs. Benefits are the projected annual savings; costs are the recurring operating costs; and the cash flow is the net income after taxes plus non-cash charges. The keys are to determine cash flow and how and when it will offset the initial expenditure. The basic questions to ask with *every* justification method are:

- *Benefits.* What's to be gained from the purchase of advanced manufacturing technology? Will additional sales or savings result? Quantify your answer.
- *Costs.* What's the upfront cost of the expenditure? What are the recurring costs such as maintenance and other expenses? Again, quantify the answer.
- *Opportunity cost.* What's the cost to the company for not making this expenditure? For example, if cash can earn 10% after taxes, the cash itself has an opportunity cost of 10%. Thus, if equipment is purchased for cash, the opportunity cost is 10% of the cost used to acquire the items. And the opportunity cost of equipment in use is the profit lost due to the unavailability of the equipment for other purposes.
- *Time value of money.* What else could the company do with the money? A capital outlay made in one year can't be compared directly with another year because time gives them different values. Thus, the cash flow stream for a new expenditure must be converted to a base year to effectively assign a time value to it. This cost of capital is what the company would pay to use the capital on an alternative purchase and it reflects the rate the firm decides it can receive from pursuing a different project.

Exhibit 1. What computer integrated manufacturing can do for the factory.

Advanced manufacturing technology will characterize the factory of the future. In this regard, computer integrated manufacturing (CIM) has many applications:

• **Order management**	Allows for faster delivery and responsiveness to customers and to customer orders through electronic data interchange (EDI). In essence, customers will secure and lock in supplier capacity for the product.
• **Computer-aided design (CAD)**	Allows the computer to assist in minute details and specifications of a customer order or to simulate variations of that order.
• **Manufacturing resource planning**	Allows the production schedule to be simulated and integrated using one information base to direct the operations on the plant floor to balance supply and demand.
• **Computer technology**	Allows different hardware and software to be integrated and to communicate with one another. Provides the foundation for both artificial intelligence and expert systems.
• **Computer-aided manufacturing (CAM)**	Allows for factory machinery to be programmed through numeral controls (NC), tape preparation, and computer numeral control (CNC).
• **Robotics**	Allows for the minimization of human activity in the areas of pick/pack, and excessive lifting, transporting and manufacturing operations.
• **Automated guided vehicle system**	Allows for driverless forklifts and automated storage and retrieval systems. As JIT becomes more imbedded in future manufacturing disciplines, the role of computerized material-bundling equipment will become more vital.
• **Group technology**	Allows for the coding and classification system to group various families of parts, to aid in both inventory use and part standardization.
• **Vendor scheduling**	Allows for improved scheduling of customer orders to improve delivery and internal processing. In the future, orders will be booked directly via EDI into a vendor's upcoming production schedule.

There are four basic techniques to determine what the "hard" benefits are from advanced manufacturing technology:

1. Payback period
2. Return on investment
3. Net present value
4. Internal rate of return

Let's see how each approach works in a basic example: Assume Acme manufacturing wishes to purchase a numerical control stamping machine for $50,500 to help control operating costs. The sophistication of this machine means no new annual operating costs will be incurred. The annual savings resulting from this expenditure are expected to decrease from $25,000 (overtime expenditures) to $4,000 over the four-year life predicted for the equipment. Acme set a 10% discount rate as the minimum return expected on investments. Therefore

Initial cost = $50,500
Annual recurring costs =   0
Annual savings = $25,000 (year 1)
                                        25,000 (year 2)
                                        10,000 (year 3)
                                          4,000 (year 4)

Estimated life =   4 years
Discount rate =   10%

PAYBACK PERIOD METHOD

The payback approach attempts to calculate the amount of time to recover the initial capital outlay for cash flows generated.

$$\text{Payback} = \frac{\text{Initial cost}}{\text{Cash flow}}$$

When the cash flows are unequal, the annual cash flows beginning with year one should be added and a determination made as to when the expenditure will be recovered.

$25,000 (year 1)
25,000 (year 2)
  500 (1st quarter year 3)
$50,500 initial cost

Therefore, payback is in three years. A general rule is if payback occurs within one-half to one-third of the equipment's lifetime, the purchase should be accepted. In this case, three years is 75% of four years; therefore, the proposal would be *rejected*.

RETURN ON INVESTMENT

Return on investment (ROI) is a ratio that attempts to determine the financial gain from the project compared with the initial capital costs incurred.

$$ROI = \frac{Benefits - depreciation}{Initial\ costs}$$

$$Therefore: Depreciation = \frac{\$50,000}{4\ year\ life} = \$12,625\ per\ year$$

$$Benefits = \frac{Sum\ of\ cash\ flows}{Estimated\ life}$$

$$= \frac{\$25,000 + \$25,000 + \$10,000 + \$4,000}{4}$$

$$= \frac{64,000}{4} = \$16,000\ per\ year$$

$$ROI/year = \frac{\$16,000 - \$12,625\ per\ year}{\$50,500} \times 100\%$$

$$= 6.7\%\ return\ on\ investment$$

Since 6.7% is less than the minimum requirement set by management of 10% on investment, a proposal using this technique should be *rejected*.

Exhibit 2. How to calculate net present value of a CIM investment.

Year	Savings	Costs	Cash flow	PV of $1	Discounted cash flow at 10%
0	0	($50,500)	($50,500)	1.000	($50,500)
0-1	$25,000	0	25,000	.909	22,727
1-2	25,000	0	25,000	.826	20,661
2-3	10,000	0	10,000	.751	7,513
3-4	4,000	0	4,000	.683	2,732
Total	$64,000	($50,500)	$13,500		+$3,133 NPV

NET PRESENT VALUE

Net present value (NPV) is a discounted cash flow method that relates the flow of monies and the timing of such investments over the life of the project. NPV attempts to adjust cash flows to base year zero in order to ensure that all funds are compared against the same benchmark. (See exhibit 2.)

In this case, the proposed project recovers all the initial costs; plus it yields an additional $3,133 return. Moreover, under this example, the 10% opportunity cost of the firm's capital is met. Consequently, the proposal should be *accepted.*

INTERNAL RATE OF RETURN

The internal rate of return (IRR) is that interest rate at which the cash flow stream equals all the costs of the proposed investment. The IRR technique requires a trial and error approach that finally hits on the solution. While more difficult to compute than NPV, its intent is to find the maximum rate of interest the project could pay on the investment—and break even. (See exhibit 3.)

Since the IRR is 13.73%, which is greater than the desired 10% minimum rate of return, the project would be accepted using this technique.

Exhibit 3. How to calculate the internal rate of return on a CIM investment.

Year	Benefits	PV of 1 at 10%	Discounted cash flow	PV of 1 at 13.73%	Discounted cash flow
0	0	1.000	($50,500)	1.000	($50,500)
0-1	$25,000	.909	22,727	.879	21,982
1-2	25,000	.826	20,661	.773	19,328
2-3	10,000	.751	7,513	.680	6,799
3-4	4,000	.683	2,732	.598	2,391
Total	$64,000		$ 3,133 NPV		0 NPV

JUSTIFICATION MYOPIA

As shown, these techniques offer the CPA a wide variety of options and result in different conclusions about whether to accept or reject a project. However, if you're using these techniques within your advanced manufacturing technology justification process, beware of their shortcomings:

- *Payback.* This technique gives only an indication of the time needed to recover an investment. The approach tends to consider only cash flows up to the payback period. It fails to look beyond that period to determine what future cash flows will or won't be. The payback method is best used as a device to determine when an investment will be satisfied rather than as an indicator of the potential value of an investment.

- *Return on investment.* ROI takes into account the depreciation of the investment over time and gives the user a better tool than payback. While the ROI approach can place capital expenditures with varying lives on a comparable basis, it doesn't consider cash flows. Thus, it is limited in evaluating long-term, large-scale projects. If ROI comes to less than 15%, time value techniques should be used.

- *Time value techniques.* Both NPV and IRR are better techniques than payback and ROI for justifying advanced manufacturing technology. Both methods consider all *hard* costs associated with the investment, including the cost of capital. With NPV, the user selects the alternative project that yields the highest net present value. IRR, as an extension of NPV, compares the proposed project's return with the discount rate appropriate for the company. IRR, in essence, ignores the company's current discount rate and determines the rate of return of the total cash flows.

Unfortunately, using these techniques and managing strictly by the numbers does not take into account the *strategic importance* of the investment to the company. NPV and IRR are geared to long production runs of standard products. Under CIM, however, manufacturing is geared to increased flexibility, improved quality and innovative expansion of products. Thus, accountants must rethink and refine these time-honored cost justification approaches. Besides the hard benefits calculated, each company now needs to add the *soft* benefits available under CIM.

JUSTIFICATION FOR CIM

The justification process for advanced manufacturing technology in a CIM environment must be viewed differently from the traditional process for three reasons:

1. *Project size.* CIM investments are projects without end. Investments made today eventually will be replaced by new technology. Most benefits from CIM accrue with time as advances in both hardware and software take hold.
2. *Project components.* Since CIM requires various successful installations of advanced manufacturing technology, benefits will accrue due to the synergism of various pieces on the shop floor. The integration of advanced manufacturing technology long term is what makes CIM a self-liquidating expense.
3. *Identification of CIM soft benefits.* The installation of advanced manufacturing technology in a manufacturing environment can provide significant intangible benefits that traditional accounting justification methods don't recognize. These include

   • Improved flexibility on the shop floor
   • Reduced manufacturing lead time
   • Faster delivery of new products to market
   • Improved product quality
   • A more skilled and better trained workforce
   • Improved product design
   • Optimal customer service

While these benefits may be hard to quantify individually, collectively they can both reduce operating costs and stimulate additional sales. The key to these soft benefits is to understand that a CIM environment allows for fewer levels of management and thus better use of corporate assets—both human and mechanical. The result to the company is improved decision making and significant improvement in profitability.

AT A GLANCE

• Computer integrated manufacturing generally refers to a network of computers and machines run by people to achieve optimal manufacturing productivity.

• The installation of CIM can provide significant intangible benefits, including improved flexibility on the shop floor, reduced manufacturing lead time, faster delivery of new product to market, improved product quality, a more skilled and better trained workforce, improved product design and optimal customer service.

• The first step in the cost justification process is to explore the four traditional cost justification methods—payback period, return on investment, net present value and internal rate of return.

• The payback approach attempts to calculate the recovery time for the initial capital outlay through cash flows generated. It's best used as a device to determine when an investment will be satisfied rather than as an indicator of the potential value of an investment.

• Return on investment (ROI) is a ratio that attempts to determine the financial gain from the project compared with the initial capital costs incurred. While the ROI aproach can place capital expenditures with varyng lives on a comparable basis, it doesn't consider cash flows.

• Net present value (NPV) is a discounted cash flow method that relates the flow of monies and the timing of such investments over the life of the project.

• Internal rate of return (IRR) is that interest rate at which the cash flow stream equals all the costs of the proposed investment in advanced manufacturing technology.

• Both the NPV and IRR are better techniques than payback and ROI for justifying advanced manufacturing technlogy. Unfortunately, using them and managing strictly by the numbers does not take into account the strategic importance of the investment to the company.

• While traditional cost accounting methods do not account for these benefits individually, collectively they can reduce both operating costs and stimulate additional sales.

• New techniques must incorporate long-term planning that pulls in the soft benefits available with advanced manufacturing technologies.

HOW TO GET STARTED

An investment in CIM through the purchase of advanced manufacturing technology must be looked at not merely as an accounting exercise but as a *strategic policy decision*. Remember, with CIM the traditional cost justification techniques provide only an appropriate starting point. It's important to approach the new manufacturing environment with a different perspective— a perspective that looks at the long-term benefits to the company using CIM. Here are four steps to follow:

1. *Investigate CIM alternatives today.* There are several advanced manufacturing technology options available that can make an immediate impact on company profits. Investigate them and take appropriate action. Waiting until the state-of-the-art technology becomes completely adopted within a market could cause your company or client to lose competitive advantage.

2. *Develop a CIM project team.* Pull together a CIM project team that will investigate and report the new technologies in the market. By staying abreast of evolving technology in manufacturing, you can strategically advise how to best allocate funds now for future growth.

3. *Realize CIM requires a long-term focus.* Always, when introducing CIM into a company, attempt to link together various aspects of the business. Realize the investment of advanced manufacturing technology requires risk, but that risk can be minimized when various aspects of the plant can be integrated into one long-term strategic process.

4. *Develop tomorrow's skills today.* The skills required for the adoption of CIM or the installation of advanced manufacturing technology need to be available for benefits to materialize. CIM requires a better educated workforce and a commitment by management that training will be budgeted and implemented. Only through the integration of man and machine can CIM be really profitable.

A NEW VISION

The factory of the future is around the corner. Short-term cost accounting justification techniques, while valid in the first half of the century, are losing impact as more and more plants automate their manufacturing process. New techniques must incorporate long-term planning that pulls in the soft benefits available with advanced manufacturing technologies. Without this vision of the future, the factories of tomorrow will be no more than a showcase for the indecisiveness of the past.

10

CORPORATE ACCOUNTING PRACTICE IS OFTEN BARRIER TO IMPLEMENTATION OF COMPUTER INTEGRATED MANUFACTURING
ERIC BOLLAND AND SALLY L. GOODWIN

There's an ambush waiting for anyone who thinks that a production process can be automated by showing top management the benefits of automation. Even the best laid plans for incorporating computer integrated manufacturing technologies into the work place can be thwarted by corporate practices and traditions that are so commonplace they are ignored by automation advocates. Yet they are there, and their longevity alone suggests their powerful influence on corporate decision-making concerning computer integrated manufacturing.

More recently, as firms recognize that they must automate production to compete in the world market, the difficult obstacle of current practice remains to be overcome. In many cases, the greatest challenge to automation is not external but internal, and, unless those who want to automate understand and defeat this obstacle, the effort to incorporate automation is doomed from the start.

BARRIERS TO AUTOMATION

The troublesome barrier to automation in this instance is traditional cost accounting. By this, it is meant all those accounting activities which are aimed at three primary outputs: to produce pricing information, to provide inventory values and to control costs.

Costs, revenues, productivity and profit information are additional objectives. Since these are crucial pieces of information to any company, financial activities are understandably important.

Still, how the financial information is interpreted is equally crucial. Readers are likely quite familiar with instances in which a cost reduction

Reprinted from *Industrial Engineering,* July 1988, vol. 20, no. 7; Norcross, GA: Institute of Industrial Engineers, 24-26.

effort led to lower quality end products.

Cost accounting can be misused if emphasis on improving one measure ultimately results in overall product degradation. It can be misused in determining if an automation investment should be made as well, especially if simple, single measure financial analysis tools are used to decide if an automation investment should be made or not.

These simple tools generally fail to detect and measure the many benefits of automation. This article will review the evolution of cost analysis techniques and introduce a recommended method, net present value cost benefit analysis. The basic steps necessary to do this kind of analysis will also be described.

SIGNIFICANT OBSTACLES

Just how significant is the cost justification barrier as viewed by managers and production heads?

We recently posed this question to a number of our business associates and discovered that an inability to financially justify a computer integrated manufacturing investment dominated other concerns such as expense, risk, lack of interest and a poor understanding of computer integrated manufacturing as an explanation for not going ahead with an automation project. We believe this is an indication of the depth of a very significant obstacle to automation.

The problem reflects a conflict between disciplines as much as methodologies. Finance and engineering personnel clearly have different types of education. Financial analysis tools are not familiar to engineering managers. The opposite is also true. However, engineering managers should know something about cost analysis techniques and the origin of these methods to better make their cases for automation to corporate management. Without this understanding, they may be at odds with their own finance departments.

Put in mechanical context, the prospective robot arm may cross swords with the accountant's sharpened pencil. In this situation, many a prospective automation project has been cut down because engineering managers have been unfamiliar with the language and techniques of cost analysis.

A major explanation for differing perspectives on cost justification of automation projects is historical. Accounting systems were well established before automation became a production factor. The older accounting systems did not anticipate automation and, consequently, treated automation investments the same way any other investment was considered. These systems were fully in place four decades ago and they were aimed at measuring mass production of few, very uniform goods where the cost of labor was the major component.

Modern production has been radically transformed from earlier times. These changes include greater foreign competition, shorter product life cycles, lower unit labor costs, rapid technological change and the introduction of flexible manufacturing systems.

IMPACT ON COSTS

All of these factors have had an impact on manufacturing costs. The most dramatic impact may be in the changes between overhead costs and direct labor costs. As shown in Figure 1, overhead now dominates as a part of value added. This change means that the high cost element of manufacturing is in equipment, not labor.

For those intent on introducing computer integrated manufacturing, there is a special challenge in justifying the high initial cost of automation equipment and the financing of the automation investment. It is at this stage where the most traditional and most popular financial analysis tools fail to help the manager argue for the investment.

The two most popular tools, payback and average rate of return, tend to disfavor very large, risk-prone investments such as automation systems where the cash benefits come back slowly over time and cannot be easily measured.

There are other problems with these methods as well. Payback, which is obtained by dividing the initial investment by the annual cash inflows from use of the equipment, ignores any benefits past the period in which the costs are recovered.

If the equipment is "paid back" in 10 years, eleventh year and beyond benefits are not included. It also ignores the timing of the cash inflows from the investment. When you obtain a cash inflow is as important as if you get it at all.

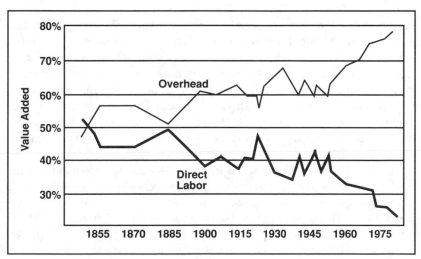

Figure 1. Overhead dominating as value added element.

119

Average rate of return on investment is the most popular and traditional tool. It is obtained by dividing yearly cash inflows from an investment by the investment cost. It is expressed as a percentage and does have the advantage of relating cash benefits to the investment. But, like payback, it ignores the timing of the cash inflows. Also, the scale of the investment is not figured in.

A low cost automation project may have a higher rate of return than a higher cost project. In a strategic evaluation, the higher cost project may be desirable, however, even though it may be eliminated on a cost analysis basis.

BEST TECHNIQUE

Automation investments are best analyzed by using discounted cash flow techniques which incorporate the idea that benefits derived from automation must be adjusted by the cost of capital for the company, tax impacts and cost of financing the investment. This offers a more realistic picture of the present and future costs and benefits of an automated system.

Discounted cash flow takes into account the amount and timing of cash inflows from an automation investment so it is superior to payback and rate of return. Because it produces a single figure, the total of cash inflows and outflows over the lifetime of the equipment, produces a much more precise measure of the worth of an automation investment. This dollar figure can be compared to other corporate investment opportunities and an optimal investment choice can be made.

One discounted cash flow method, which has been used effectively to determine if an automation investment should be made, is the net present value cost-benefit analysis. This method is far less complex than it may sound.

To do this, the costs and benefits of an automation investment are placed along a horizontal line. They are put on the line when they occur. The benefits of the automated system are calculated and shown as cash inflows. These might be the annual labor cost savings from automated equipment, annual scrap reduction savings, inventory cost savings, product quality savings and utility savings. These annualized benefits are added to the tax benefits (depreciation plus interest at the corporate tax rate) and the total is summed on a year by year basis. Principal and interest payments are shown the same way as cash outflows.

It should be noted here that this instance assumes the automation equipment is paid for with borrowed money. The difference is found between cash inflows and outflows and the present value interest factor is applied to each year's cash total. The present value interest factor is found in finance texts. It is related to the company's cost of capital and length of time. The adjusted yearly cash flows are then summed to produce a net present value dollar value for the automation investment.

120

The result of the analysis can be compared to a similar analysis which calculates the net present value of continuing current operations. If the net present value of the new automation system exceeds current operations, then the new system should be adopted.

The net present value cost benefit analysis can also be used to compare different courses of action. For example, a $300,000 automated machine could be compared with a $200,000 control system. The alternative with the greatest net present value would be selected.

CRITICAL STEPS

There are a few critical steps in this process. One is selecting the right discount rate to be used. This can be done in consultation with your finance department.

Another important step is the translation of automation benefits into yearly cash flows. Suppliers can help project these cash flows but you must be cautious about overly optimistic projections. Another important factor in the analysis is the lifetime of the equipment.

The cash inflows and outflows are paced over the equipment's useful life. This lifespan can be obtained from prospective suppliers. You can also obtain initial cost figures for equipment from the supplier.

The computation of the net present value involves figuring a loan amortization schedule if the purchase is financed so that year-by-year interest payments can be calculated for tax benefit purposes. Next, the yearly tax benefits are calculated (interest plus depreciation) and then the time line is set up with yearly cash inflows and outflows.

Once the basic information is obtained, the calculations are straightforward. Engineering managers can use a sophisticated and proven financial analysis tool to justify automation projects.

Net present value cost benefit analysis also works well with modern production methods and is clearly better than popular but deceptive alternatives such as payback and rate of return.

AN EXAMPLE

The three methods mentioned here all produce very different results. This is true even if the same amount is invested in automation equipment in every case. For example, suppose that $300,000 is invested in an automation cell. If the investment is financed at an interest rate of 10%, the useful life is ten years, the corporate tax bracket is 34% and the annual depreciation is $30,000, then the results are as follows:

1. Payback = 10 years
2. Average rate of return = 10.5%
3. Net present value = $147,780 (at 15% discount factor)

Same investment, three different answers. Which method should be used? Method three is the most rigorous. It is the recommended alternative.

11

INDIRECT COSTS TAKE ON GREATER IMPORTANCE, REQUIRE NEW ACCOUNTING METHODS WITH CIM

DILEEP G. DHAVALE

M anufacturing overhead, or factory burden, has often been misunderstood by factory personnel. In the past, this "necessary evil" has represented only a small portion of the total manufacturing cost. With the advent of computer integrated manufacturing systems (CIMS), however, this is no longer the case.

Manufacturing has undergone significant changes in the last few years, and studies indicate that the trend is for change to continue at a rapid rate into the nineties.

However, the people who keep track of how well the manufacturing department is doing or how much it costs to make a superduper widget or a run-of-the-mill widget essentially have not changed their methods of tracking cost since the methods were first used—at the turn of the century. Obviously, the manufacturing technology and competitive environment that existed at the turn of the century or even later were dramatically different from what exists today.

This continued use of outdated accounting methods in CIMS environments makes the resulting overhead numbers particularly misleading at a time when the very survival of many companies will depend on accurate and realistic data being available to managers who make important decisions on equipment purchases, product discontinuation, product pricing, sales promotion, etc. In today's fiercely competitive manufacturing environment, there is no room for errors, especially errors that could have been avoided by using better cost accounting methods.

To understand the problem of inaccurate overhead in CIMS, let us recall that the cost of manufacturing a product has three components: (1) direct labor; (2) direct material; (3) all other costs, or manufacturing overhead. The

Reprinted from *Industrial Engineering*, July 1988, vol. 20, no.7; Norcross, GA: Institute of Industrial Engineers, 41-43.

direct labor and material costs can be determined from work tickets and material requisition forms, respectively.

To determine the amount of overhead to be charged to any job, first all components of the overhead—such as indirect labor and material, depreciation of factory machinery and buildings, utilities, insurance and taxes, allocated costs from service departments, and factory administration and supervision—are accumulated in one pool and distributed to each job based on the number of hours of direct labor used in processing the job.

This approach of computing each product's share of the overhead cost is totally inadequate in an automated manufacturing setting. In conventional job shops, the overhead measured as percentage of total manufacturing cost is relatively small, anywhere from 10 to 40%. However, the overhead becomes the largest of the three components in CIMS because of the higher depreciation costs of numerical control (NC) machines, computers, microprocessors, automated transportation systems, etc.

In addition, the direct labor requirements of a CIMS are substantially lower than those of a job shop. This helps to push the percentage of overhead even higher, to the range of 70 to 90% of total manufacturing costs.

Not only are the direct labor hours reduced in a CIMS, but they are no longer easily identifiable and assignable to the jobs. One of the advantages of a CIMS is the flexibility of lot sizes. No longer is it necessary to process lots in predetermined sizes. Instead, lots of any size, even size one, can be launched if there is a need.

Processing on an NC machine can be in any order as long as the machine is equipped with appropriate tools in its magazine and the job does not need any special dies or jigs, etc. An operator may be assigned more than one machine to tend at a time.

It is easy to see why operators find it very difficult to allocate their time correctly to different units of different jobs being processed simultaneously on different NC machines under their control.

This all means that in a CIMS even the smallest error made in properly assigning direct labor hours is magnified several times in computation of the overhead. Note that direct labor hours required with a CIMS are much fewer than in a job shop; in addition, the overhead pool is much larger in a CIMS. Hence each direct labor hour now carries a much, much larger amount of overhead charge with it.

There is, however, a more fundamental argument against direct labor hours being used as allocation base for the overhead. Compare two machines, one an expensive machine and the other a low-cost machine. The expensive machine will add a larger amount to the overhead pool due to high depreciation expense, and also consume more overhead resources in the form of maintenance, indirect material, power, etc. The higher price of the expensive machine may be due to a higher production rate and/or more automation (i.e., less direct labor) and/or greater precision. For the sake of comparison, assume the higher price is due mainly to automation. Then it is clear that the expensive machine will consume more overhead resources, but since it uses fewer direct labor hours, it will be charged (or the jobs processed on it will be charged) less overhead than the low cost machine.

This of course is totally inappropriate and unfair. The low cost machine is subsidizing the jobs manufactured on the expensive machine, because those jobs are allocated artificially low overhead.

On the other hand, the jobs on the low cost machines are charged higher overhead than they should be. This problem is further exacerbated if machines of totally different direct labor usage characteristics, such as NC and conventional machines, are put in one single overhead pool.

The above discussions provide us with the following pointers about how overhead should be computed:

• Stop using plant-wide overhead pools; instead, accumulate overhead cost into smaller pools. Ideally, overhead should be pooled for each machine center. Recent studies report many companies still continue to use plant-wide or large department-wide pools.

• Stop using direct labor hours as the allocation basis for overhead cost. Consumption of the overhead items in a CIMS does not depend on the number of direct labor hours used. In fact, that relationship is inversely proportional. The continued use of direct labor hours will totally distort the overhead allocation.

Instead of direct labor hours, machine hours would be an appropriate allocation basis, especially when the overhead costs are pooled by the machine centers. Again, studies report that companies continue to use direct labor hours to allocate overhead costs.

• Direct labor hours and their cost are no longer significant in most CIMS. The direct labor cost should be made part of the overhead. Then the manufacturing cost would have only two components, direct material cost and transformation cost. The transformation cost includes all other manufacturing costs, including direct labor cost.

Changing the name from overhead to transformation cost would be advisable to eliminate misconceptions about the overhead cost. Furthermore, the term "transformation cost" correctly describes the nature and purpose of the cost pool.

Overhead costs are no longer insignificant compared to direct labor and direct material costs, and can no longer be ignored and treated lightly. In a CIMS the overhead cost is the largest component, usually much bigger than the sum of the two direct costs. It is essential that the overhead costs be accurately allocated to products so that product cost can be correctly determined. Accurate product costing data will help managers make better decisions about product mix and efficient use of expensive manufacturing equipment so that their companies can prosper in highly competitive manufacturing markets.

12

ECONOMICS IN THE
FACTORY OF THE FUTURE
MARIANN JELINEK AND JOEL D. GOLDHAR

One factor delaying the implementation of computer-integrated manufacturing is a great gap in economic thinking. Much present-day thinking about production economics rests firmly on assumptions built into the economies-of-scale notion and leaves out any real consideration of potential diseconomics of scale. Even more important, such thinking ignores advances in technology and strategic imperatives. Both are crucial for properly evaluating the revolutionary impact of computer integration in manufacturing.

The new production economics grows directly from the economies-of-scope logic. Where the economies-of-scale logic emphasizes stability and change, the economies-of-scope logic stresses flexibility and integration. This article outlines some key features of the new economics relating to productivity, quality, flexibility, and international competition—features that must be taken into account for sensible evaluation of advanced technologies. The authors also suggest some ways to assess CIM benefits.

Today's managers have grown up under a strict discipline based on economies of scale: it's thought that bigger is better in virtually any circumstance. For the better part of a century such ideas seemed valid in the U.S., and many other countries followed the U.S. example. Perhaps more important, the development of technology has been guided by assumptions of economies of scale, encouraging profitable rigidity and discouraging expensive change. And standard evaluation criteria like return on investment (ROI) payback and net present value (NPV) typically assume that change involves replacement of individual machines an assumption that reinforces the short-term focus because it permits consideration only of incremental, additive benefits. This limited incremental change is characteristic of the older systems and their mature technologies.

Reprinted from the Winter issue of *CIM Review* (New York: Auerbach Publishers).
© 1986 Warren, Gorham & Lamont Inc. Used with permission.

The widespread application of computers and communications technology—in the form of computer-aided design/computer-aided manufacturing (CAD/CAM) computer-aided engineering (CAE) and CIM systems—to manufacturing changes the fundamental nature of the factory however. Because the factory's capabilities, constraints, and economics are changing, methods of evaluating equipment for replacement also must change. Comparing the characteristics of older technologies with those of newer ones will highlight the difficulty.

OLD-FASHIONED ECONOMICS

Traditional economies-of-scale thinking assumes that per-unit cost automatically decreases as factory size increases (i.e. that bigger is better). Because change is expensive, older factories encourage standardization, central control, and stable, unchanging products with long production runs. Stability and resistance to change become the norm for production. Because factories and production processes changed slowly for years, such stability is assumed to be good.

In the stable environment typical of older factories (and the vast majority fall into this category) variable costs are emphasized often to the exclusion of other costs. Inventory is used as a buffer for uneven demand, smoothing production and protecting against input disruptions. Because long production runs are seen as desirable, few product variants are produced. Such thinking led to calls for a world-standard car for instance, and for extensive product standardization and worldwide homogeneity as markets became increasingly global.

However, increases in scale entail costs. Holding inventory is expensive. Long production runs carry the costs of such activities as coordinating production activities and distributing products. Larger plants are more vulnerable to accidents, supply disruption, product obsolescence, and technological change. For example a large factory is more difficult to manage, simply because it covers more floor space. And because more employees typically are involved, communication and supervision become more difficult.

Even more important are issues of survival. Though today's economy is increasingly global, markets are not standardized, but increasingly specialized and fragmented. Product life cycles are shorter, and products change more frequently. Global competitors have relatively free access to markets around the world—so domestic markets on virtually every continent are increasingly held to global standards for quality, cost, product design, and competitive production technology. The minimum standard performance required for survival is substantially higher than it was a few years ago.

A large inventory stored for future use may become obsolete before it can be sold. Perhaps more important, rigidly specified equipment that is incapable of responding to changing needs may quickly become worthless. A massive commitment to older-style, rigid production equipment designed to run high volumes represents substantial risk. It assumes that the product will be in demand long enough to amortize the equipment costs and that newer methods will not supersede the equipment or its economics. An excellent example of this problem is the expenditure of millions by U.S. automakers on single-purpose high-volume, equipment, which locked them into unchanging products and processes. Because the cost of the equipment was so high and changing it so difficult, the automakers were very slow to respond to changing tastes and demands, with serious consequences for market share and cost positions.

Fundamental Assumptions

Economies of scale assume that changeover costs are high and therefore to be avoided; thus, longer production runs of standard products will lower per-unit cost and rigid manufacturing makes sense. Actual costs for changing over include lost production; the time and money required to physically shift the equipment and adjust, clean, and reset it; and additional waste incurred in fine-tuning equipment after it has been reset. It is ordinarily assumed that once equipment is set up, continued running will be more economical than changeover. This assumption largely ignores the additional costs of long production runs discussed.

Traditional financial measures for evaluating proposed investments in advanced production equipment reflect these basic assumptions. The short-term biases of ROI, payback, and NPV are built in but often unnoticed. Accounting methods that treat fully depreciated equipment as having little or no fixed cost reward the manager who continues using the equipment, in effect discouraging efforts to upgrade and replace older equipment with advanced technology. Typically, new equipment costs more and its benefits are future benefits.

Unfortunately, traditional accounting methods that consider the time value of money give little or no consideration to the strategic opportunities and threats that technological advances present. Such methods are based on the assumption that money in hand is worth more than money promised in the future. By implication, a cost deferred is preferable to a cost incurred. Although this is often true and sometimes useful, the concept is often extended to a point where present activities are seen as bearing little or no risk and new activities are seen as risky. Such views form the basis of economies-of-scale thinking, and they inhibit change. Put bluntly, although advanced technologies offer life-saving advantages for mature industries, traditional financial analysis criteria assume the new equipment simply does a little more a little faster.

Replacement-trigger thinking—the notion that equipment should be replaced only when worn out or unworkable—adds to the difficulty. Unfortunately, advanced automation equipment usually cannot be legitimately evaluated machine for machine. Such equipment doesn't just do old things better; often it does entirely new things or does old things in completely new ways. Thus, the full benefits of automation technology can be appreciated only through evaluation of entire systems. The important advantages of factory automation equipment—vastly increased flexibility and opportunities for responding to changes in material availability, product design, or product mix demand—all constitute important exceptions to replacement-trigger thinking. In short, it may be irrelevant whether existing equipment is still operative or has further depreciation life.

The islands-of-automation approach grows in part from replacement-trigger thinking and extends the add-a-little, change-a-little mentality of incremental advancement. If only small advances in such measures as productivity, utility, and quality are to be expected, such an approach is reasonable. But technological change today offers orders-of-magnitude shifts. Because manufacturing management continues to focus on individual machines, the overall view of the manufacturing system is missed, as are important advantages and benefits that stem from integration.

REALIZING ECONOMIES OF SCOPE

At the heart of manufacturing computerization is programmable computer control, which radically shifts the old trade-offs between volume and variety, stability and change. As computer hardware has become smaller, smarter, and cheaper, control theory has become more sophisticated and production equipment and machine tools vastly more capable. The union of computers with smart, multipurpose tools produces highly flexible process equipment capable of change at electronic speeds. Of course, not every process lends itself to such speedy change—but the range is surprisingly broad. In discrete parts manufacturing especially, economies of scope are replacing economics of scale, as the following examples illustrate.

• Ingersoll Milling Machine's Rockford, IL plant uses a completely computer-integrated manufacturing system to produce 25,000 different prismatic parts. Half of the 25,000 will never again be manufactured, and 70 percent are made in lots of one.

• Hughes Aircraft's El Segundo, CA flexible manufacturing system (FMS) uses nine machining centers plus a coordinate measuring machine, a towline conveyor, and a supervisory computer system to do the work of 25 stand-alone machining centers. The installation cost about 75 percent of the investment cost of comparable traditional capacity, operates at 13 percent of the labor cost, and will generate its output at 10 percent of the machining-time cost.

• Vought Corporation began work on a $10 million flexible machining center in Dallas in July 1984. The plant will produce 600 designs one at a time in random sequence and is expected to save $25 million in machining costs by reducing the 200,000 hours required by conventional methods to 70,000.

• Mazak Corporation's Florence, KY plant produces 180 different parts ranging in weight from a few pounds to three tons with only two operators in its FMS. The company hopes for a 30-day delivery schedule on machine tools, in contrast with the six months or more typical in the U.S.

As these examples illustrate, advanced manufacturing technologies greatly increase flexibility. But speed, quality, and precision are also increased. Change is low in cost because a computer program can reliably execute any designated sequence of actions without downtime or other inefficiencies typically associated with change. If tool changes can be made at electronic speeds, almost no production time will be lost for changeover.

With such flexibility available, inventory buffers are no longer needed and turnaround time can drop dramatically. This, in turn, permits a firm to offer both a broader product line and speedy parts replacement at little cost. Setups that used to take hours can take minutes as a result of computer programs and microprocessor sensors and controls.

The underlying assumptions here are those of economies of scope, not scale. Variability and responsiveness to change, not rigidity and standardization, are at the heart of computer-based manufacturing operations. Exhibit 1 highlights the contrast between economies of scale and economies of scope.

The Information Basis of Manufacturing Automation

Some of the greatest advantages of computer applications are integration benefits. The economical use and reuse of information directly attacks the troublesome overhead costs that plague conventional factories. The benefit of common data bases for CAD, CAM, CAE, group technology (GT), and flexible manufacturing systems comes from not having to reinvent the wheel. Not having to regenerate or reenter information that was entered earlier or that can be derived from information already entered increases efficiency.

Machine scheduling, production and shipping records, inventory control, and material requirements planning (MRP) rely on information generated in design, in order entry, or in both. Major advantages can be realized by integrating this information and sharing it among functions, thereby reducing the needless duplication of information and of the activities necessary to regenerate it.

	Economies of Scale	Economies of Scope
Fundamental Assumptions	*(Old-style technology)*	*(CIM environment)*
	Experience curve	Truncated (or expanded) life cycle
	Task specialization	Multimission firms
	Work as a social activity	Unmanned systems
	Separable variable costs	Joint costs
	Product standardization	Product variety
	Flexibility and variety are expenseive	Flexibility and variety create profits
Desirable Operating System Characteristics	Centralization	Decentralization
	Large plants	Disaggregated capacity
	Balanced lines	Flexiblity
	Smooth flows	Surge and turnaround ability
	Standard product design	Many custom products
	Low rate of change, high stability	Innovation and responsiveness
	Inventory as a decoupler	Product tied to demand
	Focus as an organizing concept	Functional range for repeated organization
	Job enrichment and enlargement	Responsibility tied to rewards
	Batch systems	Flow systems

Exhibit 1. Comparison between economies of scale and economies of scope.

CAD provides a logical starting point for illustration.

The information entered in initial design (e.g., material requirements, dimensions, and component parts) affects inventory, purchasing, process planning, and scheduling. Once this information is captured on a CAD system, it can be adapted, increased, or modified much more easily than it can be recreated. Once a given design is on the CAD system, it can easily be modified, since only the new portion must be redone. This may mean that only 20 percent of custom parts actually require redesign. Even for custom-designed products, adaptation of past designs is often sufficient to produce the needed product. Thus, the use of CAD-assisted variants radically reduces the new design effort required, as evidenced by reported productivity gains of 10, 20, or even 40 to one.

Similarly, the premise behind GT is that products grouped into families according to commonalities in shape, materials, and production processes are manufactured more efficiently. Computers make sophisticated data systems like GT possible by speeding accurate information handling. GT coding permits the efficient retrieval of prior designs and facilitates both computer-aided process planning (CAPP) and the establishment of more efficient manufacturing cell organization on the shop floor.

On the factory floor, CAM systems perform machine monitoring and adjustment as well as controlled materials movement. CAM systems reuse the data generated in the design process (though often in a somewhat changed format) to generate machine instructions for parts manufacturing.

CHANGING FINANCIAL ANALYSIS PRACTICES

Clearly, traditional financial methods are inappropriate for evaluating new technologies. Common accounting practices often allocate overhead costs on the basis of direct labor hours, although direct labor content has substantially declined in recent years. Today, direct labor may account for less than 10 percent of costs. (For automobiles today, the figure is about 8.5 percent; for discrete metal parts, on the average, it is less than 12 percent.) This allocation distorts true manufacturing cost performance and distracts management attention from ballooning overhead, staff, and other indirect costs.

How important are the distortions resulting from these accounting practices? One gross indicator is found in total employee levels. In 1980, Ford Europe was arguably the most efficient of the Western automakers. That year, Ford Europe manufactured 1,500,000 cars and trucks, using 140,000 employees. In the same year, Mazda manufactured 1,100,000 vehicles with just 22,000 employees. Comparable differences in overall efficiency—influenced by sharply differing organizational practices—contribute to the price gap between Japanese compact cars and those manufactured by U.S. automakers, which is reliably estimated at between $1600 and $2400 per landed vehicle.

These problems are not unique to automotive manufacturers. McKinsey Consultants estimates that cost differentials of 30 to 50 percent are common between U.S. and far eastern manufactured goods—and that the figures are even worse for many European manufacturers.

Many evaluation methods, such as ROI and NPV, give too much weight to short-term benefits and costs through the simplistic use of concepts relating to the time value of money. These evaluation methods assign no cost to lost opportunities and no benefit to potential strategic advantages. Indirect financial advantages of effective manufacturing performance are ignored. Thus, although quality and inventory control are of increasing importance today, they are invisible in most equipment investment evaluation methods. ROI analyses, developed some 60 years ago in a very different manufacturing setting, are simply inadequate for estimating these advantages, particularly where the analysis is narrowly defined as a comparison of the return on the investment in one machine with the return on the investment in another, as illustrated in Exhibit 2.

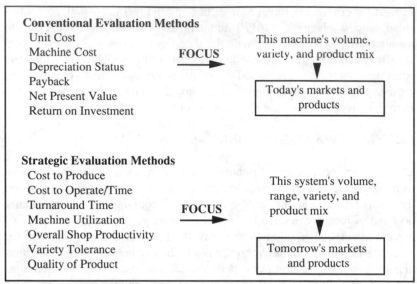

Exhibit 2. Conventional versus strategic evaluation methods.

Advantages derived from replacing a single machine, though perhaps of value, are scarcely the final goal. The greater benefit will flow from such systematic, overall changes as reductions in design time and errors with simultaneous increases in design complexity. For example, after implementing a new CAD/CAM system, Simmonds Precision realized substantial labor and cost savings in programmable control design and found itself able to perform four or even five feasibility layouts with its new equipment, in place of the single layout that was previously possible. This made it easier to predict costs and design early in the design process. Minimizing PC layers not only simplified production initially but continued to provide benefits throughout product life. In addition, while work load increased (by 220 percent over the comparison period) and complexity increased, design staff remained constant. These benefits are pervasive and persistent—and they go well beyond machine investment costs or even direct machine operation costs in the design area.

Documented Improvements

The hidden cost benefits of CIM result from the close integration, improved speed and flexibility, higher quality, and greater product variation these systems can support. Substantial savings will be realized in the costs of energy, factory floor space, and clerical and administrative staff, which are difficult to account for. Because many manufacturing cost systems do not track overhead costs directly, they are usually allocated arbitrarily (e.g., on the basis of direct labor cost distributions) and therefore are essentially invisible—until they hit the bottom line. Although this allocation may have been a useful shortcut when direct labor was a major part (e.g., 60 percent) of manufacturing costs, it is extremely misleading when direct labor costs drop to 20 percent or less, as is typical today.

Invisible too, are such factory floor benefits as reduced raw materials and work-in-process inventory (often reduced by half or more) and the consequent increases in inventory turns. Although these benefits of CIM may be hard to quantify, they are real—as evidenced by the following accounts of some leading manufacturers' experiences.

General Electric Company's Large Steam Turbine Generator plant in Schenectady, NY produces replacement parts to order, delivering them in less time than it once took to retrieve parts from stock. The guaranteed replacement and quick delivery made possible by the flexibility of CIM provide substantial strategic advantage in a fiercely competitive market.

Elsewhere, General Electric's North American appliance business has achieved major quality improvements with better warranty performance, lower waste, and smaller, more tightly controlled facilities. These improvements are significant, despite General Electric's long and well-deserved reputation for excellent management.

In some areas, General Electric has done away with blueprints entirely— as have some other firms. Instead, design information is electronically filed, electronically modified, and electronically transferred from the designer to the production floor. In addition to improving speed, accuracy, and precision, this method eliminates the cost, space, and personnel formerly associated with blueprint control—and the difficulties of ensuring that only the latest blueprints are in fact used in production.

A Canadian pharmaceutical manufacturer uses a direct order entry line to initiate production scheduling, inventory adjustment, invoicing, and shipping. This has dramatically improved response to customers and decreased inventory, despite the company's batch mode of production. Expedited shipping and billing (within 24 hours of order entry) has speeded customers' payment as well.

Grundfos, a highly efficient Danish pump manufacturer facing raw material supply difficulties, turned to automated parts stamping to reduce waste. In addition to direct savings, the firm gained welcome relief from the hazards of erratic supply, because a given inventory quantity went farther. Payback was under one year, and the company was encouraged to further its automation efforts. The addition of sophisticated production monitoring, scheduling, and control capabilities has multiplied these benefits.

General Dynamics Corporation discovered that eliminating costly, repeated redesign of parts could cut the number of different parts from 2891 to 541, with considerable improvements in efficiency and greatly reduced cost.

Flexibility such as these manufacturers' systems provide is highly desirable, particularly since it is achieved without sacrificing quality or incurring additional changeover costs. Flexible manufacturing allows manufacturers to explore the benefits of using alternative materials, new designs, and product tailoring or product mix shifts to gain and extend the firm's position in markets. Small market segments or niches not economical under old technologies are quite practical when varied products can be cost-effectively manufactured in random sequence in batches of one.

Such capabilities are reported by Ingersoll Milling, Mazak Corporation, and John Deere among others. Volkswagen produces cars with left- and right-hand drives in random sequence Traditional equipment, unable to respond to market opportunities because of its rigidity, is increasingly less preferable as markets fragment and product life cycles decrease. Strategic opportunity is the issue, not per-unit or per-machine investment cost or operating cost

ACCOUNTING FOR INTEGRATION BENEFITS

CIM benefits are substantial and rest heavily on advantages not present in traditional equipment or recognized readily by traditional accounting methods. These benefits are not simply additive or incremental improvements on a fairly standard, unchanging base. Instead, they are major changes that can be realized in three key categories.

- *Basic improvements in manufacturing performance.* Lower cost and better quality, increased speed, reduced waste and materials usage, and reduced work-in-process and raw materials inventory.

- *Strategic benefits and improved responsiveness derived from basic improvements.* Greater adaptability to change, which makes it possible to enter new markets while serving older ones; higher quality as a means of defending market share; and greater flexibility, which provides protection against the risks of market change.

- *Integration benefits that multiply the usefulness of information derived from initial design and initial order entry, machine monitoring, and electronic data transfer.* Lower cost, fewer errors, easier information transfer, spread of CAD or GT benefits throughout manufacturing operations and company management, and competitive advantages.

Any single benefit—such as improved unit production costs—may be valuable, the overwhelmingly unrecognized multiplied effects of integration and strategy benefits are far more important. Because the costs of overhead and inefficient operation are so often inadequately tracked by accounting systems, the benefits of eliminating these are difficult to articulate.

The advantages of integration and strategic opportunity are so great, however, that they must be addressed. Flexibility, quality, speed, and integration are directly relevant to strategic survival in the global competitive environment of today and tomorrow. It is no longer a question of whether to replace older technologies; instead, the question is whether survival is possible if new technologies are not acquired.

New evaluation methods must transcend the 1920s logic of ROI and the simplistic use of NPV in order to properly assess strategic advantages, integration benefits, and the cost of maintaining older positions. For manufacturers around the world, economies-of-scope logic provides a far more reliable guide to the new technology.

SECTION IV
PLANNING INTEGRATED SYSTEMS

The vision of totally integrated manufacturing design, planning, inventory control, numerical control (NC) programming and accounting systems has proven to be an extremely difficult task. Given the proliferation of different types of computers, different operating systems, different databases, and different communications protocols, truly integrated systems currently do not exist.

A simple answer, which is often promoted, is that a single vendor develops the ultimate system which integrates all of the key business functions. The vendor-supplied, turn key system would run on compatible computer equipment, use compatible file and communications formats, and solve everyone's problems. No vendor, to date at least, has been able to do this. It does not appear that any single vendor will be able to provide this type of integration in the near future.

Many companies have had considerable success in developing systems which support their needs. The significant cost required to coordinate across different functional areas within the company, different computer and software vendors, and various external and internal consulting groups make these extremely expensive endeavors. The articles in this section provide insight into how the pieces of the puzzle fit together.

At least seven major programming modules must be integrated. These modules include accounting, production planning, inventory planning, production scheduling, computer aided design, process planning, and NC parts programming. The integration of accounting, production planning, inventory planning, and scheduling has been the major focus of the MRP II systems which have already been widely implemented. Links between the MRP II system and engineering design, process planning, and NC programming are not well developed. Additional indirect functions, which may be supported in an integrated environment, include cost estimating for new products, job costing for products in production, computerized machinability data to help determine optimal cutting conditions, computer assisted work standards, computer assisted line balancing, and group technology coding and indexing.

The first article, by Michael Bohse and George Harhalakis titled "Integrating CAD and MRP II Systems," describes the integrated data requirements of these two systems. Problems of data duplication and concurrency in dynamic environments are discussed in the paper. The use of "attributes" tagged to computer-aided design (CAD) drawings is an approach that is readily implemented using existing technology and is described in the article.

Possibly the most difficult aspect of developing an integrated system is the storage of design data. Current CAD systems use either wire-frame (line oriented) or solid model schemes for storing graphics description data. Current standards for the exchange of wire frame data exist in the form of the Initial Graphics Exchange Standard. This specification falls far short of the information needed for the development of computer aided process planning systems and automated NC programming systems. Detailed three-dimensional shape and surface feature information is required. Andrews Atkinson describes approaches to solving this representation problem in his article titled "Manufacturing Part Features: CIMs Technological Common Denominator." Atkinson also describes the product development cycle time reduction possible through the use of concurrent engineering concepts.

An area key to the success of integrated systems and where there has been significant progress, is in data communications. Celia Joseph describes, in "Using LANS to Automate the Factory Floor," the current state of Local Area Networks (LANS), which provide the backbone for data sharing. The FieldBus, Bitbus, MAP/TOP, Mini-MAP, and Ethernet standards are described and compared based on performance characteristics. Those who are unfamiliar with the "alphabet soup" of telecommunications terminology will find this article interesting.

One of the most interesting facilities in the United States where research is conducted in the integration of manufacturing systems is the Automated Manufacturing Research Facility at the National Institute of Standards and Technology; the designers of this facility have intentionally used many different technologies. The article by Richard Jackson and Albert Jones titled "An Architecture for Decision Making in the Factory of the Future" describes work at the facility. The insights gained from this facility are valuable to solving the problems of truly integrated manufacturing. Periodically, the facility is opened to the public for tours. Readers of this book would find a visit interesting.

13

INTEGRATING CAD AND MRP II SYSTEMS
MICHAEL E. BOHSE AND GEORGE HARHALAKIS, PH.D.

Computer-aided design (CAD) and manufacturing resource planning (MRP II) systems provide an ideal starting point for integrating design/development and operations management functions. Many firms have implemented one or both of these systems independently, but with little thought to their integration. The basis of the integration is part specification and product structure information, which is essential to both systems. This article details the common features of CAD and MRP II, describes how a combined CAD-MRP II system could function, and pinpoints the advantages of sharing information between the two systems. This article also suggests methods for achieving CAD-MRP II integration and discusses expanding the CAD-MRP II system to a computer-integrated manufacturing (CIM) system.

The data elements common to CAD and MRP II include part specification data, found in the part master record (PMR) and bills of material (BOMs) as depicted in Exhibit 1. Although these elements serve somewhat different functions in each system, much of the same data is used by both systems. Part specification involves the documentation of parts, both purchased and manufactured. In an MRP II system, the PMR is the collection of information documenting each part; it contains information used in the procurement, manufacture, or assembly of components such as:

- Part number
- Part description
- Revision number
- Drawing number
- Make or buy code
- Unit of measure

Reprinted from the Summer issue of *CIM Review* (New York: Auerbach Publishers). © 1987 Warren, Gorham & Lamont Inc. Used with permission.

143

- Vendor information (for purchased parts)
- Lead time
- Cost
- Required quality level

PMR information is held in the PMR module of the MRP II system. In addition, many of the information fields (e.g., part number and part description) are also maintained by the CAD system as a means of documenting and cataloging design drawings.

The BOM for a product is a family tree structure that identifies the component parts, their quantities, and their relationships. Parts or assemblies on a given level in the BOM are said to be the "parents" of the "children" (i.e., subassemblies or component parts) on the next lower level. A well-structured BOM models the manufacturing and assembly of the product by establishing the logical sequence of manufacturing operations.

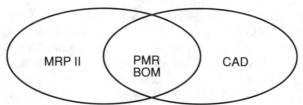

Exhibit 1. The intersection of CAD and MRP II.

In the MRP II system, the BOM serves as the guide to production activities and material purchases. Within the material planning and inventory control module of the MRP II system, the requirements for end-product production (as determined by the system's master production schedule) are carried through the various levels of the BOM to determine the required quantities for each assembly and component and for raw material; need dates are also determined, using the lead time and vendor information in the PMR file. Inventory records are then checked for current stock and pending orders of items to determine the net requirements of each. For purchased items, purchase orders can be automatically generated. For manufactured items, work orders are released to the shop floor control module of the MRP II system for more detailed scheduling and execution.

In the CAD system, the BOM is used for documentation purposes, representing the explosion of a product into its components and subassemblies. The CAD BOM defines the product structure for the rest of the organization.

CREATION OF THE PMR AND BOM

Before a part is released from the CAD system, it is assigned a part number and given a description. In addition, the designer usually includes other information (e.g., revision number, estimated cost). Typically, this information from the CAD system is manually entered into the MRP II system's PMR file, along with additional information (e.g., vendor sources, lead times). Entering and maintaining the same basic information in both systems wastes time and increases errors.

Traditionally, the BOM was constructed by the designer, who reviewed each detail and assembly drawing to generate a list of needed components and materials, including consumable items (e.g., welding rods, adhesives, protective finishes). This process was extremely time-consuming, considering that even a relatively simple project often required reviewing more than 100 drawings. Complex assemblies required more time because the drawings had to be reviewed repeatedly to achieve accurate quantity counts and ensure that no items were overlooked. While some of today's CAD systems better facilitate BOM construction, considerable effort is still generally required.

Once the BOM is created by the designer, a paper copy of the BOM information is generated and manually entered into the MRP II system so that the production control and purchasing functions can begin the activities required to produce the new product. This transcription of data from the CAD to the MRP II system is redundant and time-consuming and increases the likelihood of errors. Furthermore, from the very entry of a BOM into the MRP II system, the possibility exists that the MRP II BOM will differ from the CAD BOM. Keeping track of the inevitable engineering changes throughout a product's life is complicated by the need to enter and maintain data in each system independently. Not only is the chance of data error increased at each step, but the engineer is denied quick access to MRP II inventory information that would be useful in determining effectivity dates for changes.

Sharing PMR and BOM Data

To eliminate the redundant effort and higher error rates that result from maintaining PMR and BOM data in both CAD and MRP II systems, an integrated CAD-MRP II system should be developed. Common data would be maintained in this system and would be available to either application, eliminating transcription errors resulting from redundant data entry; the data for both CAD and MRP II would always be current and consistent. Part specification data from CAD drawings would be used at the time of the drawing's release to establish a PMR for the part, which would be completed by MRP II users. A preliminary BOM would be automatically generated by working through the explosions of the product and its subassemblies. This first-run BOM could be edited by CAD or MRP II users to better represent the manufacturing sequence.

Engineering changes would be greatly simplified by the integrated system. During the design change process, the designer would be able to access inventory and pending order information about a component before determining the change's effectivity date. Once changed and given an effectivity date, the modified BOM or PMR data would be immediately available for MRP II application to prepare in advance for the changeover. A flagging system would alert users of the need to acknowledge or approve changes originating from CAD or MRP II applications. This is especially important in the event of design changes necessitated by MRP II constraints (e.g., a change in a supplier's part).

The integrated system would also enable MRP II users (e.g., shop floor personnel) to view useful CAD geometrical information on a high resolution monitor (as opposed to an expensive CAD terminal) as the need arises.

The goal of this system is to achieve accurate and timely exchange of information between CAD and MRP II. The use of paper for information transfer could be virtually eliminated; paper would be needed only for permanent record keeping. Because information is shared, however, accuracy of the data is essential.

CAD-MRP II INTEGRATION REQUIREMENTS

CAD and MRP II have not yet been integrated in any commercial system for many reasons. As noted by Burgam, each "technology is moving too fast for the systems integrators to follow."[1] Keeping up with the changes has made it nearly impossible for software firms to break away from their traditional specialties and address the more complex concerns of integration. To complicate the problem, MRP II and material planning systems have traditionally been designed for mainframe computers, while most CAD/CAM systems have been intended for minicomputers; thus, the internal architectures, programming languages, and data representations differ. This trend seems to be changing, however, with the introduction of several MRP II systems for minicomputers and even microcomputers.

Another problem is the reluctance on the part of CAD advocates to get involved with MRP II because of its historically poor success rate (typically only 25%).[2] The primary reasons for this poor success are insufficient user education, inadequate implementation strategy, and lack of top management commitment.[3]

Interestingly, while many CAD implementations also fail to live up to their full potential,[4] this problem is less often recognized since CAD systems generally are not complete failures.

Although the concept of CAD and MRP II integration is easy to grasp—common information is shared by the two applications to avoid errors and wasted time and to improve the control of product structure information—the physical integration presents many problems. The most apparent of these are the data base structure and the required system capabilities. Further, since CAD-MRP II is only a starting point for CIM, consideration must be given to the addition of other systems.

Data Base Considerations

There are two primary methods of structuring the CAD-MRP II data base: the use of a single, central data base for all functions, or the use of multiple data bases with some interface between them. Each structure has its advantages and disadvantages, and the final choice will have to provide the best compromise between these. Some of the major data base considerations—of data bases in general and specific to multiple data bases—are summarized in Exhibit 2.[5]

Exhibit 2. Some major data base considerations.

Considerations with multiple data bases:
- Heterogeneous hardware
- Heterogeneous software
- Heterogeneous models
- Data conversion
- Data consistency

General considerations:
- Size
- Heterogeneous data
- Heterogeneous users
- Update difficulties
  - —Integrity constraints
  - —Automatic update propagation
- Performance requirements
- Graphic I/O requirements
- Numerical calculation requirements
- Ease of modifying data base
- Control of security integrity and privacy
- Distributed data

Multiple data base considerations. Multiple data base concerns relate to the complexities of transferring data from a given data base on a given computer to a different data base, possibly on a different computer. Even if the data bases are on the same computer, the transfer of information must reflect the different data base configurations. When the data bases are on different computers, the additional barrier of different computer architectures must also be addressed. In either case, custom programming is required to ensure an accurate conversion of data between the data formats of two or more systems.

Another significant concern is data consistency. With several data bases containing the same information accessible to various users, the interface must be able to monitor and control modifications from all possible points and make the necessary changes to the same data in all appropriate data bases.

General considerations. In addition to the concerns specific to multiple data base configurations, there are many important general concerns. The first of these is size. The combined data from several large computer systems may easily run into hundreds of millions of pieces of information, even for a medium-sized manufacturer; thus, large amounts of storage and close and careful control will be required.

The heterogeneity of data and users also challenges the systems integration effort. Throughout a manufacturing operation, there are many different types of data—including text, numerical, and graphical information—which must be handled by an integrated system. To complicate matters, different users requiring the same information often require different data formats and arrangements to meet their special needs. Thus, an integrated system must provide several user interfaces to cater to the various user requirements.

One of the major concerns in data base integration is the problem of updating data within the system and data-integrity constraints. Since a given piece of information may be modified by users of several systems, means must be provided not only to ensure that all users will have immediate access to the new information but also to evaluate the impact of changes on other information throughout the system. Thus, the data base management system must be aware of the detailed data relationships so that changes to related information can be made automatically (e.g., changing a production schedule when an order due date is changed), or messages can be sent to appropriate personnel for further action. When the integrity of one or more systems is temporarily violated due to incomplete or inconsistent data, a freeze on related activities may be necessary until the conflicts are resolved.

In addition to satisfying technological problems, the data base must satisfy the users' performance requirements. Data must be quickly accessed, even when the data is distributed over several geographic locations. The system must be able to handle the special loads induced by graphical information as well as the heavy numerical calculations required for engineering analysis. For an extensive integrated system, these requirements will necessitate large-scale computing power that can be achieved with one large system or, more likely, with a network of smaller machines. When the organization's needs change somewhat, the data base should provide a means for adapting to the change without extensive modification.

Finally, the data base must provide for data security; because the entire organization will be using the same data, this security is imperative. A detailed authorization system should be maintained within the system so that users have access only to the extent necessary to perform their work (e.g., read only, read/modify).

The key to successfully creating an integrated system is that, regardless of the particular data base structure, the user should be aware only of a single, all-encompassing data base.

Suitability of a Single Data Base

A single data base for the integrated system would provide the most efficient means of communication; data would be stored only once, though it would be accessible to CAD and MRP II users for reading and modification as appropriate. No duplication of data would occur. Exhibit 3 demonstrates this principle. On the negative side, a single data base would require redesigning considerable portions of both systems, which might result in a data base that is too large and slow to be practical. Further, adding other systems would be difficult, as it would require more modifications to the data base.

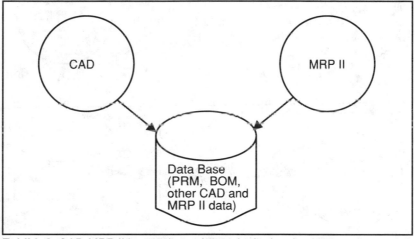

Exhibit 3. CAD-MRP II integration using a single data base.

Suitability of Multiple Data Bases

The second alternative is to use separate data bases for each component and link them using some form of communication. While this is less efficient than a single data base in some respects, it is considered by many to be the only real alternative. Bridging different data bases, which will have some redundant data, requires custom programming to define the systems' interrelationships and special care to ensure that updating will be performed with as little human intervention as possible. However, multiple data bases have several advantages. First, by developing a custom interface that defines the common data and interaction procedures, virtually any two systems can be integrated. This allows the selection of the most suitable CAD and MRP II systems, regardless of the software vendors. Second, as it becomes practical to add other CIM components to the CAD-MRP II integrated system, new interfaces can be defined to handle the required interactions.

In light of these considerations, the multiple data base appears to be the most practical alternative. The integration of CAD and MRP II using this approach is shown conceptually in Exhibit 4. The required interface revolves around the BOM and PMR data. The interface would be an independent system used to define the interaction or interoperability of CAD and MRP II under all circumstances. It would provide the conduit for data exchange between the two data bases as well as the logic for propagating changes throughout all affected areas. For those actions requiring human intervention, messages would be conveyed to the appropriate personnel.

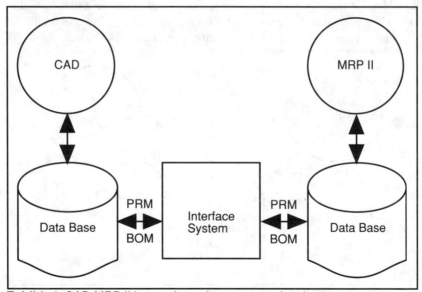

Exhibit 4. CAD-MRP II integration using separate data bases.

With this approach, it is possible to make use of currently available packages. Though more complex, the use of an interface should also allow CAD and MRP II to operate on separate computers, with the interface system operating on either computer or on a third computer. The redundant data resulting from this approach can be tolerated, as long as the interface ensures data consistency.

System Requirements
Generally, any MRP II system using a BOM and PMR file would be an acceptable candidate for integration with CAD. However, selecting a suitable CAD system is more complicated because many CAD systems cannot sup-

150

port the automated generation of BOMs, even with the custom programming (short of redesigning the system). The following items describe some of the features that help facilitate BOM generation.[6] As CAD systems become more sophisticated, a growing number of systems will support at least the most essential of these requirements—the capabilities of associating attributes with each entity. Without that capability, there is little hope of integrating CAD and MRP II; unfortunately, there are still several older systems on the market that do not support that capability.

Attributes. A method for assigning characteristics or attributes (e.g., part number) to a drawing entity must be established for automatic BOM generation. After an attribute is attached to the entity, it should remain inseparable throughout the life of the part or until an intentional change or deletion is made.

Entity selection. A CAD system should offer a simple method for selecting the entity that needs to be addressed. For example, some systems provide the user with visual feedback that verifies entity selection as specified by a CAD system input device (e.g., light pen, cursor, tablet status). The visual feedback (e.g., blinking, brightness level, color changes) ensures that users attach the proper attribute to an entity. Visual feedback becomes even more necessary for complex drawings.

Attribute attachment. The user should be able to attach a multiline attribute to the entity selected because many items are difficult to describe with a single line. Line-length limitations may force the designer to use abbreviations that may be misinterpreted by other users. For this reason, a system should have an 80-character attribute line and special characters available to describe items properly. Special characters include percent signs, quotation marks, and parentheses for attaching notes. Special characters are not available to the designer who uses a system that allows only alphanumeric representation in the attribute string.

Attribute editing. A CAD system should provide the capability for editing and updating existing attributes to accommodate design improvements and part number changes. Using a CAD system that does not have an attribute capability is inefficient because the existing attribute must be deleted and a completely new one generated if only a few characters need to be changed.

Attribute display. A CAD system should allow attribute information to be displayed as desired for both plotting and graphics terminals needs. While attaching the appropriate attributes to each part, the designer should have the option of viewing the attributes and verifying that all are in place and correct or of removing the attributes from the display for drawing clarity.

151

Variable positioning. The user should be able to position the attribute information anywhere on the drawing and reposition the attribute when necessary. Repositioning the attribute should not affect its attachment to the entity. Variable positioning of the attribute is essential for enhancing legibility as the drawing becomes more complex and crowded.

Attribute file generation. A CAD system should offer a method for generating an attribute file (similar to a symbol library) so that the designer has access to previously generated attributes. The ability to generate an attribute file that has already been entered into the system reduces the designer's typing effort.

Symbol library enhancement. The user should be able to attach attributes to symbols in the symbol library. For example, if a symbol library of items commonly used for a required project has been constructed, the designer should not have to add the attribute for each item every time it is used in a drawing. Instead, the system should allow the designer to attach attributes to the symbols in the library, thereby decreasing drafting time and ensuring that the same attribute is always used for the same item or piece of equipment.

Attribute grouping. A CAD system should allow attributes to be grouped so that the BOMs for assemblies and subassemblies can be listed separately. The attribute grouping capability is especially useful when subassemblies are manufactured by different vendors or shops.

FUTURE DIRECTIONS

Integrating CAD and MRP II is only the first step in the development of computer-integrated manufacturing Eventually, not only CAD and MRP II but all of the software and automation systems involved in production will be integrated. From forecasting and long-term planning to distribution and after-sales service, common information will be shared among all users in a business. A completed CIM system may be arranged with MRP II as the central hub to coordinate activities and information flow among the various functions.

In such a system, a designer will be able to sit at a CAD terminal and design a product using data from marketing surveys and research. The product structure information will be shared with MRP II, and the design data will be shared with a computer-aided process planning system, which will use group technology and artificial intelligence to automatically develop detailed process plans for product manufacture. The process plans will then be shared with MRP II and a computer aided manufacturing (CAM) system. The MRP II shop floor control module will schedule the various processes in conjunction with other shop floor activities, and the CAM system will use computer-controlled machinery, robotics, and automated material handling systems to help execute the schedules. Progress will be continually monitored to ensure on-time delivery or provide adequate warning when deadlines cannot be met.

THE IMPORTANCE OF PLANNING

Planning for integration is crucial to success. Analyzing needs, arriving at a conceptual model of information flow through the organization, and developing an implementation plan may take anywhere from several months to several years. French provides a list of various considerations to explore during this phase;[7] some of the most important are:

- The potential impact on every functional area of the organization should be examined and likely problems, penalties, and benefits, both short- and long-term, should be identified.

- The leaders of each functional area should be allowed to share their concerns and ideas with those in charge of planning so that a consensus can be reached as to why the project should proceed from the viewpoint of a given function.

- Companywide concerns and opportunities, as well as those specific to each functional area, should be identified and listed.

From this list of concerns and opportunities, a plan can be developed, which would include funding needs, personnel, and time requirements; the plan should allow for inevitable delays and mistakes. Once generated, it is important that the development and implementation plans be discussed with each functional area so that its involvement can be clarified.

The actual implementation of the plan may extend another several months to several years. The most important factor for success is that implementation be done gradually and with minimal disturbance of existing operations. From the initial CAD-MRP II nucleus, other CIM components can be integrated when technology permits and the organization is ready. Where areas will be altered drastically, the current system should be maintained until the operation is running trouble free under the new system.

As portions of the integrated system become operational, the system should be continually evaluated to uncover any problems and to determine the system's effectiveness. Potential changes should be carefully studied before mailing any alterations.

FOOTNOTES

1. P. Burgam. "Marrying MRP and CIM," *CAD/CAM Technology*. 2(1983): 25-27.
2. Burgam, pp. 25-27.
3. G. Harhalakis. "An integrated production management system for engineered equipment" (Ph.D. diss. University of Manchester, Institute of Science and Technology, Manchester England, 1984).
4. T. G. Gunn. "CAD/CAM/CIM: now and in the future." *IE&CS*. 58(1985): 59-64.
5. M. Melkanoff. "The CIMS database: goals, problems, case studies, and, proposed approaches outlined." *Industrial Engineering*. 16(1984): 78-92.
6. C. P. Bauer. "Automating bill of material generation." *Computer Aided Design, Engineering, and Drafting*. New York: Auerbach Publishers, 1984.
7. R.L. French. "Managements looking at CIMS must deal effectively with these issues and realities." *Industrial Engineering*. 16(1984): 70-77.
8. The authors wish to acknowledge the Systems Research Center (NSF Grant NSFD CDR-85-00108) of the University of Maryland for partially funding this research as well as the National Science Foundation for its direction and contributions (NSF Grant NSFD DMC-85-04922).

14

MANUFACTURING PARTS FEATURES: CIM'S TECHNOLOGICAL COMMON DENOMINATOR

ANDREWS ATKINSON

Significant progress has been made during the 1980s in the development of computer-integrated manufacturing (CIM). This article documents the efforts of key US industrial leaders to implement CIM and identifies the next strategic development steps required to establish CIM as the most important industrial technology of the 1990s.

Manufacturing parts features are now generally recognized by industry experts as the technological link between computer-aided design (CAD) and computer-aided manufacturing (CAM)—the prerequisite for concurrent engineering. There is a subtle but distinct difference between the part geometry defined by the design engineer and the geometric attributes that the manufacturing engineer is concerned with in removing material to create the geometry of the final design.

Automated access to detailed machining technology data and analysis algorithms by designers, planners, and numerical control (NC) programmers will have a major impact on part quality and manufacturing productivity because it will improve the accuracy of data selection and allow an in-depth assessment of design and manufacturing alternatives. Direct benefits can be measured in the reduction of the initial planning and programming time, planning and programming rework time, direct machining time, and the rework itself.

These advantages are not only beneficial and justifiable in today's manufacturing environment but a prerequisite to tomorrow's technology of integrating engineering, part design, manufacturing engineering, and manufacturing into complete production systems.

The desired approach to this technology is to design and construct a system that compiles a machining plan from a set of manufacturing part

Reprinted from the Winter issue of *CIM Review* (New York: Auerbach Publishers). © 1990 Warren, Gorham & Lamont Inc. Used with permission.

features. These manufacturing part features are the fundamental building blocks of a machined part. Regardless of the particular selections of commercial engineering, design, and part programming systems, the manufacturing part features will ultimately be the technological link between part geometry and the manufacturing operation used to create that geometry.

MACHINING TECHNOLOGY AT BOEING

The level of machining and tooling knowledge among machine operators, programmers, and process planners has been falling for years, and companies face the problem of capturing what machining process knowledge they have.

In July 1982, Boeing Military Airplane Co. (in Wichita, KS) decided to tackle the problem by developing a companywide (and later corporate-wide) machining data base to incorporate the cumulative knowledge of its master machinists. It then discovered a second problem—when 20 machining experts were given a simple part, each came up with a different machining plan that had different speeds, feeds, cutting parameters, and logic.

The company realized that building a machining and tooling data base would be a major undertaking. Boeing established a small team of machining technology committees at several of its companies to develop a system to capture, standardize, and optimize the metal-cutting technology data required for detailed planning of machining operations. Working with Metcut Research Associates Inc. (in Cincinnati) as the software vendor, this team built an operational system.

Building a Data Base

Today, more than six years later, the committee at Boeing Military Airplane Co. has almost completed its machining and tooling data base. Ninety percent of new jobs machined in-house are run on the basis of tooling and machining parameters selected by planners using the Machining Technology System. The system does not make its machining recommendations simply on the basis of Boeing's accumulated experience but combines that experience with the machining and tooling experience and machining principles incorporated by Metcut into its MetCAPP expert machining system.

A Knowledge-Based System

The following modules in MetCAPP are divided into those that require the user to enter information and those in which the software carries out selections and computations to arrive at a decision, which becomes the output:

• *Machine-tool selection*—Includes the size, power, rigidity, and other features of the 210 metal-cutting machine tools.

- *Workpiece-materials selection*—Includes the hardness and heat-treated condition of all major classes of materials.
- *Manufacturing feature descriptions*—Prompted from interactive dimension screens.
- *Cutting tool selection in order of productivity*—Taken from an inventory that includes 18 cutter types (just one of those types, milling cutters, contains 5,000 configurations).
- *The pass-logic calculations*—Performed identically and in standardized fashion for all users because it requires no user input.
- *System output*—Comprises detailed machining plans that are ready for the shop.

The first part of the system was installed in 1984 and addressed end milling. In 1987 face-milling, hole-making, and lathe-turning portions of the system were installed. Today, 95% of all cutting operations are covered. The following are the three major benefits of the MetCAPP system:

- The system solves the problems that it was designed to solve by capturing the machining and tooling skills of its master machinists— Therefore, even plans prepared or run by inexperienced machinists, and tapes generated by new programmers, are much less likely to have mistakes than they were before.
- Because it's consistent, accurate pass-logic is the same for all users; regardless of their level of expertise, it provides a standardized machining practice.
- It optimizes the selection of tools, cutting paths, and NC tapes—The internal cut logic overcomes the occasional conservatism of a machinist or programmer and makes the machine work to its capability. Furthermore, automating much of the routine work of machining planning has allowed Boeing Military Airplane Co. to form a 15-person shop floor optimization group, which looks for ways to use the system to improve its machining practices. Cycle times on a sampling of two dozen parts optimized by the MetCAPP system has been improved 5% to 63%—a big productivity boost. [1]

By-product benefits of the MetCAPP system are also significant. NC-program tryout time has been significantly reduced. Eventually, the historical data stored in the system will enable Boeing to standardize and reduce its tool inventory.

EXPERT SYSTEMS IN MANUFACTURING

Expert systems can be used for diagnosis, monitoring, analysis, interpretation, consultation, planning, design, instruction, explanation, learning, conceptualization, control, prediction debugging, and repair. Currently, the main application areas for expert systems in manufacturing are process planning, diagnostics, and scheduling. A major impetus for developing such knowledge-based systems for metal-cutting technology is the declining availability of experienced machinists and planners in the face of ever-increasing manufacturing complexities.

The Evendale Component Manufacturing Operation of GE Aircraft Engines (GEAE) is a case in point. According to John M. Roth, a systems analyst at GEAE, its manufacturing operations must continually deal with rapidly changing component-parts designs that must be produced from a variety of high-temperature alloys that are increasingly difficult to machine.

"This problem is further exacerbated by the need for productivity gains that can be met only through the implementation of advanced, application-specific cutting tools, materials, and methods," says Roth.[2] Perhaps the greatest challenge of all is dealing with these requirements in the face of a dwindling supply of experienced process planners.

System for Selecting Tools and Methods

The challenge is being met through the use of the General Electric (GE) Machining Optimization System, an expert system to aid NC methods specialists in the selection of cutting tools, machining parameters, and cutter-path logic. This system is based on MetCAPP; Metcut Associates helped with its implementation.

MetCAPP deals with operations planning, which specifies the detail parameters for the individual operations within a part's process plan. A process plan typically refers to the collection of all planning activities required to convert a single part design into a manufactured product, and operations planning is often considered a subset of process planning.

Computer-aided process planning (CAPP) schemes have developed along two basic approaches, the variant and the generative. The variant approach depends on capturing historical planning information in a computerized data base and providing an efficient means for retrieval and editing by the planner. In a variant CAPP system, group-technology schemes for classification and coding are used to identify parts families and standard plans. Each parts family comprises similar parts with enough common attributes to prescribe a common manufacturing method, or standard plan, for all of the parts in that family.

Avoiding Past Errors

The shortcoming of the variant approach is that retrieving standard or historical data tends to institutionalize current practices at the expense of the introduction of new or innovative methods. In contrast, the generative approach to process planning uses an intelligent computer system that has captured the logic and decision-making ability of experienced process planners. The generative approach incorporated in MetCAPP develops decision logic for each operation type, uses this logic to analyze a problem being faced by the planner, and recommends a current solution incorporating the latest technology. The system consists essentially of an information-gathering module, a knowledge base of machining rules, a controlling program, and a data base of machinability and tooling information.

The information-gathering module consists of interactive screen-driven decision trees to identify the workpiece material, the part feature to be machined, and required machine-tool capabilities for the operation to be planned.

The knowledge base of machining rules contains algorithms, decision tables, and heuristic features for selecting the proper cutting tool, cut sequence, and machining parameters for the operation. The controlling program governs the module sequence, user interface, and calls to the data base, which contains both machinability data (e.g., speed and feed recommendations and empirical constants) and facilities data (e.g., available machine tools and cutting tools).

To plan an operation, the system first generates the necessary cutting-tool characteristics based on the chosen work material, part feature, and machine tool.

Analysis Performance

The set of feasible tools for the operation is then analyzed to find the most productive, economical tool that can perform the operation within such constraints as rigidity and surface finish. The system uses rules and numerical heuristic features to rank the tools by such factors as cost, machining time, metal-removal rate, and rigidity. Once a cutting tool is selected, MetCAPP applies cut-sequencing rules to establish entry, roughing, and finishing passes to produce the particular part feature. The rules are based on a facility's standard machining practices—for example, minimizing the total number of passes or making all rough passes of equal size.

Changing Rule Performance

Embedded in the rules are variable numerical parameters that can be modified to change the rule's performance as new data and technology become available. Such parameters may include the maximum allowable ratio of cut depth to cutter diameter for end milling or the recommended depth of pass for finish-turning a certain alloy. A typical set of rules may be to:

- Minimize the number of passes required by using maximum tool capacity.
- Load tools equally for each of the passes to obtain a more consistent tool life.
- Use the most rigid tooling possible to minimize deflection, reduce the possibility of cutter breakage, and increase metal-removal rates.
- Use the smallest insert that can make the cut in the least number of passes to reduce tooling cost.

The selection of feeds and speeds for individual passes is based on data tables containing guidelines for various machining operations and materials. These guideline parameters represent data known to be acceptable for the particular production environment. The parameters can be updated through feedback or actual performance data so that the latest improved data is available at all times to all system users. The system also applies rules to modify guideline feeds and speeds when the operation-description codes indicate severe machining conditions (e.g., such warning messages or suggestions as reducing feed in concerning pass because of severe cutting force).

The initial version of the GE Machining Optimization System was developed through a series of interviews by Metcut personnel with GE process planners to extract their planning logic and knowledge. "Our implementation team then carried out a series of walkthroughs and modified the system in an iterative manner to fine-tune it to our needs," recalls Roth.

Although the system was initially designed as a stand-alone tool for the Evendale casings operation, it has since been expanded for use in other production areas. Interfaces to tool engineering and CAPP systems are now under development. The ultimate goal, according to Roth, is the development of the GE Machine Optimization System as the tooling, methods, and machining-selection module for the overall manufacturing-process environment envisioned for the Aircraft Engine Business Group.

John Radzikinas, the GE Machine Optimization System project manager at GE Aircraft Engines, states that the goals of the system are to:

- Provide an integrated data base for manufacturing technology.
- Capture and retain manufacturing planning experience and knowledge.
- Serve as a focal point for the dissemination of manufacturing and quality technology.
- Serve as a consistent, on line, real-time training device for new planners.
- Reduce manufacturing losses.
- Improve shop efficiency and reduce manufacturing planning cycle time by consistent and improved methods.
- Provide applications across all engine programs.
- Improve the competitiveness of machined part manufacturing areas.

160

Roth says the most immediate benefit from the system has been the development of routines for coding, storing, and retrieving cutting tools.

These extremely detailed formats have facilitated standardization efforts and provide the capability to use the logic of the best process planners and tool engineers in the everyday selection of cutting tools.

The best available logic for sequencing operations, specifying machining passes, and process tolerancing is captured by the expert system, which uses the power of the computer to make the iterations necessary to calculate the optimum machining condition for a chosen metal-removal operation. All the advanced tools of interactive graphics, group technology, data base management, and process planning will be provided in one expert system.

BUILDING A PROCESS PLAN

Building a process plan typically consists of breaking a part down into the operations needed to produce the part and routing it to the proper locations and workstations to perform those operations. Descriptions of the operations and other notes are usually necessary to describe details and provide instructions. As the plan is developed, the machines, tools, and operations needed to produce the various features must be documented. Finally, estimates of times needed to produce one part or a part lot are calculated for scheduling and cost-estimating activities. The result is a plan that can be used by anyone to produce the desired part.

MetCAPP uses a large data base of information and a rule-based expert machining system to help the planner build process plans. The same steps that are used to produce a plan manually are followed, but most of the information that was looked up in reference books and tables when plans were produced manually is provided by MetCAPP. In addition, expert machining assistance is always available to help select the proper tooling and to determine the machining techniques needed to produce features on a part.

Developing Parts Features

MetCAPP develops information for machining specific parts features. This approach leaves the process planner in control of the sequence of operations to machine a part. An example of how to decompose a part into its various features for machining is covered in this section as an aid to developing this technique.

A typical part is shown in Exhibit 1 in its finished form, ready to be broken down into its component features for machining. The MetCAPP Feature Dimension Screen, which lists the full set of features that support manufacturing, is also shown.

The first step in machining the part consists of reviewing the available MetCAPP feature descriptions to find one that can be used to rough the

Exhibit 1. Component-part features.

Finished Part

Feature #3

Feature #1   Feature #2

Screen Number	MetCAPP Feature Dimension Screens Part Feature	
T2.M1	Flat Rectangular Surface—Open, Cutter Axis Parallel	M1
T2.M2	Flat Rectangular Surface—Open, Cutter Axis Perpendicular	M2
T2.M3	Flat Rectangular Surface—To a Shoulder (Step)	M3
T2.M4	Flat Rectangular Surface—To a Shoulder and Corner	M4
T2.M5	Through Spot	M5
T2.M6	Rectangular Pocket—Open End (Not Fully Enclosed)	M6
T2.M7	Rectangular Pocker—Fully Enclosed	M7
T2.M8	General Peripheral Milled Form	M8
T2.M9	Milled Conical Form	M9
T2.M10	Milled Dovetail Form	M10
T2.M11	Milled T-Slot Form	M11
T2.M12	Milled Chamfered Edge	M12
T2.M13	Milled Rounded Edge (Corner Rounding)	M13
T2.M14	Contour Milled Surface—Two-Axis Profile or Contour	M14
T2.M15	Contour Milled Surface—Multiaxis Linear	M15, M16
T2.M17	Plunge Milled Spotface or Counterbore—Full Diameter	M17
T2.M18	Plunge Milled Spotface or Counterbore—Partial Diameter	M18
T2.M19	Milled L-Shape Cross Section	M19
T2.H1	Single Diameter Hole	H1
T2.H2	Double Diameter (Step Drilled) Hole	H2
T2.H3	Tapped Hole—Blind	H3
T2.H4	Tapped Hole—Through	H4
T2.H5	Front Counterbored Hole	H5
T2.H6	Back Counterbored Hole	H6
T2.H7	Front Countersunk Hole	H7
T2.H8	Back Countersunk Hole	H8
T2.T1	Straight Turning—Through	T1, T3
T2.T2	Straight Turning—To a Shoulder	T2, T4
T2.T5	Facing—Through	T5
T2.T6	Facing—To a Shoulder	T6
T2.T7	Contour Turning	T7
T2.T8	Internal Holemaking Operations (Drill, Bore, etc.)	T8
T2.T9	Groove	T9, T10
T2.T11	Form Turning	T11
T2.T12	Cut Off	T12
T2.T13	Threading—External	T13
T2.T14	Threading—Internal, Blind	T14
T2.T15	Threading—Internal, Through	T15

majority of the stock from the part. For this part, the feature appropriate for roughing, as illustrated in Exhibit 2, is a flat rectangular surface. After the wall and floor of the part have been machined, the slot can be added with the milled T-slot form feature, as illustrated in Exhibit 3. In the final step of this process, the counterbored holes are added using the front counterbored hole feature (see Exhibit 4).

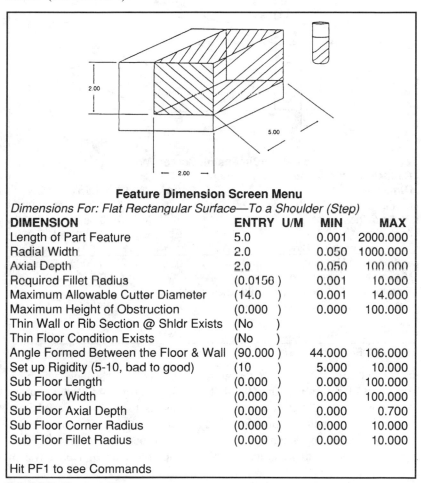

Feature Dimension Screen Menu

Dimensions For: Flat Rectangular Surface—To a Shoulder (Step)

DIMENSION	ENTRY U/M	MIN	MAX
Length of Part Feature	5.0	0.001	2000.000
Radial Width	2.0	0.050	1000.000
Axial Depth	2.0	0.050	100.000
Required Fillet Radius	(0.0156)	0.001	10.000
Maximum Allowable Cutter Diameter	(14.0)	0.001	14.000
Maximum Height of Obstruction	(0.000)	0.000	100.000
Thin Wall or Rib Section @ Shldr Exists	(No)		
Thin Floor Condition Exists	(No)		
Angle Formed Between the Floor & Wall	(90.000)	44.000	106.000
Set up Rigidity (5-10, bad to good)	(10)	5.000	10.000
Sub Floor Length	(0.000)	0.000	100.000
Sub Floor Width	(0.000)	0.000	100.000
Sub Floor Axial Depth	(0.000)	0.000	0.700
Sub Floor Corner Radius	(0.000)	0.000	10.000
Sub Floor Fillet Radius	(0.000)	0.000	10.000

Hit PF1 to see Commands

Exhibit 2. Feature #1.

CONCURRENT RESEARCH AND DEVELOPMENT

Product development is traditionally a linear process in which the design activity first focuses on the product's functional requirements and manufacturing, then addresses such activities as testing, producing, and inspecting. This limits the amount of information available for later stages during product

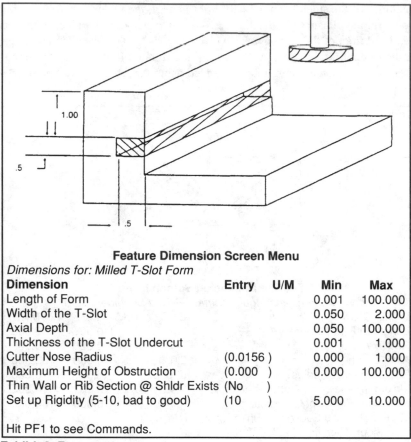

Feature Dimension Screen Menu

Dimensions for: Milled T-Slot Form

Dimension	Entry	U/M	Min	Max
Length of Form			0.001	100.000
Width of the T-Slot			0.050	2.000
Axial Depth			0.050	100.000
Thickness of the T-Slot Undercut			0.001	1.000
Cutter Nose Radius	(0.0156)		0.000	1.000
Maximum Height of Obstruction	(0.000)		0.000	100.000
Thin Wall or Rib Section @ Shldr Exists	(No)			
Set up Rigidity (5-10, bad to good)	(10)		5.000	10.000

Hit PF1 to see Commands.

Exhibit 3. Feature #2.

design and usually results in redesign requirements by subsequent activities. The intent of an effort at the 4950th Test Wing Design and Manufacturing Operations at Wright Patterson Air Force Base is to research the inherent problems of technology limitation, study the associated design process, and develop a design-by-feature system capable of performing simultaneous design for producibility and inspectability. The objectives of such a system are:

• Lowered product life cycle cost
• Reduced product development time
• Improved product quality

Two aspects of the design through manufacturing cycle are being addressed. The first is the development of a data structure to capture producibility

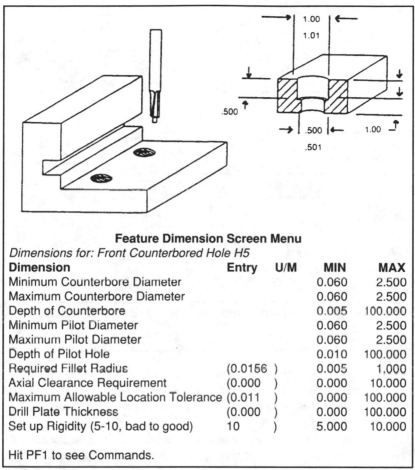

Feature Dimension Screen Menu

Dimensions for: Front Counterbored Hole H5

Dimension	Entry	U/M	MIN	MAX
Minimum Counterbore Diameter			0.060	2.500
Maximum Counterbore Diameter			0.060	2.500
Depth of Counterbore			0.005	100.000
Minimum Pilot Diameter			0.060	2.500
Maximum Pilot Diameter			0.060	2.500
Depth of Pilot Hole			0.010	100.000
Required Fillet Radius	(0.0156)		0.005	1.000
Axial Clearance Requirement	(0.000)		0.000	10.000
Maximum Allowable Location Tolerance	(0.011)		0.000	100.000
Drill Plate Thickness	(0.000)		0.000	100.000
Set up Rigidity (5-10, bad to good)	10)		5.000	10.000

Hit PF1 to see Commands.

Exhibit 4. Feature #3.

and inspectability knowledge. This knowledge must be coupled to the design features (e.g., topology, geometry, and material information) to allow a qualitative evaluation of the design. Once the design is producible and inspectable, the second step is to generate software automatically to perform fabrication and inspection using numerically controlled machine tools and to coordinate measurement equipment.

The goal is to advance the state of the art in simultaneous engineering by demonstrating the concurrent design of a product with the associated manufacturing processes (limited to fabrication and inspection). An important goal of this effort is to construct a system that provides not only simultaneous design for producibility and inspectability but a significant reduction in the product development time with improved product yield (i.e., quality) as well.

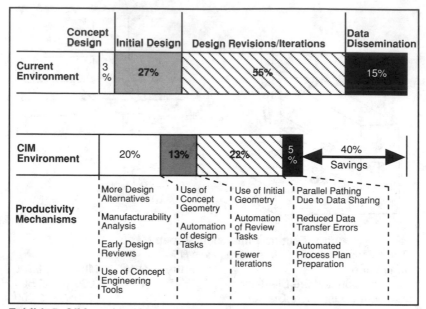

Exhibit 5. CIM product development cycle time reduction.

The first phase of development will focus on developing a manufacturing feature set on a particular class of products produced by the 4950th Test Wing. The Metcut manufacturing features will be evaluated as a part of the development effort.

In the second phase, the manufacturing features will become the basis for a feature-based design system (for design for producibility and inspectability) that will allow automatic process planning and numerical control and other programming functions to be generated from the design and manufacturing features. This will require the development of a systematic way to decompose the part design geometry into a series of manufacturing features that are ordered in a logical manufacturing sequence.

Research commenced in October 1988 to identify and examine the 4950th Test Wing manufacturing operations and identify specific programs based on existing and planned equipment capabilities and a representative class of products to be addressed within this effort. It was expected that by the fall of 1989 work would begin on developing a prototype feature-based design system capable of evaluating manufacturing features for producibility and inspectability.

CONCLUSION

CIM provides a competitive edge to practitioners excelling in the application of technology throughout the product life cycle. An example of product development reduction time is shown in Exhibit 5. This translates to a leadership position in product development, manufacturing processes, automation planning, and facilities design. The result is a strategically refined product and process development cycle with less investment and greater flexibility achieved within a short period of time.

FOOTNOTES

1. F. Mason, "Data base substitutes for lost skill," *American Machinist & Automated Manufacturing.* April, 1988.
2. J. Roth, "Artificial intelligence, a tool for smart manufacturing," *American Machinist Automated Manufacturing.* August, 1986.

15

USING LANS TO AUTOMATE THE FACTORY FLOOR
CELIA A. JOSEPH

This article surveys local area networks (LANs) for factory communications, which are rapidly changing in response to the need for integrated, automated manufacturing systems. The article begins with the requirements that factory LANs must fulfill and then focuses on the aspects of factory LANs that make them unique and on factory-floor LANs in particular. It covers the requirements for factory-floor LANs and the currently applicable standards, summarizes the main media and transmission techniques now in use, and concludes with a look at some of the upcoming changes in factory communications.

To implement CIM, many different types of automation and communications are needed. CIM can be divided into four main functional areas: business data processing, computer-aided design, computer-aided manufacturing, and flexible manufacturing systems.

Several models of manufacturing functions exist; one of the most prevalent is the reference model for factory automation developed by the International Standards Organization (ISO) presented in Exhibit 1. Because different parts of the organization have different requirements, different LANs are typically used to meet these functions. A hierarchical LAN architecture, which permits different LANs to be used as needed, is growing in popularity. Exhibit 2 shows how different LANs could be used to meet specialized needs. For example, the enterprise LAN could be a TOP LAN, the factory backbone LAN could be a MAP broadband LAN, the section LANs and cell LANs could be MAP carrier-band LANs, and the controller-to-device connections could be made with a FieldBus LAN. All of these types of factory LANs are discussed later in this article.

Some of these communications needs can be met by common office

Reprinted from the Summer issue of *CIM Review* (New York: Auerbach Publishers). © 1990 Warren, Gorham & Lamont Inc. Used with permission.

Exhibit 1. ISO reference model for factory automation.

Level	Hierarchy	Control	Responsibility	Basic Functions
6	Enterprise	Corporate Management	Achieving the mission of the enterprise and managing the corporation	• Corporate Management • Finance • Marketing and Sales • Research and Development
5	Facility or Plant	Plan Production	Implementing the enterprise functions and planning and scheduling the production	• Product Design and Production Engineering • Production Management (upper level) • Procurement (upper level) • Resource Management (upper level) • Maintenance Management (upper level)
4	Section or Area	Allocate and Supervise Materials and Resources	Coordinating the production, supporting the jobs, and obtaining and allocating resources to the jobs	• Production Management (lower level) • Procurement (lower level) • Resources Management (lower level) • Maintenance Management (lower level) •Shipping • Waste Material Treatment
3	Cell	Coordinate Multiple Machines and Operations	Sequencing and supervising the jobs at the shop floor and supervising various supporting services	• Shop Floor Production (cell level)
2	Station	Command Machine Sequences and Motion	Directing and coordinating the activity of the shop floor equipment	• Shop Floor Production (station level)
1	Equipment	Activate Sequences and Motion	Performance of commands to the shop floor equipment	• Shop Floor Production (equipment level)

LAN products. The enterprise and plant- or facility-level requirements, for example, could potentially use office LAN products. Other needs (e.g., those of the cell, station, and equipment levels) will require more specialized facilities. These three levels, which support factory-floor production, differ

170

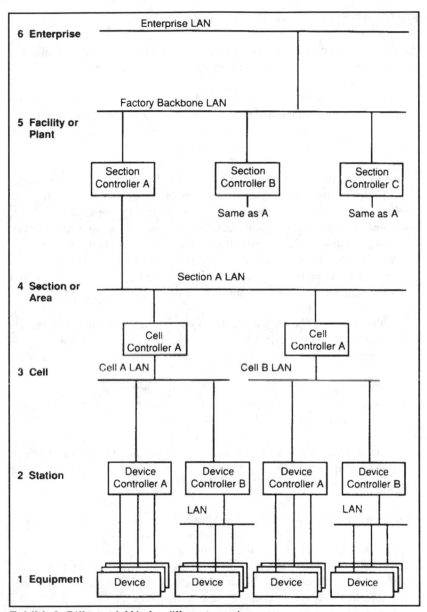

Exhibit 2. Different LANs for different needs.

the most from office communications. Integration, as in CIM, also means that these two extremes—the office and the factory floor—must communicate. The remainder of this article will focus on factory-floor LANs.

FACTORY-FLOOR LAN REQUIREMENTS

Factory floor production has several features that may require special communications capabilities. These features include the following:

- *Environment*—Dirt, dust, and water are obvious enemies of electronic components. Electromagnetic interference can induce voltages in network components that can interfere with the electrical signals used to transmit data.

- *Real-time processing*—This requirement usually translates into two basic needs: deterministic response times and clock synchronization throughout the network. Some believe that office-type systems are not applicable here, because of the variability that can be induced by changes in network resource loading or the probability-based nature of the network protocols. Real-time communications also requires that the communications components use the same concept of time; however, time synchronization across LAN components can be difficult to achieve.

- *Fault tolerance*—The communications equipment, protocols, and associated manufacturing applications must be able to withstand and recover from faults.

- *Priorities*—The ability to ensure rapid response times or high throughput may require giving some applications priority over others in accessing and using communications resources.

- *Special applications*—Two examples of these are messaging between manufacturing controllers and their associated devices, and graphics-data exchange between CAD/CAM systems and controllers.

FACTORY-FLOOR LAN STANDARDS

Because of the simple nature of many factory floor manufacturing devices (e.g., sensors and actuators), the first generation of factory communications products were developed to provide a cheap, rugged, and simple means of communications between these devices and their controllers.

When manufacturing devices become more sophisticated, however, these communications products will be too inflexible and limited in their functions. Furthermore, factory-floor communications systems have faced the same problems as other communications systems; growing needs have led to a proliferation of vendors offering unique solutions. Linking the proprietary products from different vendors was difficult and expensive, and as with office communications, the need for interoperable products from different vendors has led to the growing development of standards.

Several standards are being researched and developed to provide for different factory-floor needs. Some standards differ greatly in the factory communications functions they provide. To contrast these standards, they are compared in the following discussion with the ISO factory reference model in Exhibit 1 and with the ISO open systems interconnection (OSI) reference model for communications.

The standards that this article covers are FieldBus, Bitbus, and MAP/ TOP. Also included is Ethernet, because its widespread use makes it a de facto standard. Exhibit 3 compares these standards with the ISO OSI communications reference model. The shaded areas show the areas of the OSI model that are pertinent to that standard.

FieldBus

FieldBus is the name of a standard initiated by the International Electrotechnical Commission (IEC) PROWAY Working Group to standardize communications for industrial LANs. In the factory LAN hierarchy in Exhibit 2, FieldBus

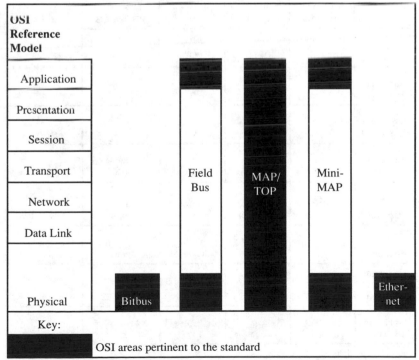

Exhibit 3. Comparing the ISO OSI seven-layer reference model with other standards.

would be used between the devices at level 1 and the device controllers at level 2. It provides functions equivalent to the OSI physical, data link, and application layers. The main goal of FieldBus is to simplify the complexity of current point-to-point cabling between devices and controllers and to provide improved communications capabilities.

Several other standards organizations are working on standards similar to FieldBus. These include the Factory Instrumentation Protocol (FIP) in France, Process FieldBus (PROFIBUS) in Germany, MIL-STD-1553 developed by the US Air Force and US Navy, and the Instrumentation Society of America's ISA SP-50 FieldBus. Exhibit 4 compares several features of these standards with each other and with Bitbus, which is described in the next section.

Most of these standards have many characteristics in common because they address fairly similar requirements, primarily those involving replacement of existing 4-20 milliamp (mA) systems. For example, the ISA SP-50 FieldBus focuses on two sets of requirements, called Hl and H2. Hl is a digital replacement for existing 4-20 mA systems. It is intended for short distances, operates at low speeds, and uses low-cost wire in a star topology. H2 is a higher-performance system suitable for logic applications. It uses a bus

	ISA SP-50 FieldBus	MIL-STD 1553	FIP	PROFIBUS	Bitbus
Speed	≤100K bps	1M bps	3M bps	9.6K-500K bps	62.5-375K bps
Hamming Distance	*	2	3	2 or 4	1
Broadcast Supported	*	Yes	Yes	Yes	No
Message Length	*	2-64 bytes	2 bytes	246 bytes or fewer	2-248 bytes
Control	Peer-to-peer controller	Central arbitrator	Single bus multiple masters	Master-slave	Master-slave
Encoding	*	Manchester	Manchester	Non-return-to-zero	Non-return-to-zero inverted
Maximum Number of Stations	256	31	60	32 or 122	28
Maximum Distance	750 m or 1,900 m	6 m	1 km	0.4 km to 2.4 km	13.2 km/900 m
Note: * To be determined.					

Exhibit 4. Comparison of FieldBus and Bitbus systems.

topology and provides support for longer distances, higher speeds, and peer-to-peer communications. Some expect the H2 FieldBus to become a low-cost subset of IEEE 802.4. H2 will contain protocols equivalent to the OSI physical, data link, and application layers. Its application layer will be based on the ISA dS72.02 for a process-control application layer.

As shown in Exhibit 4, many details of the ISA standard are yet to be determined. ISA's FieldBus standardization is not likely to be completed before the early 1990s. Other standards, such as MIL-STD-1553 and FIP, are completed.

Bitbus

Bitbus is a serial protocol for the rapid transfer of very short control messages (2 to 248 bytes) among nodes in a control network, based on Intel's 8044 microcontroller. Bitbus is a low-cost method for connecting distributed intelligent devices to a central host in an electrically harsh environment. It is sometimes considered another type of FieldBus network because, like FieldBus, it connects devices to device controllers—so it serves levels 1 and 2 of the ISO factory reference model. Its functions equate to those of the physical and data link layers of the OSI communications model. Some believe that Bitbus's lack of an application layer is a significant drawback.

In contrast to FieldBus, Bitbus operates only in a single-master, multiple-slave arrangement; it is not suitable for peer-to-peer communications. Bitbus runs on twisted-pair wire and can operate at 62.5K bps to 13.2 kilometers or at 375K bps to 900 meters. Its protocol is based on a subset of RS-485 and IBM's synchronous data link control (SDLC).

Related to Bitbus is IEEE Project P1118, which is developing a standard for a microcontroller system serial control bus. So far, the project has produced two documents: one for functional requirements and one giving a data overview and architecture. IEEE P1118 is developing a serial data communications standard for microcontroller devices on a multidrop bus. The original work used the existing Bitbus protocol as a starting point. Some believe that P1118 is a formalization of the Bitbus master-slave protocol.

MAP/TOP

The Manufacturing Automation Protocol (MAP) and the Technical and Office Protocol (TOP) are two specifications for standard communications interfaces for manufacturing. MAP and TOP can potentially satisfy all levels of the ISO factory reference model.

These specifications grew out of the work of a task force started by General Motors (GM) in 1980 to investigate the possibility of standardization, because of its continued dissatisfaction with the difficulty and expense of developing interfaces for incompatible proprietary communications systems. The first version of MAP was produced in 1982.

Boeing, faced with problems similar to GM's, adapted MAP for its own needs and produced TOP. Version 3.0 is the current version of both specifications. The MAP/TOP Users Group has frozen the specifications until 1994 in an effort to encourage vendors to develop products meeting these specifications.

MAP and TOP follow the ISO OSI reference model and support all seven protocol layers. In an effort to accommodate the process-control industry, however, MAP also has the Enhanced Performance Architecture (EPA), which includes only the physical, data link, and application protocol layers of OSI. Systems that include a seven-layer protocol stack and a three-layer EPA stack are called MAP/EPA systems. Systems with only a three layer EPA stack are called mini-MAP systems. Exhibits 5, 6, and 7 depict the protocol layers used in these specifications.

A distinguishing feature of MAP and TOP is the wide variety of applications they support. Both MAP and TOP use existing standards whenever possible, primarily using standards from ISO or the IEEE. The main applications in MAP and TOP include the following:

- *Messaging between controllers and associated devices*—This is used primarily for MAP and is based on the Manufacturing Message Specification (MMS). MMS specifies the syntax and semantics for general manufacturing messaging but does not contain application-specific information. Application specifics are being defined separately in such MMS companion standards as those being developed for robots, programmable logic controllers, numerical controllers, production management, and process control. MMS has more than 80 services providing the following functions:

  —Connection management
  —Device information sharing
  —Program upload and download
  —Program management
  —Variable access
  —Resource management
  —Operator communication
  —Event management
  —Journal management

- *File Transfer*—The ISO standard for file transfer and access method (FTAM) is used in both MAP and TOP. FTAM defines an abstract, distributed, file storage method and provides basic services for such functions as reading, writing, creating, erasing, locating, and transferring data.

OSI Reference Model		MAP 3.0
Application		Directory of Services Network Management MMS FTAM ACSE
Presentation		Presentation
Session		Session
Transport		Transport Class 4
Network		CLNS --- ES-IS
Data Link		IEEE 802.2 --- IEEE 802.4 10M-byte
Physical		Broadband or 5M-byte Carrier Band

Notes:
ACSE Association control service element
CLNS Connectionless network service
ES   End system
FTAM File transfer and access method
IS   Intermediate system
MMS   Manufacturing message specification

Exhibit 5. MAP and OSI protocol layers.

• *Virtual terminal*—The ISO virtual terminal standard lets users connect to and access heterogeneous host systems, regardless of the type of terminal used.

• *Mail*—The TOP specification includes an electronic-mail capability called the Message-Handling System. It is based on CCITT recommendation X.400 and has two services: a basic message transfer service supporting general, application-independent message transfer, and an interpersonal messaging service that uses the message-transfer service to give users electronic-mail service.

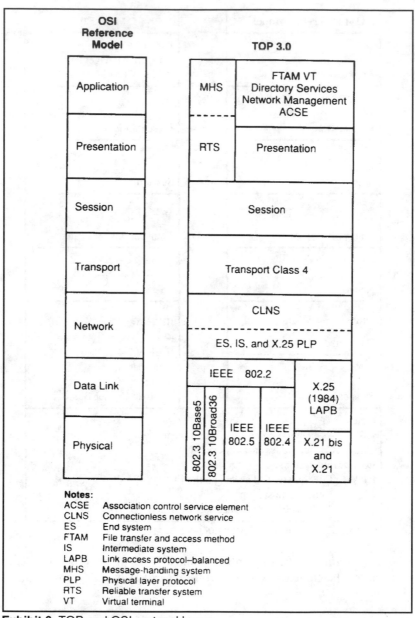

Exhibit 6. TOP and OSI protocol layers.

• *Directory of services*—The ISO directory of services standards provides for centralized or distributed directories of resources on the network. It also provides security features (e.g., controls that determine who may access certain directory resources).

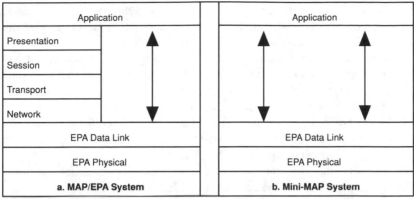

Application		Application	
Presentation			
Session			
Transport			
Network			
EPA Data Link		EPA Data Link	
EPA Physical		EPA Physical	
a. MAP/EPA System		**b. Mini-MAP System**	

Exhibit 7. MAP/ERA and Mini-MAP protocol layers.

- *Network management*—Network management's basic role is to monitor and control the resources used in a network. ISO's efforts in network management were in preliminary stages when MAP and TOP capabilities had to be defined. Partly because of this, MAP and TOP include only three network-management functions in their specifications: configuration, fault, and performance management. Furthermore, the management information protocol and service specified in MAP and TOP is an older version of the ISO Communications Management Information Service/Protocol (CMIS/CMIP). When ISO's work in defining managed objects was just beginning. MAP and TOP created their own definitions of the objects to be managed, also incorporating work from the IEEE 802 efforts.

- *Interchange formats*—The TOP specification includes several formats for standardizing the exchange of information, including the Product Definition Interchange Format (PDIF), the Initial Graphics Exchange Specification (IGES), and the Computer Graphics Metafile Interchange Format (CGMIF). These formats are particularly useful for CAD/CAM applications.

Ethernet
Ethernet is a de facto standard for factory-floor systems that provides functions equivalent to the OSI physical layer and the lower part of the data link layers (i.e., the media access control sublayer). It has been used for virtually all levels of the ISO factory reference model, although it is mainly used for the station, cell, section or area, and, possibly, facility or plant levels. It can be used in combination with any number of higher-level protocols and applications. For example, it can be found on plant floors connecting process-control devices and is also used as the basis for TOP networks.

In an Ethernet system, the control is distributed throughout the network; there is no central controller. Ethernet uses carrier-sense multiple access with collision-detection (CSMA/CD) algorithms to control access to the network medium; carrier sense means that each station on the network can detect whether another station is broadcasting. If a station senses that another station is already transmitting, it will wait until that transmission ends before beginning its own. If two stations transmit at the same time, the collision-detection algorithms ensure that all stations know that there was a collision and control which station will transmit first. Ethernet typically uses baseband modulation techniques, although broadband CSMA/CD systems exist.

One advantage of Ethernet is that it is an established technology more than 10 years old; it was the basis for the IEEE 802.3 standard. Ethernet can operate over low-cost coaxial cable. If network loads are kept at less than 10% of the total bandwidth, the probability based nature of CSMA/CD does not seem to affect factory applications. Still, many critics of Ethernet feel it is not suitable for factory floor systems. Some of its main drawbacks are its inherent nondeterminism, the fact that baseband transmissions may be sensitive to electromagnetic interference, and the fact that official Ethernet baseband cable is quite expensive compared with the coaxial cable used in broadband systems. Furthermore, if an Ethernet system is more than 80% loaded, its performance degrades to a standstill because of the number of collisions and retransmissions that occur. A research project by Digital Equipment Corp., a large vendor of Ethernet systems, has tried to dispel some of these criticisms.

Factory Transmission Techniques and Media
Two main transmission techniques are in use in factory-floor systems: baseband and broadband. Baseband and broadband techniques can be used on a variety of media including twisted-pair wire, coaxial cable, and optical fiber. The characteristics of these techniques and media are summarized briefly in the following sections.

TRANSMISSION TECHNIQUES

In baseband systems, bits are represented by low or high voltages that take up the entire transmission medium. The shifts in voltage propagate throughout the medium. Typical characteristics are transmission rates of lM to lOM bits per second and segment lengths of 1,000 meters or less. Some baseband transmission techniques, such as those used in Ethernet, are susceptible to electrical noise. Other transmission techniques (e.g., carrier band) use a radio-frequency carrier to provide superior noise immunity.

One of the main differences between broadband and baseband transmission is that broadband uses multiple frequencies to transmit multiple data streams on a single cable. Broadband provides a total bandwidth in the range of 300 to 400 MHz. which is usually divided into smaller, individual channels of from 1 to 12 MHz.

Broadband is highly immune to noise interference, which makes it a good choice for factory environments. Broadband networks can span 10 kilometers or more. Although the cable for broadband is relatively cheap, other components, such as the head-end (remodulator) and modems, can be expensive. Furthermore, the head-end can be a single point of failure.

Media

Twisted-pair wiring is usually found in telephone systems but is also the basis for Bitbus and FieldBus LANs. Noise interference can be a problem with twisted-pair wire unless it is shielded, which significantly drives up the cost. Twisted-pair wire is also limited in the bandwidth it provides and the distance it can carry signals.

The cable television industry developed coaxial cable in its effort to eliminate the weather and radio interference to which other media were susceptible. Coaxial cable shields the conductor and protects it from noise. Using broadband transmission techniques, coaxial cable can provide enough separate channels to satisfy a wide variety of applications. For example, broadband coaxial systems can simultaneously carry data, voice, and video transmissions.

Fiber optic-based systems are easily capable of transmission rates of millions of bits per second. Systems on fiber-optic networks can be kilometers apart. Furthermore, fiber-optic systems are immune to electrical interference, making them ideal for factory environments. The lack of standards for fiber-optic systems, however, hampers their current use. Other issues of concern with fiber-optic systems are the topology for use and methods of reconfiguring the network, particularly if nodes fail.

FUTURE DEVELOPMENTS

This section presents an overview of anticipated changes in factory communications. These are divided into near-term changes (what forward-thinking firms are installing), mid-term changes (changes expected in the next three to five years), and long-term changes (promising research areas).

Near-Term Changes

Rapid changes in communications technology are being applied to various needs throughout manufacturing enterprises. Some current trends are communications integration, the development of manufacturing infrastructures, and the use of microcomputer LANs for manufacturing.

Communications integration. Products to support enterprise-wide communications necessary to implement CIM are being offered by several vendors, including IBM, Digital Equipment Corp., and Hewlett-Packard. Achieving integrated communications in an enterprise requires hardware and software products in three areas: connectivity, information transfer, and common applications that use the information.

LANs, wide-area networks (WANs), or combinations of the two may be needed for connectivity throughout the organization. Information-transfer products are readily available using any one of several protocol suites (e.g., OSI, SNA, DECnet, and TCP/IP). Products also exist for transferring information between protocol suites. Common applications to permit information sharing can be a more difficult problem, because different portions of an enterprise have usually selected their information processing applications separately. The key to this problem is a common information architecture; otherwise, integrating different applications will result in a hodge-podge of translation products.

Manufacturing infrastructures. Connectivity is a vital ingredient in developing the industrial infrastructure necessary to improve the competitiveness of US industries and to reduce manufacturers' reliance on outside sources. One way such infrastructures are developing is through groups of small to medium-sized manufacturers bidding collectively on projects. The Flint River Project in Michigan is an example of one such group. This project combines the abilities of 30 to 40 smaller, more focused establishments with the marketing and engineering capacities of a central firm to form a flexible manufacturing network. For such an infrastructure to work, the organizations must coordinate their activities, ideally using both voice and data links to support the integration of such activities as design, scheduling, and production. This type of integration may not be feasible because of cost, but communications over facsimile (sometimes dubbed fax-net) is a low-cost first step.

Microcomputer LANs. A new trend is to use off-the-shelf, micro-based LANs for factory floor applications. Microcomputers are being used in growing numbers as low-cost, automated tools at the station and cell level, and as more micro-based systems are used, the need to integrate them increases. Microcomputer LANs that use off-the-shelf components are an inexpensive method of providing integrated communications at a much lower cost than specialized methods. Another advantage is that they are easy to use as gateways to other factory engineering, order-entry, and office computer networks because of the availability of microcomputer LAN products.

Mid-Term Changes
Mid-term changes will result from current research and from products that implement standards now being completed. Some potential areas for mid-term changes are new applications, mobile communications, distributed data management, growth in manufacturing infrastructures, and applications management.

New applications. Nearing completion are several application standards that can provide great utility to manufacturing enterprises. These include the following:

- *The Product Data Exchange Specification (PDES)*—PDES defines a standard for the exchange, description, and format of the data necessary to fully describe a product and its manufacturing process. More specifically, PDES definitions cover the following areas: formats for storing and archiving data, formats for product data exchange, mechanisms for exchanging product data among different applications, and mechanisms for sharing product data among several different applications.

- *The Remote Data Access (RDA) standard*—RDA provides an established way to exchange data base manipulation instructions and to exchange the resulting data, if any. RDA is based on a generic data manipulation language that can be specialized according to the type of data base (e.g., relational). Currently, the only specialized data manipulation language being developed is for relational data bases using Structured Query Language (SQL). RDA also provides transaction processing support (i.e., multiple data manipulation language operations can be grouped together). Any updates will not be permanent until the entire transaction is completed.

- *The Office Document Architecture (ODA)*—ODA is an international standard that provides definitions for the syntax of a number of commonly used document types, including memoranda, letters, invoices, forms, and reports. ODA also defines what these documents can contain and how this content is exchanged. Possible types of ODA document content are text, images, graphics (e.g., raster and geometric), and sound. ODA permits communication of the document originator's intentions regarding editing, formatting, and presentation. ODA relies on other OSI application standards for actual document transfer, so it requires the use of FTAM or the Message-Handling System.

Mobile communications. The factory of the future will most likely use some form of mobile machines, such as automated guided vehicles (AGVs). In an integrated factory, the problem with these machines is how to communicate

183

with something that moves. Current research is focusing on developing through-the-air methods of communications suitable for factory environments. Possibilities being investigated include spread-spectrum packet-radio techniques and such optical methods as those based on infrared light. Prototypes of these methods are being evaluated.

Distributed data management. As an enterprise migrates to integrated communications, its information storage methods require revision. Before integration, most organizations store information in separate repositories. The information must therefore be reentered when transferred between organizational entities. The results are highly redundant data storage as well as concurrency problems (i.e., determining which copy is the most current) when data updates are needed.

Communications integration facilitates the consolidation of information into centralized data bases, or common distributed data base servers. Consolidation information stores can reduce the overall storage and the number of information transfers needed and can solve the concurrency problem. One example of how consolidation can pay off is the Industrial Technology Institute's Network Object Server for MMS applications. The Network Object Server is a central repository for the MMS information required in a manufacturing cell; it reduces the communications needed to coordinate the actions of devices in the cell, facilitates the distribution of up-to-date data, and reduces the overall communications processing needed.

Growth in manufacturing infrastructures. As firms working collectively in a manufacturing infrastructure gain experience, their integration tools can become more sophisticated. For example, a fax-net could be gradually replaced with integrated communications using a combination of LANs and WANs.

Applications management. With the growing use of distributed manufacturing applications comes the problem of managing distributed resources. This problem is compounded if the applications are developed by different vendors. A new area of research is applications management, which seeks to adapt techniques developed for managing distributed-network resources to distributed applications.

Long-Term Changes
Long-term changes in manufacturing communications will be based on new research in manufacturing. Two promising research areas are distributed data and control integration and total communications integration.

Distributed data and control integration. Centralized data repositories may not be adequate for large, flexible, highly integrated manufacturing systems.

An architecture based on artificial intelligence concepts, one providing both distributed control and distributed knowledge bases, may be more efficient and reliable. Purdue University researchers are investigating the use of separate information management elements and decision-making or control elements. The information is managed using distributed, hierarchical knowledge bases, with one knowledge base for a particular function or group of similar functions. The decision-making or control system performs most of the tasks of a traditional control system. The information management and the decision-making or control systems will be implemented through distributed systems that are parallel yet independent.

Total communications integration. Although CIM solves many information-flow problems, it creates others. The biggest of which is how to integrate the diverse communications methods used in various parts of an enterprise. To solve this problem, ways of developing one basic communications method usable throughout an organization are being researched. Such a method must support various requirements, including both real-time and nonreal-time traffic. One potential method is to create protocols specialized for fiber optic-based systems that can handle all types of traffic.

Manufacturers must account for changes like these as they plan for improved communications and integration. Such developments as mobile communications and distributed data management should be considered as companies replace obsolete methods of factory communications with new products, standards, and media.

16

An Architecture for Decision Making in the Factory of the Future
Richard H. F. Jackson and Albert W. T. Jones

A major manufacturing research facility is being established at the National Bureau of Standards. The Automated Manufacturing Research Facility has been designed to address the need for standards and measurement for the factory of the future. A five-layer hierarchical control architecture is under development to control the various production and support activities needed to drive that factory. The proper execution of many of these activities requires the solution of one or more optimization problems. We propose a decision-making hierarchy that parallels that control architecture, describe the problems that exist at each level within that hierarchy, and discuss the work underway at NBS to address some of those problems.

Manufacturing plants contain various combinations of people, computers, and machines, working together to maximize corporate profits from the goods they produce. Many of these plants are not meeting this goal. They are plagued by several problems—large work-in-process inventories, low utilization of equipment, insufficient throughput, and excessive delays—all of which tend to have a negative impact on profits.

When computer-controlled robots, machine tools, and transporters became commercially available, many companies made large capital investments in this new equipment, hoping to alleviate these problems. They then purchased the sophisticated computer and data-base technologies needed to integrate this equipment into existing plants. The result is often referred to as computer integrated manufacturing (CIM). CIM was, and still is, expected to increase profits and lead to larger shares of the world markets.

In general, this has not happened. In fact, introducing these new CIM technologies can have a greater negative impact on profits. There are three

Reprinted by permission of Richard H. F. Jackson and Albert W. T. Jones, *Interfaces*, volume 17, no. 6, November-December 1987. Copyright 1987 the Operations Research Society of America and The Institute of Management Sciences, 290 Westminster Street, Providence, Rhode Island 02903 USA.

major reasons for this surprising phenomenon. First, integrating equipment from different vendors is far more difficult than ever anticipated. This demonstrates the pressing need for software and hardware interface standards. Second, the continued use of existing planning and scheduling strategies often magnifies the effects of the problems mentioned above. This results in very expensive equipment lying idle and makes it impossible to achieve the desired profits or rate of return on capital investments. Finally, poor data management and communication strategies have also caused undesirable delays and idle equipment.

The National Bureau of Standards (NBS) is trying to address these issues within the Automated Manufacturing Research Facility.

THE AUTOMATED MANUFACTURING RESEARCH FACILITY

The National Bureau of Standards has a fundamental commitment to promote the development of standards for automated manufacturing systems and to transfer technology to American industry. To meet this responsibility, the Center for Manufacturing Engineering at NBS has established an experimental test bed, the Automated Manufacturing Research Facility (AMRF) [Simpson, Hocken, and Albus 1982]. Industry, academia, and other government agencies have played an active role in this development effort through direct appropriations, equipment loans, and cooperative research programs.

Physically, the AMRF contains several robots, machine tools, storage and retrieval systems, two wire-guided vehicles, and numerous computers. This equipment includes donations and purchases from four different robot manufacturers, three machine tool vendors, and every major computer company. This diversity of suppliers has forced NBS researchers to focus on designing and testing uniform software and hardware interfaces and data exchange formats to address the problems involved in system integration. They have developed factory control software, a manufacturing-data-preparation system, a distributed data management strategy, a communications system, and numerous sensors. These individual hardware and software components have been successfully integrated into a small CIM system (Figure 1).

DESIGN PHILOSOPHY

The AMRF is intended to exhibit a greater degree of flexibility and modularity than any currently available flexible manufacturing system (FMS). To achieve these goals, the AMRF has adopted the following design philosophies concerning its control architecture. It is

• partitioned into a functional hierarchy in which decision making and control functions reside at the lowest possible level;

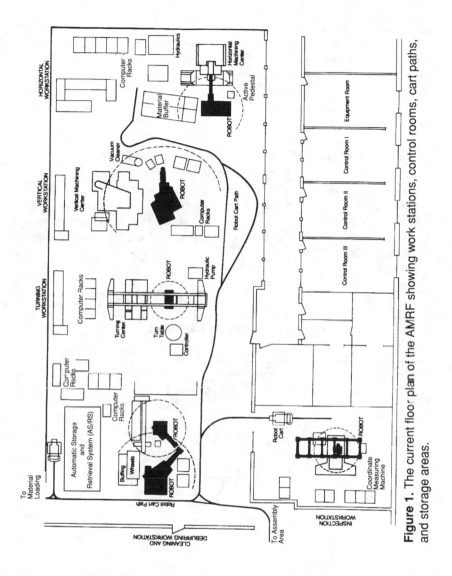

Figure 1. The current floor plan of the AMRF showing work stations, control rooms, cart paths, and storage areas.

- intended to respond in real time to performance data obtained from machines equipped with sensors;
- implemented in a distributed computing environment using state-of-the-art techniques in software engineering and artificial intelligence; and
- designed so that control processes are completely data-driven and communicate via NBS-developed hardware and software interfaces which are uniform throughout the AMRF.

189

The AMRF control architecture is based on the classic hierarchical, or tree-shaped, command/feedback control structure (Figure 3) typical of many complex organizations [Albus, Barbera, and Nagel 1984]. This approach ensures that the size, functionality, and complexity of individual control modules is limited. In addition, each control level is completely data driven. That is, the data required to perform its functions is separated from the actual control code.

Each module decomposes input commands from its supervisor into procedures to be executed at that level and subcommands to be issued to one or more subordinate modules (Figure 2). This decomposition process is repeated until, at the lowest level, a sequence of coordinated primitive actions is generated which actuates shop floor equipment [Albus, Barbera, and Nagel 1981]. The status feedback that is provided to supervisors by their subordinates is used to close the control loop and to support adaptive, real-time decision making.

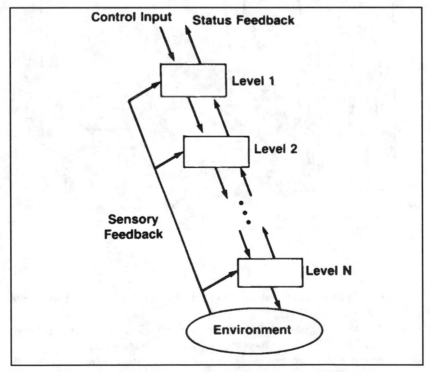

Figure 2. The information flow in a control hierarchy showing inputs and outputs to each level.

All control modules have been designed and implemented to be completely data-driven. That is, the data required to execute a command is completely separate from the control code which executes that command. Consequently, the management of that data is crucial to the AMRF.

The data management function is concerned with providing shared data to all manufacturing processes in a timely, accurate, and completely transparent manner. This function is complicated by both the manufacturing and computing environment in which it must be performed. The manufacturing environment requires dynamic and frequent updates to the data directory, data delivery paths that are separate from the existing control structure, and local but efficient storage of data for real-time operations. The computing environment consists of heterogeneous systems with different data manipulation languages, data management capabilities, formats, types, and structures.

FUNCTIONAL DECOMPOSITION

An analysis of traditional small batch manufacturing systems provided the foundation for the decomposition of the manufacturing functions into five levels: facility, shop, cell, work station, and equipment (Figure 3). A brief discussion of the responsibilities assigned to each of these levels follows. More details can be found in Jones and McLean [1986].

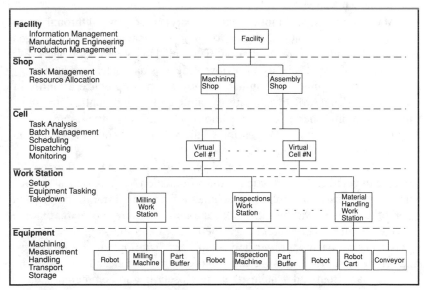

Figure 3. The five-level AMRF control architecture showing functions assigned to each level in the hierarchy.

The facility level is responsible for implementing the front office functions that are typically found in manufacturing facilities. Activities at this level are grouped into subsystems that fall into three major functional areas: manufacturing engineering, information management, and production management.

Manufacturing engineering functions are typically carried out with human involvement via user-data interfaces. This includes computer-aided design (CAD), group technology classification, and process planning. The information management activities provide user-data interfaces to support administrative and business management functions. Production management tracks major projects, generates long-range schedules, identifies production resource requirements, determines the need for additional capital investments to meet production goals, determines excess production capacity, and summarizes quality performance data.

The shop level is responsible for coordinating the production and support jobs on the shop floor. It is also responsible for allocating resources to those jobs. Two major component modules have been identified within the shop controller: a task manager and a resource manager. The task manager is responsible for capacity planning, grouping orders into batches, assigning and releasing batch jobs to cells, and tracking individual orders to completion. The resource manager is responsible for allocating the production resources to individual cells, managing the repair of existing resources, and ordering new resources.

At the cell level, batch jobs of similar parts are sequenced through work stations, and supervision is provided for various other support services, such as material handling and calibration. The cell [Jones and McLean 1984] brings some of the efficiency of a flow shop to small batch production by using a set of machine tools and shared job setups to produce a family of similar parts. The AMRF cells are dynamic production control structures which permit time-sharing of work stations. This software structure is named the virtual cell. A detailed discussion of the virtual cell concept is found in McLean, Bloom, and Hopp [1982].

The activities of small integrated physical groupings of shop floor equipment are directed and coordinated at the workstation level. A typical AMRF work station consists of a robot, a machine tool, a material storage buffer, and a control computer. Machining work stations process trays of parts that are delivered by the material handling system. The controller sequences equipment-level subsystems through job setup, part fixturing, cutting processes, chip removal, in-process inspection, job takedown, and cleanup operations.

These are front-end systems that are closely tied to commercial equipment or industrial machinery on the shop floor. Equipment controllers are required for robots, numerically-controlled machine tools, coordinate-measuring machines, delivery systems, and storage/retrieval devices. Equipment controllers perform two major functions: (1) they translate work station commands into a sequence of simple tasks that can be understood by the vendor-supplied controller, and (2) they monitor the execution of these tasks via the sensors attached to the hardware.

These constraints imply that data will, of necessity, be physically distributed around the factory. NBS researchers have proposed an architecture called IMDAS —integrated manufacturing data administration system—to manage this distributed data. IMDAS is also a hierarchical structure, but it is completely separate from the control hierarchy. And, it has been specifically designed to meet the manufacturing and computing requirements described above. A detailed description of IMDAS can be found in Barkmeyer, et al. [1986].

A NEW DECISION-MAKING HIERARCHY

Many decisions affect the actual production of parts on the shop floor. We have described the benefits of hierarchical decomposition of the control problems within automated manufacturing facilities. We propose to mimic this approach to control by decomposing the decision-making process along the same hierarchical lines.

As one moves down this decision-making hierarchy, several important observations can be made concerning the nature of these problems. First, each level must sequence through the list of jobs assigned by its supervisor, and develop a schedule of tasks for its subordinates. Second, the number of problems to be solved and the frequency with which they must be resolved increases dramatically. Third, the time available to find solutions decreases significantly. Finally, the information used to solve them becomes more abundant, complete, and deterministic. These properties will have a tremendous impact on the techniques used to solve problems at different levels within this hierarchy.

What follows is, in a sense, a laundry list of problems, some classical and well recognized, others new, arising from the introduction of new technologies into manufacturing systems. Indeed, some of the problems may seem insignificant now, but as our ability to understand and control these CIM systems increases, the marginal gain from having optimal solutions to these problems will also increase.

THE FACILITY LEVEL

The facility level has sole responsibility for the business and strategic planning functions that support the entire manufacturing enterprise. Better mathematical models are required to aid top management in assessing and justifying the potential benefits and costs of flexible automation. In addition, once the decision has been made to employ this technology, new techniques are needed in cost accounting, depreciation, capital investment strategies, and many other business functions [Eiler 1986]. Existing methodologies are unable to measure the impact of this flexibility in a meaningful way.

Another function performed at the facility level is the manufacturing-data-preparation crucial to the actual part production. Schedules must be generated for all of the activities required to complete this preparation. These schedules include both new customer requests and revisions to existing data required by changing conditions on the shop floor. In addition, new methods are needed to aid in the classification and coding of parts from CAD data, geometric modeling, decomposition of complex geometries into primitive features that can be machined and inspected, and the design, revision; and verification of process plans.

THE SHOP LEVEL

The shop level receives a list of customer requests and any assigned priorities or due dates from the facility level. The shop level sequences these requests, groups them into batches, and determines the order in which these batches will be released to the manufacturing cells on the shop floor. It then produces a schedule that indicates the cells to be used for each batch, estimated start and finish times at each cell, and the required material transfers among those cells. These plans must be updated any time a new request is issued, an existing request is cancelled or given a higher priority, or a significant problem occurs.

The shop also has overall responsibility for inventory control, tool management, capacity planning, and preventive maintenance for all equipment in the shop. These activities must be managed to support the schedules developed at this level.

An important issue to be resolved at the shop level is the future use of existing techniques, such as material resource planning and master production scheduling. In an environment like the AMRF, in which decisions are pushed down to the lowest level, these global planning approaches may no longer be applicable. However, this is still an open question.

THE CELL LEVEL

A cell controller must coordinate the activities of its subordinate work stations to complete the jobs assigned by the shop. Each job will require the services of one or more work stations including material handling and will usually have some due date and priority associated with it. The cell must sequence these jobs and develop a schedule of anticipated start and finish times and priorities for each job at each work station. It must determine which work stations will be needed and the order in which they will be needed. It must also arrange for the requisite material transfers in support of that schedule. When conflicts or delays are reported by a work-station controller, the cell must replan, reroute, and reschedule to overcome them.

Coordinating the activities at these work stations becomes more difficult when there exist shop-wide, shared resources like material transport devices. In addition, the introduction of virtual cells will also complicate the decisions at the cell level and at the shop level.

THE WORK-STATION LEVEL

Each work-station controller must coordinate the activities of its subordinates to execute a series of tasks assigned by a cell controller. Although the exact nature of the tasks are work-station-dependent, they typically consist of receiving materials, shipping materials, setup, takedown, and a list of features to be machined or inspected. The work-station controller must generate a sequence in which to perform these tasks and a schedule for each of its subordinates.

In addition, the material-handling work-station controller has several other problems it must address. These special problems are directly related to its primary responsibility of planning and coordinating the activities required to move trays of materials around the factory. It must locate the material, assign a transportation device (or devices) to pick up and deliver that material, and determine the routes it will follow in executing the task. Further, all these activities must be coordinated and monitored for possible changes and updates.

Assigning trays to batches of parts must also be addressed. This problem is complicated in an environment in which a batch size of one or two is the rule rather than the exception. In this case, a single tray could contain several batches of parts, each having a different geometry. Further complications are that deliveries to more than one work station may be combined on a single tray and that each transportation device may be capable of carrying more than one tray.

THE EQUIPMENT LEVEL

The lowest level in the hierarchy contains the equipment controllers. There are three classes of equipment: stationary robots; machine tools; and material storage, retrieval, and transport devices. The mathematical decision problems to be solved by each equipment controller fall into two major categories. The first is sequencing and scheduling. Each controller must sequence through the current tasks assigned by its supervisory work station. They may be rank-ordered, with expected completion times associated with each task. In addition, the controller must schedule and coordinate the activities required to execute these tasks. The second set of problems is equipment-dependent, and is discussed in more detail later.

ROBOTS

Robots are used primarily to locate, move, and handle materials, such as parts, tools, and fixtures. In addition, they perform housekeeping duties to remove chips during machining and assemble and disassemble fixtures. Typical subsystems are vision, multiple hands and grippers, and other actuators. In addition to the sequencing and scheduling problems discussed above, robot controllers have several, more time-critical problems to solve. They include path generation, optimal routing for traversing parts, loading and unloading materials, and tray layout.

All robots are required to maneuver through three-dimensional space as part of their routine activities. Paths must be generated to allow the robot to move from one point to another. This problem is complicated by the fact that the robot's work space is filled with obstacles. If the position of these objects remains fixed, then this problem can be solved off-line and to optimality. If, however, obstacles are constantly moving into and out of the work space or changing position within the work space, then this becomes a realtime problem. In this case, it may be necessary, due to time constraints, to replace optimality with a suboptimal yet feasible and easily generated path.

Once the robot has reached its destination, it must then carry out some specified task. It may need to pick up a part, to place a part in a fixture, insert a tool into a tool drum, or any of a number of other similar activities. Each task demands the precise positioning of the robot arm(s) before the activity can commence. The relative or absolute precision required will depend on the activity and the capabilities of the robot. For instance, a robot equipped with a vision system does not require the same precision as a robot without a vision system. This is an important problem and could be viewed as a solution to a nonlinear optimization problem in which the objective is to minimize the error in the actual or relative position.

Another area where optimization methods can be brought to bear is in the loading, unloading and layout of trays. In some respects, portions of the problems are scaled-down facility layout problems. Thus, some of the ideas from the facility layout and design literature could be useful. However, all of these problems can be complicated by the likelihood that multiple geometries may exist in the same confined space within a tray.

There is an interesting optimization problem concerned with finding optimal routes for traversing parts for inspection, cleaning, and deburring. These tasks usually require several different end-effectors such as probes, deburring tools, and so forth. The objective would be to perform these activities in a way that is optimal with respect to some measure, perhaps time, number of two-handed moves, end-effector changes, or part repositioning.

Pattern recognition for robot vision systems is another area where significant optimization problems appear. These range from simple nonlinear least-squares problems that arise from attempting to match patterns, to more complicated nonlinear least-squares problems that arise in combining small windows of bit patterns to form larger windows for faster scanning.

The robot carts that serve the work stations must address some of the same problems as the fixed-position robots; they may, however, take on a slightly different look. For example, path calculations for the robots become routing problems for the carts. The issue here is deciding which path to take to deliver or pick up trays from the work stations. If the cart can travel forward and backward, the problem becomes more complicated. The situation is further complicated by the use of multiple carts on the same path, although the coordination activity for this is performed at the next higher level. The layout of the wire-guided path is also a task that lends itself to mathematical analysis and could be studied to determine the best paths to lay down.

MACHINING CENTERS

The AMRF contains three computer numerically controlled (CNC) machining centers: horizontal, vertical, and turning. They are capable of performing several metal removal operations and limited, online inspection of parts and tools. In addition, the AMRF has a coordinate measuring machine (CMM) to perform off-line inspection of machined parts. Typically, each machining center must coordinate the activities of tool holder(s), part holder(s), spindle(s), and coolant sprayer(s). The CMM controls a rotary table, probes, and several other axes of motion. Each of these controllers is responsible for sequencing and scheduling assigned tasks. Examples of these tasks are tool and collect changes, remounting parts on pallets, chip removal, and the actual machining and inspection operations. These problems should be solved to optimality with respect to some performance measure, such as number of tool changes, number of refixturings, time in queue, or number of late tasks. Again, as noted with the robot controllers, these problems must be solved often and quickly.

Machining centers have several other problems related to the storage, selection, and use of tools. The storage problem is essentially a tool-layout problem. The placement of tools in a drum (or other similar device) can affect the total time required to machine a set of features.

Consequently, the exact arrangement of tools can be represented as an optimization problem in which the objective is to minimize the time required to gain access to the tools required to perform a set of machining tasks. This assumes that the tools have already been selected and that the order in which they will be used is also known. The solutions to these two problems become constraints in the tool placement problem. Before the actual cutting can begin, a tool path, depth of cut, speed, and feed must be generated. Finally, it is necessary to determine which tools will be kept for later jobs and which should be sent for storage or use elsewhere.

THE AUTOMATED STORAGE AND RETRIEVAL SYSTEM

Automated storage and retrieval systems (AS/RS) are used to house raw materials, in-process, and finished parts, as well as robot end-effectors, fixtures, and tools. Basically, two decision problems must be addressed. The first is to determine the optimal size and location of these devices throughout the factory: this is typically an off-line problem. The second problem is concerned with the layout of the storage areas. One would like to store all of the materials required for a particular job in a contiguous area within a single AS/RS. But, since storage areas are assigned and released frequently, this may not be possible. Consequently, this becomes a dynamic storage allocation problem whose solution will have consequences for the time required to transfer these items to the required location for processing.

MORE ON SEQUENCING AND SCHEDULING PROBLEMS

Typically, a shop manager is responsible for sequencing and scheduling all jobs on the shop floor. The result of this effort is usually a Gantt chart [Baker 1974] showing the start and finish times for each job on each machine. The manager is required to update this chart frequently to account for changes in job and equipment status.

The literature abounds with mathematical programming, simulation, heuristic, and other techniques to aid the manager in solving these problems [Jackson and Jones 1986; Graves 1981; Raman 1986]. However, because of their computational requirements and restrictive assumptions, these approaches tend to have limited applicability in a real manufacturing environment. In applications such as this, a major constraining factor is the real-time planning horizon at each level. This is the period of time over which each module is responsible for planning and updating local schedules. While this horizon may be long at the higher levels in the hierarchy, it becomes very short at the lowest level.

Several researchers, including Chiodini [1986] and Fox [1983], have tried to use expert systems to address these problems. Unfortunately, this approach has met with little success. Expert systems are expensive and time consuming to build, and they are still computationally inefficient. And, there are no scheduling experts around to create the required knowledge bases. Consequently, they cannot provide useful solutions in a timely manner.

Another recent trend is to develop hierarchical planning and scheduling systems. Several researchers [Bitran and Hax 1977; Davis 1984; Gershwin 1986; Lawrence and Morton 1986] have proposed such systems. They are restricted in scope and limited to two or three levels. We have proposed a hierarchy in which scheduling and sequencing problems appear at every level.

A PROPOSED MODELING METHODOLOGY

From a mathematical point of view, this is a new approach. Heretofore, scheduling was performed at one time for the whole system, and usually off-line. This new approach proposes that each level be responsible for generating and maintaining its own schedules. These schedules should be created quickly and only as needed. They should also obey the constraints imposed at higher levels. These constraints are in the form of priorities among jobs and start and finish times for each job. Each level within the decision making hierarchy is responsible for generating schedules for the jobs assigned by its supervisor. We will model each of these jobs as a project comprising several activities. These activities are related through a set of precedence constraints and resource requirements. Consequently, we view the scheduling problem at each level as a multiproject, constrained resource problem.

Several researchers including Kurtulus and Davis [1982] and Pritsker, Watters, and Wolfe [1969] have developed techniques to solve multiproject, constrained resource problems. In particular, Pritsker, Watters, and Wolfe modeled this problem using zero-one decision variables, subscripted by project, task within a project, and time period, that is, x_{ijt}. Using this idea, $x_{ijt} = 1$ if job j in project i was completed during time period t, and $x_{ijt} = 0$ otherwise. Objective functions are developed in their paper to minimize throughput time, makespan (time required to complete all jobs), and total lateness, or lateness penalty. Constraints are also developed to account for limited resources, precedence relations, job splitting, due dates, substitution of resources, and concurrent and nonconcurrent job performance requirements.

Direct application of this model to the five levels in the AMRF would require at least six subscripts, one for each level in the hierarchy, and one for the time period. (To be most accurate, more subscripts would be added for the lowest level to account for commands given to actuate shop floor equipment.) It should be easy to see that attempting to solve the scheduling problem at once in this way will result in a zero-one integer programming problem of tremendous proportions; certainly too large to be solved in realtime in the average shop.

The approach we are pursuing is to look at x_{it} at each level, thereby creating a schedule of activities at each level, independent of the other levels.

The resulting solution yields a set of activities that are arranged for a subsequent level processor to decompose further and to schedule. In this way, the large problem is decomposed into smaller problems that can be solved as needed by each lower-level processor in real-time.

The full mathematical implications of this approach are not yet understood. For example, a serious question arises regarding optimality of the resulting set of schedules. Moreover, it is entirely possible that, as this process evolves to ever increasing levels of complexity, and ever larger portions of the feasibility region are constrained, no even feasible solution will emerge at the lowest level. These are serious problems that must be resolved.

We will be attacking this problem empirically. Our next step is to complete the development of the model proposed above and to investigate the various solution techniques available in the literature. Then, we will implement it in the AMRF and compare the results to the full model that incorporates all variables and constraints in the AMRF.

FUTURE WORK

Future research will focus on two major areas. First, work will continue on the integrated planning and control architecture proposed herein. That architecture consists of a generic production control module that can be used at every level in the hierarchy, a process-planning system and command/feedback structures to provide data to those modules, and a data management system to store, update, and transfer that data in a timely and accurate manner. Second, we will focus on developing solution techniques for the decision problems described above. This research will be conducted in three concurrent phases. First, we must determine the information, both qualitative and quantitative, required to solve each problem. Next, we must find efficient structures for representing that information. Finally, we will attempt to marry techniques from operations research and artificial intelligence to solve each problem.

ACKNOWLEDGMENT

The NBS Automated Manufacturing Research Facility is partially supported by the Navy Manufacturing Technology Program. This is to certify that the article written above was prepared by United States Government employees as part of their official duties and is therefore a work of the U.S. Government and not subject to copyright.

REFERENCES

Albus, J., A. Barbera, and N. Nagel. "Theory and practice of hierarchical control," *Proceedings of 23rd IEEE Computer Society International Conference*. 1981: 18-39.

_____. "A control system for an automated manufacturing research facility," presented at the Robots 8 Conference and Exposition, Detroit, MI. 1984.

Baker, K. R. *Introduction to Sequencing and Scheduling.* New York: John Wiley & Sons, 1974.

Barkmeyer, E., M. Mitchell, K. Mikkilineni, S. Su, and H. Lam. "Distributed data-management architecture for computer integrated manufacturing." NBSIR 86-3312, Gaithersburg, MD: National Bureau of Standards, 1986.

Bitran, G. R. and A. C. Hax. "On the design of hierarchical production planning systems." *Decision Sciences.* 1977. 8(1): 28-54.

Chiodini, V. "A knowledge based system for dynamic manufacturing replanning." *Proceedings of the Symposium on Realtime Optimization in Automated Manufacturing Facilities.* Gaithersburg, MD: National Bureau of Standards Special Publication 724, 1986. 357-372.

Davis, W. J. "Decision making and control hierarchies for production systems," Report No. 145, PLAIC, West Lafayette, IN: Purdue University, 1984.

Eiler, R. "Cost accounting faces automation." *Managing Automation.* 1986. 1(1): 25-29.

Fox, M. "Constraint-directed search: A case study in job shop scheduling." Doctoral diss. Carnegie-Mellon University, 1983.

Gershwin, S. "An approach to hierarchical production planning and scheduling." *Proceedings of the Symposium on Real-time Optimization in Automated Manufacturing Facilities.* Gaithersburg, MD: National Bureau of Standards Special Publication 724, 1986. 1-14.

Graves S. "A review of production scheduling." *Operations Research.* 1981. 29(4): 646-675.

Jackson, R. and A. Jones, eds. *Proceedings of the Symposium on Real-time Optimization in Automated Manufacturing Facilities.* Gaithersburg, MD: National Bureau of Standards, Special Publication 724. 1986.

Jones, A. and C. McLean. "A cell control system for the AMRF." *Proceedings of the 1984 ASME International Computers in Engineering Conference,* Las Vegas, NV. 1: 353-359.

_____. "A proposed hierarchical control model for automated manufacturing systems." *Journal of Manufacturing Systems.* 5(1): 15-25. 1986.

Kurtulus, I. and E. W. Davis. "Multiproject scheduling: Categorization of heuristic rules performance," *Management Science.* 1982. 28(2): 161-172.

Lawrence, S. R. and T. R. Morton. "PATRIARCH: Hierarchical production scheduling." *Proceedings of the Symposium on Realtime Optimization in Automated Manufacturing Facilities.* Gaithersburg, MD: National Bureau of Standards Special Publication 724, 1986. 87-98.

McLean, C., H. Bloom, and T. Hopp. "The virtual manufacturing cell." *Proceedings of Fourth IFAC/IFIP.* Gaithersburg, MD: National Bureau of Standards, 1982. 105-111.

Pritsker, A. B., L. I. Watters, and P. M. Wolfe. "Multi-project scheduling with limited resources: A zero-one programming approach." *Management Science*. 1969. 16(1): 93-108.

Raman, N. "A survey of the literature on production scheduling as it pertains to flexible manufacturing systems." Gaithersburg, MD: National Bureau of Standards. NBS-GCR 85-499. 1986.

Simpson, J., R. Hocken, and J. Albus, "The automated manufacturing research facility of the National Bureau of Standards." *Journal of Manufacturing Systems*. 1982. 1(1): 17-31.

SECTION V
MATERIALS SCHEDULING AND JIT CONCEPTS

Hundreds of firms today are focusing on improving operations because of ever-increasing competition. To attain this goal, companies have defined a number of improvement projects focusing on the following:

- Shortening lead times
- Reducing waste and redundancy
- Working with customers and suppliers

Frequently, these projects are grouped together under various programs. Programs like Just-in-Time (JIT) and synchronous manufacturing are changing the way manufacturing organizations do business. These concepts are at least contemplated by virtually every major manufacturing organization focusing on improvement. Indeed, it is nearly impossible to attend a conference on manufacturing or read a journal in the area that does not allude to the technical, behavioral, and organizational aspects of JIT.

Our intention is to focus on JIT (and its variations), defining its major elements, and linking some of the action items to the materials scheduling function that manages the flow of parts in a production system. To start with, "What is JIT?" There are as many definitions as there are consultants in the world. For our purpose, JIT focuses on minimizing waste and improving the material flow through the customer/manufacturing/supplier chain. Activities focusing attention on equipment, materials, workers (direct and indirect), and inventory (raw materials, components, work-in-process, and finished goods) are at the heart of the JIT process. Some specific activities are:

- Focused factory
- Just-in-Time production
- Uniform plant loading
- Kanban production
- Minimized setup times
- Reduced lead time

Focused Factory

There are several reasons for building small plants that are specialized instead of building a large manufacturing facility that does everything (high vertical integration). First, it is very difficult to manage a large installation—the bigger it gets, the more bureaucratic it gets. This increases indirect operating costs. Second, when a plant is specifically designed for a particular manufacturing operation, it can be constructed and operated more economically than its universal counterpart. And third, it is easier to introduce change in a small organization. If the manufacturing facility already exists, then it may be appropriate to focus tasks by creating mini factories within the larger facility.

Once the facility has been focused, the task of improvement can move forward. If the production function follows a process flow approach, the control can be streamlined, allowing for more effective scheduling. Richard Box and Donald Herbe ("A Scheduling Model for LTV Steel's Cleveland Works' Twin Strand Continuous Slab Caster") describe one successful application which illustrates the amount of improvement possible in a highly focused environment for the production of steel.

Many companies process small batch jobs and send them from one department to another, and then another until the manufacturing process is complete (e.g., from the saw department to the grinding department, etc.). Each machine in those departments is usually staffed by a worker who specializes in that function. Getting a job through a shop can be a long and complicated process because there is a significant amount of wait and move time involved (usually between 80 percent and 85 percent of the total processing time). Group technology concepts can help rationalize the flow of materials, reducing time.

Good manufacturers consider all the operations required to make a part and try to group those machines together into a product focused production cell. One operator might run a number of machines, which increases the utility of the individual operator and reduces the move and queue time between operations in a given cell. Thus, not only does productivity go up, but work-in-process inventory comes down dramatically. Also, by locating operations close together, materials handling costs and delays are substantially reduced. A number of excellent articles on this subject are included for your review in Section II.

Just-in-Time Production

It specifies the production of the required units in the required quantities at the required time, with the objective of achieving zero deviation from the schedule. It means that producing one extra piece is just as bad as being one piece short. In fact, anything over the minimum amount necessary is viewed as waste, since effort and material expended for something not needed now cannot be utilized now. It is a most difficult concept for some manufacturing managers to accept because it is contrary to current practice, which is to stock extra material "just-in-case" something goes wrong.

The Just-in-Time concept applies primarily to a repetitive manufacturing process. It does not necessarily require large volumes, but is restricted to those operations that produce the same parts over and over again. Ideally, the finished product would be repetitive in nature. However, many managers have learned the repetitive segments of the business may only appear several levels down the product structure. Even so, applying Just-in-Time concepts to a portion of the business can produce significant improvements for them.

Under Just-in-Time, the lot size goal is one piece. The premise is that the manufacturing process is a giant network of interconnected work centers, where each worker would complete his or her task on a part and pass it directly to the next worker just as that person was ready for another piece. The goal is to drive all queues toward zero in order to minimize inventory investment, shorten production lead times, react faster to demand changes, and eliminate quality problems.

To assist in attaining these goals the manufacturing task must also be correctly linked to the customer and supplier chain. It is possible to improve internal operations and still lose that advantage because of poor vendor support. Therefore, vertical linking becomes very important.

The article by John Barry and Nathan Fisher ("Texas Instruments Goes All-Out in Efforts to Strengthen Its Planning Process Chain") provides a nice discussion on how Texas Instruments (TI) manages its material flow activities from part source, through factory production, and ultimately to customer delivery. The outlined framework should be a useful guide to other companies interested in improving the material coordination function within the product chain.

Uniform Plant Loading

To use the Just-in-Time production concept, it is necessary that production flow as smoothly as possible in the shop. Its objective is to dampen the reaction waves that normally occur in response to schedule variations. For example, when a significant change is made in final assembly, it creates shifting requirements in feeder operations that are usually amplified, due to lot sizing rules, setups, queues, and waiting time. By the time the impact is felt at the supply level, a 10 percent change at assembly could easily result in a 100 percent change for the vendor.

Good production managers say the only way to eliminate that problem is to make the perturbations at the end as small as possible so that work centers get ripples going through the shop, not shock waves. Japanese companies accomplish it by setting up a firm monthly production plan for which the output rate is frozen. Reducing variability in customer service is a key benefit from better loading. Mark Rose discusses how TI ("Production Planning at Texas Instruments Improves Service and Reduces Costs") addressed this problem. In particular, improved forecasts, reducing the planning horizon, careful attention to detail, and adjusting the plan at critical points were all part of the improvement actions.

Kanban Production Control System

This kind of an approach calls for a control system that is simple and self-regulating, and provides good management visibility. It is normally a paperless system, frequently using dedicated containers and recycling, traveling requisitions/cards, which is quite different from the old, manual shop-packet systems. This is generally referred to as a Kanban pull system, since the authority to produce or supply comes from downstream operations. While work centers and vendors plan their work based on schedules, they execute based on Kanbans, which are completely manual. There are normally two types of Kanban cards. The production Kanban authorizes the manufacturing of a container of material. The withdrawal Kanban authorizes the withdrawal and movement of that container. The number of pieces in a container never varies for a given part number. (It should be noted that a number of pull type systems, with and without, cards have been designed and are equally effective in managing the material flow.)

Kanban systems work best in repetitive manufacturing environment, but many firms have numerous variations or options for their products. Smart managers circumvent this issue by planning to build the same mix of products every day, even if total quantities are small. This evens the work load and provides a repetitive situation. Building the same mix of units each day must recognize that product variety must also be rationally managed. We have moved past the time of Henry Ford and the Model T where customers could have any color as long as it was black. Mixed model scheduling is critical to uniform loading. The work by Robert W. Hall ("Cyclic Scheduling for Improvement") covers this important topic. He addresses the more common make-to-stock application, as well as cyclic schedules for make-to-order manufacturing situations.

Minimize Setup Times

A critical component to improving productivity demands that small lots be run in production. This is impossible to do if machine setups take hours to accomplish. In fact, when using the traditional economic order quantity formula to determine what quantity to run, long production runs are required to absorb costly setup time. Instead of accepting setup times as fixed numbers, good managers fix the lot sizes (very small) and work to reduce setup time. Successful setup reduction is easily achieved when approached from a methods engineering perspective. Separating setup time into two segments—internal (that segment that must be completed while a machine is stopped) and external (that segment that can be completed while the machine is operating)— provides an excellent structure for improvement. Simple things, such as the staging of replacement dies (an external setup), on the average can represent half of the usual setup time.

The article by Per Johansen and Kenneth McGuire ("A Lesson in SMED with Shigeo Shingo") provides an excellent discussion on how setup time reduction is achieved. The article covers technical and organizational issues and includes a useful framework to accomplish single minute exchange of die (SMED). It starts with separating activities into internal and external tasks. Once this is accomplished, move as much as possible to the external task and then continue to simplify the external task through other methods of improvement studies.

Focus on Lead Time

On the highway, speed kills! In business, speed is often fatal to the competition. Customers want good, quick, dependable delivery, and companies best positioned to satisfy that need will make the most sales. Speed (lead time) is influenced by all the links (distribution, manufacturing, and suppliers) required to deliver a product to the marketplace.

Clearly, one of the key players is the manufacturing function. A byproduct of focusing on and reducing leadtime is waste reduction. For example, reducing the flow time of parts in the plant reduces work-in-process inventory, and thus investment. Projects to get this increased speed may involve SMED or reorganizing work centers to reduce material handling. The key is to use "time" as a yardstick to evaluate improvement.

There are many things that influence lead time and should be evaluated for improving performance. Richard Martel, in "Reduction in Lead Time Does Make the Difference in Profitable Operations," reviews a number of activities that can contribute to reducing lead time. In particular, he discusses the elimination of planned lead time in material control systems like Material Requirements Planning (MRP) that just guarantee longer lead times will be present. Such improvement projects take effort, but they have their rewards.

Conclusion

Firms must move quickly today if they are to be around tomorrow. There are no short-cuts to success. The successful firms like Toyota and Motorola show that thousands of small incremental steps are necessary to be a leader. Once the lead is attained, the game is not over. The key is in sustaining the improvement momentum, focusing on time and performance.

The articles selected for inclusion in this book should provide you with ideas that will help better integrate production systems under your management. It has been our experience that the design, planning, control, and scheduling of manufacturing systems are very interdependent tasks. For example, a plant's layout influences the material handling and flow time of products. Also, if visual inventory control is planned, careful attention needs to be expended when determining the location and arrangement of materials. The selected articles should give you insight into some of these interrelated functions and point you towards the "improvement direction."

17

A Scheduling Model for LTV Steel's Cleveland Works' Twin Strand Continuous Slab Caster
Richard E. Box and Donald G. Herbe, Jr.

In 1983, the LTV Steel Company started up a twin strand continuous slab caster to convert molten steel to solid steel slabs. Located at LTV's Cleveland Works, the caster is scheduled by a minicomputer-based system that includes a heuristic algorithm that is used to select the best casting sequences daily. The Cleveland Works has benefited greatly from the scheduling system, with its major benefit the high quality steel produced daily to customer orders. The Cleveland caster currently holds the North American monthly production record for a steel-casting machine. The caster-scheduling system annually saves the LTV Steel Company $1.95 million in combined manpower savings and increased production.

At LTV Steel's Cleveland Works, molten steel is converted to 25-ton solid steel slabs in a machine called a twin strand slab caster.* A twin strand caster has two molds that continuously cast slabs of steel simultaneously. The caster, which started up in 1983, is scheduled by a minicomputer-based system that determines the grade and quality of the steel slabs being produced on each side of the caster at any given time. The scheduling system takes into account a wide variety of considerations, including the types of steel required to fill customers' orders, the number of slabs of steel ordinarily produced from a single batch of molten steel (about 250 tons), metallurgical limitations on changes from one batch to the next, operational constraints on changing the width or other physical characteristics from one slab to the next, required maintenance intervals, and wastage when transitions are made in the grade, quality, or shape of the slabs.

The scheduling system meets the needs of all the user groups at the Cleveland Works—Operating, Quality Control, and Production Planning—

*See the glossary at end of chapter for definitions of terms special to the steel industry.

Reprinted with permission from *Interfaces,* January-February 1988, vol. 18, no. 1; 42-56. Copyright 1988, The Institute of Management Sciences, 290 Westminster Street, Providence, Rhode Island 02903 USA.

209

and permits flexibility in an environment where priorities must be shuffled daily to keep the customers happy. The system's greatest benefits have been the high quality steel produced and the large usable tonnage of steel produced daily by the caster. While the caster's design capacity was 150,000 tons of steel per month, a record 222,145 tons were produced in December 1986, breaking the North American monthly production record for a steel casting machine.

LTV STEEL COMPANY

The LTV Steel Company is a subsidiary of LTV Corporation which is a concern with subsidiaries in the aerospace and defense, steel, and energy industries. LTV Steel Company is the nation's second largest steelmaker and its largest producer of flat-rolled products. The company also produces bar and tubular steel products. It was formed in 1984 when the steel operations of Republic Steel Corporation and J&L Steel were combined following the merger of Republic Steel and LTV Corporation. The increased efficiency resulting from combining the neighboring J&L and Republic Cleveland plants is one of the greatest benefits of the LTV-Republic merger. The two fully integrated steel mills have been combined into one of the largest steelmaking facilities in the country. Of particular benefit was LTV's ability to combine the orders of both mills and more effectively utilize the capabilities of the Cleveland slab caster.

While excess world capacity in the flatrolled steel business continues to create intense competitive pressure, the flatrolled segment is noticeably stronger than other segments of the steel business. This is in large part due to market conditions, but technological improvements in flatrolled manufacturing using modern slab casters have contributed to this strength as well. LTV's Cleveland plant, coupled with its Indiana Harbor and Hennepin plants, are the most modern and efficient flat-rolled steel producing facilities in the country.

PRODUCTION OF STEEL SLABS

Basic oxygen steel-making furnaces (BOFs) and casters, operating in tandem, begin the process in which a generic product (molten iron) becomes grade- and order-specific steel products. At LTV's Cleveland slab caster, molten steel is converted to solid steel slabs that measure 9" thick, 31" to 73" wide, and 212" to 384" long. A typical 9" x 50" x 384" slab weighs approximately 49,400 pounds, or 24.7 tons. The molten steel is produced in batches of 250 tons, called *heats,* in the basic oxygen furnaces. The entire heat of steel is poured from the furnace into a ladle and delivered in the ladle to a stirring station ahead of the caster, where adjustments can be made to achieve final steel temperature and chemistry (Figure 1).

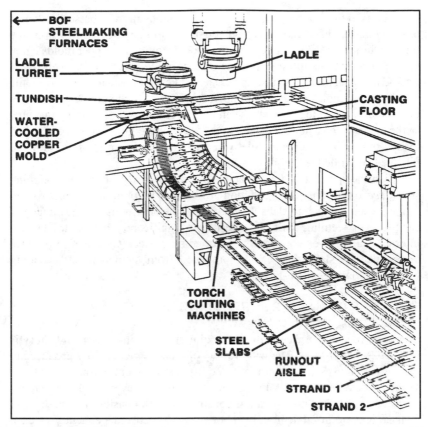

Figure 1: LTV Steel's Cleveland caster, which converts molten steel to solid steel slabs. The molten steel is produced in batches of 250 tons which are poured into a ladle, taken to a stirring station for chemical adjustments, then placed on a rotary turret that contains a second (empty) ladle. The full ladle is rotated into place over the caster and opened to allow the molten steel to flow into a basin called a tundish which holds 55 tons and serves as a buffer between the ladle and the casting machine and allows uninterrupted casting from sequential ladles. The steel flows through the caster in continuous strands that are molten at one end and solid at the other.

After the stirring station, the ladle is placed on a rotary turret which contains a second (empty) ladle opposing it at 180 degrees. The full ladle is rotated into place over the caster as the previous empty ladle is rotated out for return to the steel-making shop. A ceramic nozzle and slide gate manipulator are attached to the bottom of the ladle, the ladle is opened, and molten steel flows into a basin called a *tundish*. The tundish holds 55 tons of molten steel and serves as a buffer between the steel ladle and the casting machine, allowing uninterrupted casting of steel from sequential ladles.

The steel flows through the caster in continuous strands that are molten at one end and solid at the other end. First, the molten steel flows from the tundish through nozzles into two water-cooled stationary copper molds in the casting machine. As the steel contacting the mold walls cools, a shell forms around the otherwise molten strand of steel. The strand is withdrawn from the bottom of the mold through cooling water sprays which completely solidify the strand by the time it reaches the end of the caster. A torch cutting machine at the end of the caster cuts slabs to the desired weight. The slabs are then loaded onto railroad cars and delivered to a hot strip mill, where they are reheated and rolled into coils of sheet steel.

Slab casting is rapidly replacing the more costly process of teeming slabs. *Teeming* is the pouring of molten steel into ingot molds and the rolling of the cooled ingots into slabs. In addition to the enormous cost advantage of casting over teeming, cast slabs result in significantly better surface and internal quality when converted to finished sheet steel. Casters also produce larger, heavier slabs than can be produced from teemed ingots, yielding greater efficiency and cost savings.

THE ROLE OF CASTER SCHEDULING

The basic oxygen furnace is the first point at which in-process inventory is tied to customer orders. The wide variety of metallurgical grades produced in the furnace makes it imperative that only customer orders, not potentially sellable stock, be produced. In critical situations, however, stock is produced to prevent violating the operating constraints of the caster. The caster and furnace operate in tandem and cannot be scheduled independently of each other. The unit of production in the furnace is a 250-ton heat; while at the caster, it is a 20- to 30-ton slab. A slab produced at the caster takes on two customer-specific attributes that are not present in the ladle of steel: size and level of quality. Because of this, the caster must be scheduled first, and it drives the furnace schedule.

The basic entity that is scheduled at the Cleveland Works' caster is a *melt requisition*. A melt requisition is a customer order for a particular grade and quantity of steel that is made available for steel making based on due date. The role of caster scheduling is to select melt requisitions in such a way as to maximize on-time delivery and caster productivity while minimizing semifinished inventory. These goals often conflict with each other. Scheduling strictly for on-time delivery would result in scheduling only orders with current due dates. Scheduling strictly for productivity would result in scheduling long casting sequences of like requisitions, regardless of the due dates and inventory levels. The immense competitive pressure to deliver flat-rolled products on time leads many managers to conclude that productivity or inventory control or both must be sacrificed when they conflict with on-time delivery. Scheduling short casting sequences to pick up pockets of urgent or overdue orders, however, increases casting downtime, because the caster does not produce any steel during the times it is stopped and reset to start producing a different grade of steel. The key to overcoming this dilemma is to plan good schedules yet incorporate flexibility into the scheduling system.

THE TWIN STRAND CASTER SCHEDULING PROBLEM

A casting sequence meets all of the operating and metallurgical constraints of sequencing slabs for production and defines a sequence of heats in which each 250-ton increment of cast slabs is of the same metallurgical grade. The problem of sequencing slabs from requisitions on a single strand of a caster can be likened to a knapsack problem, where the most important orders from the order book should be included while less important future orders should be avoided. It is also similar to a traveling salesman problem in that the cost of connecting nodes (adjacent slabs) can vary greatly according to operating and metallurgical considerations.

The complexity of the problem is increased for a twin strand caster. A twin strand caster produces two simultaneous and interdependent production streams from one source, the molten steel in the tundish. This problem can be likened to two knapsack constrained salesmen traveling on two interdependent itineraries. The pool of "cities" is available to both salesmen, but their paths are mutually exclusive because a slab from a requisition order can be produced only once. Further, the two salesmen must arrive at certain cities at the same time because of heat boundary constraints. Both production streams begin with the same heat, and the sequence ends when the last heat is consumed. Therefore, the sequence must end on both strands at roughly the same time.

GRADE CHANGES

An understanding of grade changes and how they are addressed in scheduling is important to understanding the scheduling problem. A change in grade from one heat to the next in a sequence results in a segment of production, called the mix zone, that contains mixed grades. In a nonradical grade change, the two grades are similar enough that the segment containing the mixed grades can be used to fill an order.

In a radical grade change, the two grades are incompatible. The mix zone is not applicable to any order, and the objective is to minimize the size of the mix zone. This can be accomplished by slowing casting almost to a stop and cutting out and scrapping the mix zone. Another way to perform a radical grade change is to perform a *caster turnaround:* end the sequence, change the tundish, reset the casting machine, and begin a new sequence. A turnaround results in a productivity penalty, since the caster stops producing during that period.

The inclusion of grade sequencing in the already complex problem of sequencing requisitions to the interdependent production streams of a twin strand caster could result in an enormously complex problem. However, the grade sequencing dilemma has been minimized by the careful construction of over 100 cast families by metallurgists: similar grades with overlapping tolerances of temperature and chemistry are combined into castable grade families. The number of cast families is only 15 to 20 percent of the number of actual steel grades. The cast families are created in such a way that the tightest tolerance pertaining to each grade attribute is observed when the steel is melted and cast, resulting in a product that is made to the highest quality restrictions among all of the grades in the family. (Customers ordering less restrictive grades thus may receive higher quality steel than they requested.)

The casting sequences are built for one cast family at a time, with implicit grade changes that are much more optimal than would result from melting individual metallurgical grades and scheduling numerous nonradical grade changes. With the cast families, nonradical and radical grade changes have taken on new meaning. They are redefined according to similar and dissimilar cast families rather than steel grades, and they occur between sequences rather than between heats.

TIMING OF ORDERS FOR PRODUCTION

Maximizing the production of current and past-due orders is critically important to successful scheduling of the caster. The caster must be scheduled in a manner that future orders are included only when they enhance the ability of the caster to produce current and past due orders. It is also often advantageous to schedule future orders in low-volume cast families because producing only current and past due orders results in a very short sequence. The best thing to do with a low volume cast family is to produce all of it, including future requisitions, so that the cast family can be avoided for a few weeks.

SEQUENCE LENGTH

Sequence length has a major impact on production costs and is thus an important scheduling consideration. A caster turnaround takes approximately the same amount of time it takes to cast four heats. This casting downtime is time that is lost forever. Therefore, maximizing sequence length without sacrificing on-time delivery is a major objective. Of crucial importance to achieving this objective is the effective scheduling of medium volume cast families, which are neither the difficult nor the gravy portion of the product mix to schedule. Effective scheduling of medium-volume cast families should clean out all of the current and past due requisitions so that these families do not have to be scheduled more than once per week.

SYNCHRONIZING THE CASTER AND THE FURNACE

The rate at which steel is consumed on the caster depends on the width of the slabs being produced; this must be synchronized with the production rate of heats at the furnace. Casting wide slabs on both strands of the caster simultaneously causes heats to be consumed faster than they can be produced. When this occurs, the sequence may be broken because the furnace is unable to provide molten steel fast enough to continue sequential casting. Avoiding a broken sequence by slowing the casting speed can result in quality problems. If narrow slabs are cast on both strands, there is no risk of poor quality or a broken sequence, but productivity suffers. The goal is to cast widths on the two strands that maintain an aggregate casting width of 110 to 120 inches to maintain caster synchronization with the furnace. The ideal way to maintain an aggregate width from 110 to 120 inches is to schedule slab widths that run from wide to narrow on one strand and narrow to wide on the other strand.

The average casting speed is a function of cast family. Harder grade (high carbon) cast families require slower casting speeds than softer grade cast families. It is also a function of sequence length because of the effect of casting speed acceleration and deceleration over the length of the sequence. Finally, average casting speed is a function of the number of tundish and nozzle changes that occur during a sequence because of casting speed slowdowns during those events. (During continuous casting, nozzles are changed every four heats, and tundishes are changed roughly every 12 heats.)

WIDTH CHANGES

Width changes also have limitations that must be considered during scheduling. At a width change, the caster must slow down as the mold walls are moved to the next width. This results in a productivity loss and also increases the risk of tearing the strand shell in the mold. Tearing of the strand shell is termed a breakout and is an operating disaster in which molten steel runs through the casting machine, requiring a very expensive cleanup and repair to the equipment.

Although the caster is capable of producing any width, slab widths are cast only in whole-inch increments, and width changes during cast occur only in two-inch increments, both as a matter of operating policy. Width changes in less than two-inch increments will result in a productivity loss. Width changes cannot exceed two inches, or the taper in the width change slab will be too severe to be handled by the hot strip mill. The hot strip mill is capable of "squeezing" the slab and producing a width up to 1-1/2 inches narrower than the slab width. The slab can also be "spread" to a width that is up to 1/2 inch wider than the slab width. For example, a requisition with a 58.5 inch hot band width can be cast as a 58, 59, or 60 inch wide slab. An objective of caster scheduling is to minimize the amount of spread or squeeze required on the hot strip mill.

A width change slab is the first slab of a new width range and has a two-inch taper over the length of the slab. The requisitions that can be applied to this type of slab are much more limited than normal slabs. The requisition in this position on the schedule must conform to a different set of spread/squeeze rules.

PRODUCT QUALITY

A variety of events occur during the casting sequence that result in less than perfect surface quality in the end product. Reduced casting speed causes varying degrees of surface quality problems that must be addressed in scheduling. The first and last slabs of the sequence are cast at reduced speed because of acceleration and deceleration, and this results in reduced surface quality. Periodic flying tundish changes and tundish nozzle changes also cause slowdowns in the casting speed and reduce surface quality. Depending on the end use, orders vary in what is acceptable surface quality. Requisitions with the appropriate surface requirements must be provided in the casting sequence for each of the casting events that reduce surface quality.

TUNDISH LIFE

Tundish changes complicate sequencing because of the effect on cost as well as surface quality. Tundishes last for roughly 12 heats on the Cleveland caster. Since they are expensive to rebuild, a sequence length that utilizes only a fraction of a tundish life carries a heavy cost penalty.

CASTING VERSUS TEEMING

Certain sequencing objectives depend on market conditions, the configuration of other facilities within the company, and the philosophy used to requisition orders. When every requisition in the requisition data base is to be cast, caster sequencing does not involve making decisions between casting and teeming (a more costly process). However, when the requisition data base contains orders that can be cast or teemed, then the relative savings for casting versus teeming for each type of requisition must be included in the caster-sequencing objective function. Certain grades of steel have a significantly higher cast versus teem savings than other grades, based on product yield.

SOLUTION METHOD

The caster-scheduling model determines the requisitions that are to be filled in a sequence of heats, the order of the slabs produced in the sequence, and the nature of the heats needed to produce the specified slabs in the specified sequence. A heuristic algorithm is used, both because the combined problem (synchronization, sequencing, and assignment) is very complex, and also because some of the constraints are difficult to state mathematically in a form suitable for inclusion in a mathematical programming framework.

The heuristic begins by selecting requisitions to be cast without regard to the order in which they will be produced. However, the constraints are applied in such a way that at the end of this process the selected requisitions can be sequenced to meet all of the constraints concerning width changes and other criteria. The choice of requisitions is based on minimizing an objective function, described below, which is calculated at the end of each heat. In the initial step of the selection process, the heat boundaries at which the objective value is calculated are artificial (because the requisitions are not yet in the proper sequence), but the objective values are accurate and reflect the contribution of the selected requisitions prior to sequencing.

In summary, slabs are selected based on their desirability for casting, then sequenced for the caster, and lastly committed to heat lots for the furnace.

The objective function is a pseudo cost per ton for producing a given cast sequence. It is not the total cost but rather the relative savings of casting as compared to teeming. Further, the objective function contains only the components of cost per ton that determine the desirability of one casting sequence over another. It includes the following components:

1. Deoxidation practice—the savings per ton obtained by casting a requisition on the slab caster rather than teeming it into an ingot;
2. Spread and squeeze—a penalty cost per slab ton associated with the difference between slab width and desired width;
3. Slab length—a penalty cost per slab ton associated with slab lengths not cast to maximum hearth coverage in the hot mill reheat furnace;
4. Due date—a multiplier used to adjust the relative value of each requisition, reflecting the time priority of each order;
5. Turnaround cost—total expense and productivity cost of finishing one sequence and restarting the caster;
6. Yield loss—total cost of steel left in the ladles, tundishes, and so forth;
7. Width change—the productivity penalty associated with a width change; and
8. Tundish life—the cost of replacing tundishes throughout the sequence.

SELECTING THE COMBINATIONS OF STARTING WIDTHS

Alternative casting sequences are uniquely described by starting width on strand 1, starting width on strand 2, number of width changes on strand 1, number of width changes on strand 2, width change direction on strand 1, width change direction on strand 2, cast family, and number of heats. The set of alternative sequences is narrowed considerably by prescreening and reducing the number of starting width combinations (strand 1/strand 2) prior to entering sequence evaluation.

Three criteria are used to screen starting width combinations and determine whether a starting width combination is worth evaluating. The first is whether the starting width combination will result in a casting sequence that is well synchronized with the furnace shop. The second is whether the starting width combination will result in a sequence of at least the minimum requested number of heats. The third is whether the product defined by the starting width combination is sufficiently important (current business) to be considered for the current schedule.

Starting width combinations are selected by choosing a target aggregate width based on the expected average casting speed. The selected starting width combinations can be from any cast family, limited only by how tightly the cast families are screened upon input. The cast families are thus competing for consideration based on whether they have a good starting width combination to offer.

SEQUENCE EVALUATION

The purpose of the sequence evaluation process is twofold: to enumerate the most promising potential sequences, and to capture and hold detailed information on the sequence chosen to be the best.

Alternative sequences to be evaluated are initially described by the starting width combinations of strand 1 and strand 2. Sequence evaluation iterates through the set of width combinations for each number of size changes allowed on each strand. For each combination of starting width and width change, the objective value is accumulated and recorded at each heat boundary between the minimum and maximum requested number of heats. Alternative starting widths within close proximity to each other result in alternative sequences containing the same requisitions cast at different widths. This enables the selection of the sequence with the best approach to handling width gaps between requisitions, to minimizing "spread" and "squeeze" required to make ordered widths, and to applying orders to tapered slabs. The "best" sequence is thus defined by cast family, starting width on strand 1, starting width on strand 2, number of width changes on strand 1, number of width changes on strand 2, and number of heats.

Sequence evaluation consists of checking to insure that all of the constraints are satisfied, as well as calculating the objective value at each heat boundary in a sequence. Requisitions for evaluation are selected according to priorities, that is, constraints and the relative importance of requisitions. The key to the optimization process is that if the constraints are satisfied, requisitions need not be sequenced until later. Because requisitions are not sequenced while they are being selected, the most important current and past due requisitions can be selected without regard for width.

Requisitions are assigned to the strand that has the least cumulative casting time on it. Control passes back and forth between the strands, gradually building a sequence. The strands are allowed to compete for the same requisitions when the desired widths match the slab widths of both strands. Large requisitions are split and consumed geometrically, with half of the slabs being consumed, then half the remaining slabs, and so on. These techniques avoid scheduling unwanted product on one strand in order to get desired product on the other strand. The constraints that must be satisfied during the sequence evaluation include:

1. Surface quality conditions
2. Tapered slab rules
3. Synchronization of the consumption rate of the caster and the production rate of the furnaces
4. Requisitioned widths that fall between the starting slab width and the ending slab width
5. Desired distance between width changes
6. Slab length restrictions of the hot strip mill reheat furnace
7. A combined tonnage on both strands that falls between the minimum and maximum number of heats specified
8. Sequence ending simultaneously on both strands at the last heat

Two special situations that are triggered through user specified input are handled in the sequence evaluation process:

1. Creating a sequence with a specified ending width on one or both strands—here the sequence is evaluated backwards and then "flipped."
2. Cleaning out a cast family—every requisition in the cast family is scheduled and the last partial heat is finished with stock.

CAST SEQUENCE BUILDING

The first step in constructing a casting sequence is to calculate a rank for each requisition. The rank reflects the desired relative position of each requisition in the casting sequence. The requisitions are then sorted on the rank, which is the priority (requisition related parameters in the objective function) within slab length within specified surface requirements. This creates a pool of requisitions to be drawn on from the top down when building the casting sequence.

The casting sequence is then constructed, drawing on the ranked and sorted pool of requisitions. The resulting sequence contains, within each width range on each strand, requisitions in descending order of required surface quality. This means slabs that fail to be cast at the desired level of surface quality (due to casting abnormalities) can be assigned to orders with lower requirements and the schedule rearranged "on the fly."

WIDTH SEQUENCES

An intermediate step is required to build a heat sequence. Because width changes can fall anywhere in the heat, steel consumption rates are complex to estimate. A sequence of strand 1 and strand 2 widths is built from the casting sequence with the casting time of each unique combination captured. This allows us to calculate exact steel consumption rates at any point in time, making it possible to construct a heat sequence.

HEAT SEQUENCE

The heat sequence is built from the width sequence, using the consumption rate at each width to create complete 250-ton heats. The overall steel consumption rate of the heat sequence is compared with the furnace production rate while the sequence is being built. When the caster is consuming steel more slowly than the furnace can produce it, the cumulative lag between the caster and the furnace eventually reaches a point where the furnace is one heat ahead of the caster. At this point, a teemed heat to be poured into ingot molds is inserted in the sequence of cast heats. When the caster is consuming steel faster than the furnace can produce it, the cumulative lag time is computed and included in the relative times output. This tells the furnace shop how far in advance it must begin melting the first heat of the sequence in order to end the casting sequence in synchronization with the caster.

IMPLEMENTATION

The scheduling system and model were put in place at the time of start-up of the Cleveland caster in October 1983. The ease with which the model gained acceptance provided the most compelling lesson learned from this project. Any opportunity to design and install such a system with a new facility should be seized, as it is far more difficult to fight the planning inertia ingrained in existing manual systems. The Cleveland caster and its scheduling methods were new to all involved, there was no competition with other like facilities in the company at the time, there was no old way of scheduling the caster, and this totally new scheduling system grew out of a total team effort to make the caster a success.

Under these circumstances, pressure to support the model and enhance it was strong. Several features of the current model were not in the original version installed at caster start-up. They are part of it today because they were essential to its continued use. Those features include linking slabs, tapered slab restrictions, the low-volume cast family "clean out" mode, and a variety of width controls.

The scheduling system is used by various people and departments. The quality control department maintains the data base to provide data on aim casting speed, tundish life, and detailed operating practices for the scheduling model. Industrial engineering, production planning, and operating people can change various default scheduling parameters. Each department has access to the system and controls those scheduling parameters that have been assigned as its responsibility. Production planning enters transactions on the system to modify requisitions. Operating and production planning people also use the system to create numerous reports that track delivery performance and help develop and modify the caster horizon plan. Metallurgists use the system to retrieve quality-related statistical data from the production history data base.

Production planners can accept the general scheduling default values and let the system pick the best sequence available, or they can override any of the default parameters and make a more specific request. They can constrain the request for a sequence at any level, down to precisely the desired sequence in terms of cast family, starting and ending widths, and number of heats.

SAVINGS AND BENEFITS

Estimating the benefits of the scheduling model is extremely difficult because there has never been another way of scheduling the Cleveland caster. The most tangible benefit is the record-shattering production tonnage performance of the caster, almost all of which is produced to customer orders. Stock is created by the scheduling model only when it helps to get more orders out the door. The production statistic other than tonnage that is most closely related to the high tonnage performance is the number of heats per sequence. While production of stock makes high tonnage a shallow victory, frequent caster turnarounds (low heats per sequence) make high tonnage impossible.

While some sequences can be accomplished with a less sophisticated approach, the model has been particularly useful at producing reasonable schedules from very unreasonable cast families. Only a few of the over 100 cast families can be considered "gravy" cast families. The rest take their turn, day in and day out, getting shoehorned in with a minimum of stock created.

By using the cleanout feature to maximize the sequence length and minimize the frequency with which the given family must be scheduled and using the width controls to create linking sequences from the gravy cast families, the planners and operators have learned to avoid caster turnarounds in even the most complex situations.

A very conservative estimate of the model's effect on heats per sequence is put at 10 percent better than without a model. This is borne out by the Cleveland caster's average 22.7 heats per sequence for the period October 1986 through December 1986, compared to its targeted goal of 15.0. The 10 percent improvement in sequence length translates into $1.74 million annual savings. Combined with the manpower savings described by the Production Planning Department, the total annual savings are estimated at $1.95 million.

Other benefits derived from the scheduling model include:

- Quick response to unexpected situations. The planners are frequently required to derive complex sequences at the last moment because something happened to prevent production of the sequence that was planned.
- Strict adherence to the complexities of sequence evaluation and sequence building, day in and day out. A phenomenon that has been observed in the course of installing several planning and scheduling models is that complex operating rules and restrictions on scheduling are frequently not adhered to, or even forgotten, when a unit is scheduled manually. These rules and restrictions are encoded in the model and adhered to rigorously.
- The penalties of poor scheduling or missed opportunities to produce current or overdue business are cumulative. A missed item today may mean a short sequence is required tomorrow to pick up that missed item or face losing a customer entirely. The ability of the model to sequence low volume cast families, coupled with the ability of the mechanized system to track requisitions and partial requisitions, tends to minimize missed opportunities. Manual scheduling, even on a mechanized order tracking system, frequently means that the scheduler has to perform mental gymnastics to remember all of the important orders that he has tucked away somewhere.

CONCLUSION

While the Cleveland caster scheduling model has been successful and satisfying to work with, one lesson we learned from this project came from the very negative business environment it evolved in. The pressures to deliver product on time have been enormous, and the pressures to produce customer orders and not stock have been equally enormous. Attempting to balance and synchronize twin strand sequences under those pressures day in and day out without the use of a scheduling system and model would have created an unmanageable situation.

Our most positive feelings towards this project come from the Cleveland caster having shattered domestic and North American production records. While this is in part due to the exceptional performance of individuals in the basic oxygen furnace shop, caster, and production planning, the accomplishments of the caster could not have been achieved without the scheduling model. It has, with enhancements, kept up with the outstanding performance of the individuals running the shop.

Finally, from a management sciences standpoint, we learned an important lesson about the inertia of planning systems. We have been involved in the design and installation of several planning models, and it is painfully obvious to us that implementing such a system at the time a new facility is started up is the time to do it, even if the system later needs enhancement. From a management science practitioner's point of view, it would be very counter-productive to allow a manual system to evolve in a new facility that clearly needs a planning model.

Robert S. McCormick, Superintendent of Slab Caster said: "During start-up, the scheduling model proved invaluable as we went through our learning curve of operating a caster. Mannesman Demag, the machine builder for the caster, considers the start-up performance of the Cleveland caster to be unsurpassed by any Demag facility without previous caster experience."

"The design tonnage of the caster is 150,000 tons per month. We have not only achieved our design tonnage but surpassed it by nearly 50 percent. Without a dynamic tool such as the scheduling model, this type of performance would not be possible. The model has provided high quality casting sequences, resulting in a 1.4 percent increased capacity utilization which translates into an annual savings of $1.74 million. Additionally, we derive tremendous benefits from the scheduling model in the form of customer delivery performance and inventory control."

Russell W. Maier, President of LTV Flat Rolled and Bar Company stated: "I feel the assignment of benefits to the scheduling model have been understated. I estimate the benefits are at least 2-3 times greater than that reported. It should be noted that the caster complex is currently exceeding design capacity by more than 40 percent which translates into cost savings of $30 million per year. This improvement could not have been achieved without the scheduling model."

GLOSSARY

Abnormalities: Casting abnormalities are events such as casting speed slowdowns for width changes, tundish changes, and so forth that occur during the casting sequence and may reduce the surface quality of the slab.

Aim casting speed: The proper withdrawal rate of slabs from the caster, expressed in lineal inches per minute. It is established by metallurgists to obtain proper surface and internal quality and to avoid operating problems. The rate varies with the grade and temperature of each heat of molten steel.

Average casting speed: The overall average slab withdrawal rate during a casting sequence, reflecting slowdowns from aim casting speed during a variety of casting events, such as width changes, that occur during the sequence.

BOF: Basic oxygen steel-making furnace.

Casting sequence: Uninterrupted sequential casting of multiple heats (ladles) of steel into a set of steel slabs that conform to operating and metallurgical constraints.

Heat: A batch of molten steel, approximately 250 tons.

Hot strip mill: The rolling mill that reheats and rolls steel slabs into hot bands, steel strips that are typically 0.100 inches thick and 50 to 60 inches wide.

Ladle: A ceramic lined open container used to transport and hold a heat of molten steel. A mechanical nozzle in the bottom is used to pour the molten steel.

Melt requisition: A customer order that is made available to be included in the caster schedule because of its due date.

Spread/squeeze: The cast slab width may differ from the ordered hot band width; this difference has to be "spread" out or "squeezed" in on the hot strip mill, within certain constraints.

Strand: The steel as it moves through the caster from its molten state at the tundish to its solid state at the torch cutting machine.

Surface critical: Steel sheet or strip product that must be produced from slabs that were cast under ideal conditions on the slab caster (no casting abnormalities allowed) because of the end use of the product, for example, exterior automotive body panels.

Surface quality: The presence or absence of flaws in the surface of steel sheet and strip. The incidence of these flaws is extremely sensitive to steel making and slab casting (or ingot teeming) operating practices.

Tapered slab: Slab produced during a width change on either strand of the caster. It is wider at one end than the other, with a taper of two inches.

Teeming: The process by which molten steel is poured into ingot molds. The cooled ingots are then rolled into slabs. This process costs more than slab casting.

Tundish: A basin immediately above the casting machine that holds 55 tons of molten steel, used to buffer the flow of steel from the ladle into the casting machine. A tundish over a twin strand caster has two mechanically operated nozzles in the bottom, one over each strand mold.

Tundish change: Delicate procedure of quickly swapping tundishes roughly every 12 heats in the sequence to prevent build-up of impurities that can reduce surface quality.

Width change: Movement in or out of the hydraulically controlled end plates of the casting machine molds during casting to change the width of slabs being produced.

18

TEXAS INSTRUMENTS GOES ALL OUT IN EFFORTS TO STRENGTHEN ITS PLANNING PROCESS CHAIN
JOHN BARRY AND NATHAN FISHER

Manufacturing organizations must concentrate on servicing their customers in a faster, more effective way in today's highly competitive environment. Getting the right product to the right place at the right time at the least cost requires a very efficient flow of products and information along the customer/distributor/manufacturer/supplier chain. The development of a successful planning process to support this chain has been a major effort of the Industrial Automation Division of Texas Instruments (TI) located in Johnson City, TN. TI's facility in Johnson City is part of TI's Information Technology Group and manufactures programmable logic controllers (PLC). TI's PLC business is characterized by high mix printed circuit board assembly lines with over 750 devices having dynamic run rates ranging from zero to over 3000. This high mix environment presents some real challenges throughout the manufacturing and planning processes.

In 1985, TI began a strong thrust in the material management area. Through analysis of the planning process, it became evident that the planning process did not completely link together the required functions to allow products and information to flow smoothly (Figure 1). After setting an objective and determining primary drivers, the first step was to properly align the functions and develop formal communication links (Figure 2). Once the chain was linked, TI put in place several programs to shorten and strengthen the bonds of communication between functions through lead-time reduction and improved relationships (Figure 3). The programs of flexible planning, a material planning tool, lead-time management, a production planning tool, build-to-backlog and auto-replenish, production scheduling tools, and channel management—a customer service tool—are the subjects of this series (Chapters 18 and 19). Each program will be defined starting with the supplier

---

Reprinted from *Industrial Engineering*, December 1990, vol. 22, no. 12; Norcross, GA: Institute of Industrial Engineers, 41-45.

227

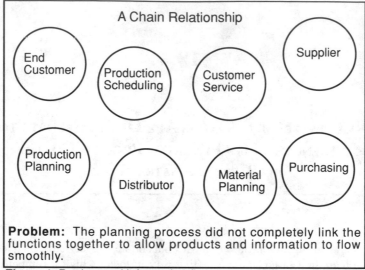

A Chain Relationship

End Customer

Production Scheduling

Customer Service

Supplier

Production Planning

Distributor

Material Planning

Purchasing

Problem: The planning process did not completely link the functions together to allow products and information to flow smoothly.

Figure 1. Product and information flow.

(flexible planning) and working through the chain to the end customer (channel management). Flexible planning is covered here.

For five years the focus of the Johnson City site was on manufacturing cycle time reduction. As this goal became reality the emphasis shifted to customer on-time delivery and an acceptable customer service level. Texas Instruments realized they could now produce a finished product quicker and deliver faster; however, the customer on-time delivery remained stagnant at 83% in terms of quoted leadtimes.

Today's manufacturers are concentrating their efforts on customer service more than at any time in the past, creating an inconsistency with their preference for low inventories. Excess raw material can reduce a company's profitability, but not having the product that the customer wants, when he wants it, can eventually close a business. With this in mind, Texas Instruments Johnson City, TN, decided to develop a plan that would provide an acceptable customer service level at the lowest possible inventory cost.

Material planning had operated for years with little change in methodology. They planned purchased material by using a forecast that attempted to satisfy 100% of the future demand. A traditional ABC analysis was used to plan the delivery of "A" parts weekly, "B" parts monthly, and "C" parts every three months. Investments in warehouse safety stock limited any shortcomings. This safety stock was calculated by using the historical demand variability of each piece part. This resulted in excess stock in the warehouse not needed to improve customer service.

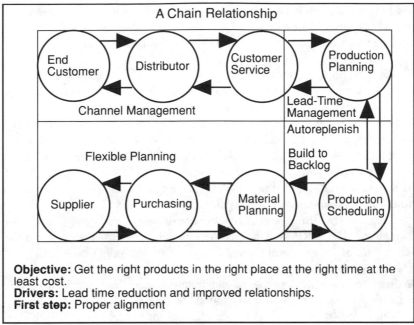

Figure 2. Communication links.

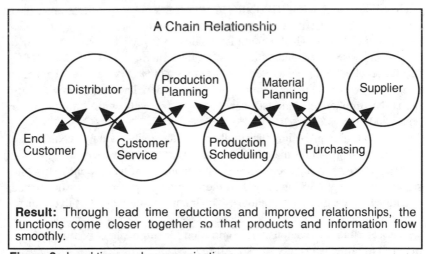

Result: Through lead time reductions and improved relationships, the functions come closer together so that products and information flow smoothly.

Figure 3. Lead time and communications.

DEVELOPING THE PLAN

The plan began by incorporating a basic philosophy of, "build only what you need, when you need it." Reductions of manufacturing cycle time improved on-time delivery, but an unaccepted service level remained. Through constant analysis came the realization that lack of performance by suppliers would limit the service level. The key to future success was raw material availability. A new focus on improving all supplier relationships and their efficiency became the critical ingredient toward the goal of 100% on-time delivery and order acknowledgment within standard lead-time.

In analyzing the industrial controls business, it was determined that eight week lead-times could be provided 97% of the time, without incurring additional inventory. This could be accomplished if TI had the ability to fluctuate its demand to the supplier in an action window six to eight weeks from the delivery date. Thus TI would increase or decrease its requirements from the supplier, building only what was needed to satisfy the customer.

By breaking down the raw material lead-times, TI found that only 15% of its raw material had a lead-time of less than eight weeks. The supplier lead-time was an important part of future material flexibility.

Supplier lead-times have characteristics of being very dynamic and hard to regulate. The MRP system plus the scheduling of raw material and the scheduling of manufacturing are all affected by the purchasing lead-time. This lead-time was the only element in the process that was not controllable. In order to reduce the dependence on purchasing lead-times the decision was made to implement a new strategy called "flexible planning."

Flexible planning uses a runrate planning methodology to reduce supplier lead-times by providing long-term demand visibility to the supplier in exchange for scheduling flexibility in the 6-8 week out time frame. The runrate can be described as the historical monthly norm of actual sales demand of a device. This demand is updated in the MRP system every two weeks and instead of generating a plan that attempts to provide a 100% service level, a plan is generated that provides a 60% service level. This plan is exposed to suppliers via a runrate purchase order. This longterm visibility helps the supplier to plan his business cost-effectively with a minimum of peaks and valleys.

In addition to providing the supplier with the visibility they need, TI also eliminated their plan for maintaining safety stock in the warehouse. TI would no longer expedite suppliers because the quantity on hand went below the safety stock level. No longer would there be air shipment boxes of unused expedited material in the warehouse. The intent of safety stock is to compensate for unpredictable demand. Since TI schedules are firm inside of six weeks and all units scheduled are committed for shipment, expediting of raw material to replenish safety stock is eliminated.

In order to achieve at least the 97% service level that customers require, TI also calculates device by device the variance from the norm (standard deviation), and incorporates this into the plan at six weeks. This variance stock can be described as one and one-half standard deviations of demand from the runrate. This one time demand appears in material planning and scheduling, but it does not materialize in the factory as a build requirement or,

230

to purchasing, as a buy requirement. Adjustments to the runrates are requested by material planning 6-8 weeks from the delivery date (our flexible planning window) and only when the variability in demand is greater than a 97% service level (too much material) or less than a 60% service level (not enough material). The TI plan outside of 8 weeks represents the norm (60% service level) of the customer demand.

METHODOLOGY EVOLVES

What TI has implemented is a methodology that eliminates wasted material by accurately linking actual customer orders to material receipts. They have closed the loop so that what is requested by the customer is reflected through production planning to material planning to purchasing to the supplier. Two parameters are required by the supplier: the maximum visibility they would like to have for a runrate purchase order and the minimum visibility required to provide TI with flexibility in the 6-8 time frame. Visibility can be in terms of time (i.e., when visibility reaches three months, purchase another three months) or quantity (i.e., when visibility reaches three months order amount and schedule releases). Suppliers make their least cost decision of inventory cost, freight cost, and set-up cost and communicate to TI the method of runrate visibility they desire.

The result is material flexibility in the six through eight week window that allows TI to reach a 97% service level without added expense. The material in the channel, whether it be in the TI warehouse or at the supplier, is less than 100% of the demand. Quantity is no longer the issue; the time of the release is now evaluated. The thought process changed from managing quantity to managing time. The supplier defines this "time" through the purchase order reorder point (minimum visibility requirement) and the replenishment visibility time (maximum visibility). TI will adjust the runrate to reflect variations in the norm demand when replenishment of a purchase order occurs.

MATERIAL VOLUME CONTROLLED

This flexible planning method is not an effort to shift the burden of raw material inventory to the supplier, but one which controls the volume of material in the procurement pipeline. It is a plan to maximize the number of vendors that provide inventory flexibility, on-time delivery, and 100% quality. Purchasing's involvement and support are essential in establishing long-term commitments with suppliers. Through stronger supplier relationships total costs are reduced. The reduction of lead-times, by providing more visibility, is proving to be the best way around the customer service level-versus-cost issue.

During the first year and a half of flexible planning, TI has discovered savings through less paperwork, more consistent order sizes, fewer price increases and less expediting. The customer service level in terms of quoted lead-times has improved to 97% while raw material inventory has decreased by 18%. Leadtime has become less of a material planning factor and some strategic suppliers have signed corporate option agreements. The plan demands that TI continuously examine the runrate and keep suppliers informed of changes in TI business to avoid obsolescence.

Future enhancements to flexible planning will include additional lot sizing rules to facilitate price breaks due to shipping costs, purchase order change notice costs, and payment discounts. Also under consideration is the use of electronic transmission of orders and forecasts to suppliers.

19

PRODUCTION PLANNING AT TEXAS INSTRUMENTS IMPROVES SERVICE AND REDUCES COSTS
MARK ROSE

T he production plan is the crucial linkage between the demand for a company's products and its ability to supply those products at the right time at the least possible cost. The production plan has two critical objectives. The first objective is to maintain a customer service level consistent with the total business strategy. The second objective is to achieve the desired service level at the least possible cost. Cost can be reduced by eliminating excess inventory and providing a credible plan from which manufacturing and procurement can work with maximum effectiveness and productivity.

THE PROBLEM

Prior to 1985, the demand forecast was compiled by the Texas Instruments marketing organization and was usually an optimistic projection which would ensure an excellent level of service. The production planning group netted the forecast against finished inventory levels and the current production plan to yield the new production plan.

The frozen planning horizon was sixteen weeks, which meant that once the production plan was set, changes could only be made beyond the sixteen week window. The frozen horizon ensured that material, labor, and machine schedules could be developed for the upcoming months. Supplier lead-times were mainly in the 12-18 week range and manufacturing cycle times were in the 4-8 week range. Any units scheduled within the frozen horizon were pushed through to finished goods to avoid excess raw material and work-in-process inventory. The MRP system was scheduled once per month to avoid excess system costs and changes to material requirements for suppliers.

Reprinted from *Industrial Engineering,* January 1991, vol. 23, no. 1; Norcross, GA: Institute of Industrial Engineers, 33-36.

While this process was fairly easy to execute and gave everyone a stable plan for the coming months, the factory's flexibility to react to customer requirements was severely limited. The combination of a volatile demand forecast, the long frozen horizon, and cyclical demand patterns led to periods of high inventory and manufacturing shutdowns followed a few months later by periods of poor service level, severe expediting, and excessive overtime in manufacturing (Figure 1). Each month traumatic changes to the production plan were required which caused dissension between groups over how soon in the plan the changes could be made and why the plan was always "wrong" in the first place.

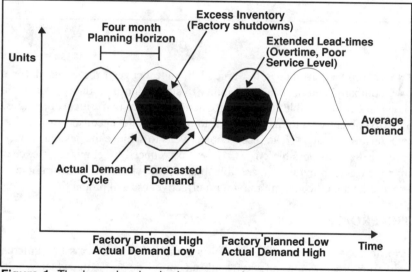

Figure 1. The long planning horizon created a four-month lag between the actual and forecasted demand. This lag resulted in cycles of high inventory and poor service.

Over the next five years several changes were incorporated into the production planning process which improved service levels to their highest ever while reducing inventory and other costs to their lowest ever. Changes were in the following areas:

• Improvements in the demand forecasting process
• Reduction of the frozen planning horizon
• Commitment to a "pull" system of planning
• More frequent adjustments to the plan

The accuracy of the demand forecast was improved drastically by simply placing ultimate responsibility with the production planning group. Since the group already was responsible for inventory and service level, the plan's accuracy naturally became very critical. In addition, analysis of each product's sales history determined its past demand trendline (or moving average), the slope of the trendline, the variability of its demand around the trendline, and any cycles that were present (Figure 2). Interestingly, the trendlines were very stable with gradually changing slopes but with very volatile cycles of demand. Further study showed that the major cause of the volatility was the instability of the product's lead-time (Figure 3). It was apparent that if the lead-time could be stabilized, the demand would become less volatile.

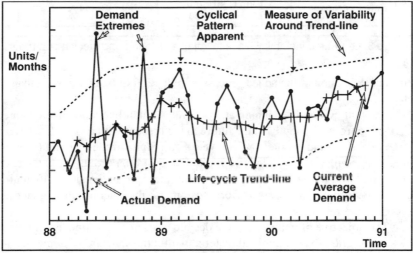

Figure 2. Statistical and graphical analysis of demand yields important information on trends, cycles, and variability.

THE FROZEN PLANNING HORIZON

The frozen planning horizon, formerly sixteen weeks, was reduced to eight weeks for increases to the schedule and to three weeks for decreases to the schedule. The improvement was made possible by cycle time reductions in every group. The largest reduction came from the implementation of "flexible planning" in the material planning group which reduced raw material lead-times to eight weeks or less. "Flexible Planning" is an agreement in which the supplier agrees to provide material flexibility at 6-8 weeks in return for visibility provided by long-term purchase orders. The amount of flexibility required is determined by the variability of the demand. Also, gradual reduction of manufacturing cycle times to three weeks or less was achieved through

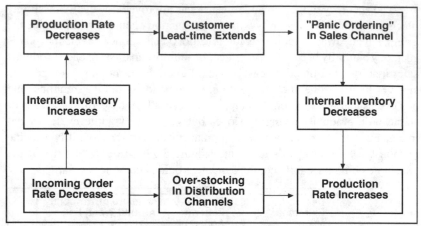

Figure 3. Lead-time instability leads to volatile ordering and stocking patterns.

elimination of non-value added processes, reduction of batch sizes, kanbans, etc.

The pull system of planning at TI operates much like a pipeline (Figure 4) running from six months in the future to the present with a valve located at three weeks out and another at eight weeks out. Some of the material (shown in red) in the pipeline is already committed to customer orders while the rest of the material (shown in blue) is not committed, in anticipation of future orders. As orders are received from customers, the uncommitted material becomes committed.

The objective of maintaining the desired customer lead-time is achieved by keeping enough uncommitted material within the standard customer lead-time to accommodate new orders as they are entered.

The objectives of delivering shipments on time and minimizing cost are achieved by ensuring that only material committed to customer orders passes through manufacturing and into finished inventory.

In Figure 4, the valve at week three is controlled by the production scheduler who cuts any uncommitted material from the schedule before it is delivered to manufacturing. The valve at week eight is controlled by the production planner and the material planner who employ the "flexible planning" agreement with suppliers to add material to the schedule to improve service level or delete material from the schedule to avoid excess inventory.

Tight control of inventory results in improved quality, flexibility, and responsiveness. Uncommitted material which has not been delivered to manufacturing can still be diverted to other products, keeping material and labor resources flexible to react to customer needs. Shifts in demand are detected immediately. When demand occurs at a greater than normal rate, the uncommitted material within the customer lead-time decreases and sends up a flag to

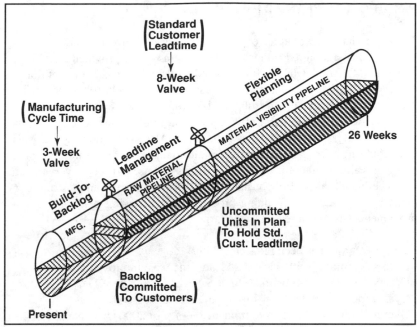

Figure 4. The pull system pipeline runs from six months into the future.

add more material. Therefore, lead-time stability, the biggest factor in demand volatility, can be improved.

In contrast to the tangible advantages already mentioned, the most important advantage of the pull system is credibility. The pull system lends credibility to all the planning information used in the factory. Credibility in the manufacturing schedule will quickly result in better performance to that schedule. Every time the manufacturing line misses a schedule, units go overdue to a customer and the line will get immediate feedback from production planning. This can be painful for a short time, but performance to the schedule will improve immediately. In a similar manner, the pull system lends credibility to material planning information. Any part shortage which shows up to purchasing within the three week "window" is holding up a customer order. No more second guessing of the schedule is necessary. No more expediting for three days only to find that the requirements for the part disappeared. The pull system always highlights the important problems— those that affect customer satisfaction.

PRODUCTION PLAN ADJUSTMENTS

The other changes would have been ineffective if the MRP system was still run only once a month. Fortunately, the systems group provided a real-time, "what-if" MRP tool, which effectively reduced the average amount of time to analyze the effects of a change to the plan from 2-4 weeks to 2-4 hours. The "what-if" tool is actually an isolated MRP run for one device that costs less than five dollars per run and provides a quantum-leap improvement in the ability to analyze desired changes to the plan. Also, semi-monthly full MRP runs could now be justified easily. Small changes being made more often eliminates almost all of the traumatic changes that used to occur every month.

The industrial controls business at TI is showing continuous improvement in its production planning process. The following performance improvements have been realized thus far:

- Total inventory has been reduced by 45%
- Orders committed within standard lead-time have improved by 26%
- Orders delivered on-time to customers have improved by 77%
- Cycle time from order entry to shipping has decreased by 40%
- Overdue units have decreased from an average of 2000 to an average of 400
- Orders completed on-time to the manufacturing schedule have improved by 50%
- Orders delivered on-time from suppliers have improved by 66%

The four concepts—improvement of the demand forecast, reduction of the frozen horizon, commitment to a pull system, and frequent adjustments to the plan—are interdependent. The planning process is not successful if even one is neglected.

Using all four concepts simultaneously will help to achieve the goal of providing the necessary customer service level at the least possible cost.

20

CYCLIC SCHEDULING FOR IMPROVEMENT
ROBERT W. HALL

E normous improvements are possible by synchronizing manufacturing tasks sequentially within a short lead time and by creating cycle times by which many different kinds of work can be fitted together like clockwork. Actually achieving close synchronization requires utmost effort to improve every aspect of a manufacturing organization. A concept central to the improvement is the creation and use of cyclic schedules. The paper discusses how and why these relationships exist.

INTRODUCTION

Scheduling is part of the total process of manufacturing. Three basic purposes of scheduling are accepted as obvious: (a) matching the production process to the demands of the market, (b) coordinating operations, both those internal to the firm and those taking place at suppliers, and (c) stimulating improvement in operations. Improvement can be either through making good use of operations as they are, or by stimulating a "learning curve effect," changing operations by a number of measures with the fastest learning rate possible. In a "JIT company," the learning curve effect is likely to be called continuous improvement.

Any method of scheduling must deal with operations in their current state, both in physical development and in organizational development. The method of scheduling reflects the current status of manufacturing development. A schedule must be within an organization's capability to execute or it is meaningless.

Many academic discussions of scheduling regard the physical production processes and the company organization as given. A common example is job shop scheduling optimizations. These usually attempt some optimal combi-

Reprinted with permission from *International Journal of Production Research,* 1988, vol. 26, no. 3; 457-472.

nation of on-time job completion, queue times, throughput times and costs, while assuming that operations are independent of each other and parameters are fixed. The shortfall of these studies is that the assumptions themselves limit the possibilities for improvement.

The "JIT framework" contains little limitation in thinking except the difficulties of actually making improvements—execution. Although the appellation "JIT" does not suggest it, the objectives are broad and the scope of improvement activity covers an entire manufacturing organization. Scheduling is but one part of the whole. The objectives are to simultaneously make improvement in a number of ways:

- *Eliminate waste.* Do not do anything unnecessary in any part of the company. Eliminate activity that does not add value to the customer.

- *Improve quality.* This begins with a firm intent to improve customer satisfaction, and extends from there into details of operations. No one "does JIT" without careful attention to quality.

- *Decrease leadtimes for all kinds of activities.* Material throughput time, supplier leadtimes, customer leadtimes, tooling preparation, engineering (design) changes, setup times and new product introduction. Sometimes lead time reduction in all these ways is expressed as an increase in flexibility.

- *Increase skill and employee morale.* These improvements occur only if both managers and employees are enthused about increasing employee skill and responsibility. From a management perspective, this is probably the hardest aspect of JIT.

- *Decrease costs.* If the first four objectives can be attained, this one will be also.

Since inventory is a waste, one objective is to decrease it, but companies make little progress if they believe that the only objective of JIT is to eliminate inventory. The true method to attain all these objectives is powerful organizational development to constantly attack the problems which prevent them from being realized.

A manufacturing company shot through with problems also has difficulty scheduling. Schedules become complex when allowances must be made for high defect rates, machine breakdowns, absenteeism and the like. Smoother manufacturing processes are easier to schedule—less rescheduling. In conjunction with a programme of process improvement, a schedule can contribute to the problem solving effort.

REPETITIVE MANUFACTURING

Improvement derives from learning about a product and production process in detail, and learning occurs by repetition. Schedules which stimulate improvement provide for as many operations as possible to be done repetitively. Repetitive manufacturing is:

1. Making the same items over and over—repeatedly if not frequently. Then potential exists to produce by a rhythm, or repetitive pattern.

2. Making items by a repetitive process, even if the products themselves are not in a standard sequence, or even if no two products are exactly alike.

Managements sometimes want to concentrate on the unique aspects of their production processes rather than on the potential to make the maximum amount of work repetitive. Some think that unless one produces identical autos or refrigerators in volume, JIT is not possible. However, with the complexity of current automobiles several details of one being assembled on a line may be unlike any other.

The key is to develop as repetitive a process as possible in any kind of manufacturing. Even large aircraft produced at a rate of one per month are made by a basically repetitive process although the cycle times between completions is long. The benefit comes from learning how to take advantage of cycles to improve both products and processes. A schedule can help create the time cycles, but the real objective is the improvement activities. Those activities stimulated by cycles can be roughly grouped into two classes: (a) cycle time analysis for improvement, and (b) cycle times used to synchronize operations as much as possible.

Cycle Time Analysis for Improvement

Improvements can be in methods, layout, technology, quality, skill—anything. A simple example of cycle time analysis is illustrated by a single operator with a cell of two or three machines making the same part over and over. While carefully observing the method and circumstances, time ten cycles or so. Review occurrences during the longest cycle which might in any way be prevented from happening again. Look for the differences in the shortest cycle which might be incorporated in every cycle.

By constantly studying activity cycles, two kinds of improvement are obtained. First, the average time to execute each cycle can be reduced, which is a productivity improvement (or potential productivity improvement). Second, the variance in cycle times is reduced, which means that work is done more consistently, and consistency is strongly related to quality (by adherence to standard methods).

This kind of analysis can be done in a crude way by operators timing themselves and keeping mental note of the methodological variations of each cycle, or it can be done by video camera or instrumented reviews of even automatic cycles. In practice, however, the major problems seem to be not ability to observe, but to actually make changes which create the improvement.

Any activity done in cycles can be studied and improved in this way. Suppose that a schedule calls for a machine to be set up about the same time each week at about the same time to make the same part number. The setup procedure can be studied on a weekly cycle, just as running operations are studied on a work cycle. Much effort to reduce setup times can be summarized as converting the setup procedure to a regular, repeating, standard routine, constantly seeking to remove the waste time.

Throughout much of a manufacturing company, operations can be studied by cycle time analysis: machine maintenance cycles, tooling work cycles, transport cycles. Even non-production work: order processing, billing, even the periodic development of schedules themselves. The improvement work itself is the important part, and the cyclic scheduling only contributes to that, albeit in a vital way.

Improvement comes by studying fundamentals of products and processes, and by working to make changes in several ways. A few of them are:

1. Flow charting material through one or more full throughput cycles through a plant. Tooling, a material handling device, or a measuring instrument can likewise be flow charted through a cycle of its use. Eliminating wasted steps reduces lead times (and often inventory besides).

2. Looking for *quality cycles* in each process. This can be done by examining mean times between failures of equipment, as is often done for predictive maintenance. Better to examine control charts or other measurements to study causes of longterm deviations from "normal" patterns. Cycle times from machine and tooling maintenance can be based on the results.

3. Synchronizing as many activities as possible so as to eliminate "dead" time between activities.

These are simple methods to improve. Because they are simple, many people can use them. The cycles of work provide that opportunity to many people.[1]

Synchronize Cycle Time Development
Create cycles of work which fit together, i.e. harmonic cycles of interlocking activities. This thinking is the opposite of believing that an overall operation

should consist of suboperations kept decoupled, buffered and wholly independent. The suboperations include those of supplier companies.

Eliminate randomness from operations. Queuing models and other stochastic approaches used for scheduling assume that operations are subject to random events. Rather than just react to randomness, try to develop both operations and a schedule that stimulate regular timing in performance.

Synchronization is the matching of repeating cycles of activity. Cycle lengths may differ, but if all are multiples of one another, they fit nicely into a pattern.

Regular timing removes randomness from operations—or assumes that it can be removed. Actual execution by synchronized timing depends on development of both people and equipment for it. Some of the cycles which affect manufacturing are from accounting or sales rather than production itself. For example, most factories are subject to surges in shipping at the ends of months or quarters because management wants more billings at the end of an accounting period, or because customer delivery times correspond to the times when sales quotas are due.

If repetitive production is possible, look for the basis to develop a uniform-load schedule for end items. If an end-item schedule can be constructed (and actually held) so that as many materials as possible are consumed at a uniform rate, these materials may also be fabricated and delivered at a uniform rate.

A steady, uniform pattern of material use forms the simplest basis for performing many production activities in a cyclic, repetitive pattern. Much direct work can be made subject to repetition. Some examples are: setups, tooling refurbishment, preventive maintenance, material handling, material transport (between plants), quality checks and calibrations, personnel schedules (use of almost all labour), engineering changes, trials of new production, and training and improvement activities.

Why should engineering changes be done on a cycle? Because once production is synchronized and flowing smoothly, there is little reason to disrupt it with a routine change. A safety-related emergency is a different matter. Hold the engineering changes until the schedule period is done and changes must be made anyway. Then implement the engineering changes as a group.

This cycle of work makes it easier to plan an effective date for an engineering change to be executed. (It also helps the calculation of the run-out times of old parts, which is additionally simplified if inventories of old parts are minimal.) Engineering, tooling and other groups also have specific target dates. The implementation of a significant portion of manufacturing activity is made much less random in timing, and more effective. Besides, it is easier to know when a change actually became effective, which is sometimes an issue.

Usually, the lead uniform-load schedule is an assembly schedule, but sometimes it is something different, for instance, a packing schedule or a material handling schedule gathering parts to ship (the product being a single-piece part). The Kanban system of shop floor control, in all its variations, works by drawing materials into a lead process governed by a uniform-load schedule. The uniform load schedule is a master schedule from which planning for materials takes place, but it is also more than that.

The development of many different activities functioning by synchronized cycle times is not very difficult if everyone is imbued with the cycle time concept, the thought that the cycles or their activities should fit into the cycle times of the processes they serve. Given that, production supervisors in fabrication areas know only the cycle times of use for the parts they provide and the material handling schedules by which material will be called for, or brought to them. From that they can derive the work cycles their operations need to perform in order to mesh into the whole.

Developing everyone to understand the cycle time concept is an important early step in mastering JIT in a repetitive production environment. Once it is understood, a simple lead schedule provides the basis for many different people to plan the synchronizing of their work. Setting the lead schedule is something like writing the melody for a musical piece. When the music is played, execution of the lead schedule keys the harmony from the supplying operations. It works when both personnel and operations have been developed to stay on the beat.

The development of the cycle time concept to simplify planning and control can hardly be separated from the development of the people and the overall production process which make it work. If potential for repetitive production is present, evolution toward a more and more cyclic schedule and synchronization is only one aspect of total refinement of the operations themselves.

Such a system of scheduling is not suddenly installed. It evolves as the problems of producing a product line are understood and overcome. Cyclic activities lend themselves to progressive improvement.

Continued further, cyclic scheduling of repetitive, low-variance operations creates the conditions for simple automation, sometimes in indirect work areas as well as direct. Simple automation costs less and usually functions more reliably.

BALANCING PRODUCTION FLOWS

Production cannot continue at the same overall output level forever. Market demand varies from period to period. One option is to balance all operations at a fixed cycle time and vary the total time worked. Another is to build ahead when market demand is down, stashing inventory somewhere in hopes demand will pick up. Neither approach is as satisfactory as flexibility to adjust output rate to the current level of sales.

If operations are to remain synchronized, operations must be easily rebalanced at different rates (cycle times). There are two major cases:

Variable Work Cycle Operations (Usually Manual)

The desire is to increase production rate by adding people to an operation and to decrease it by subtracting people. Besides low downtimes, low setup times and so forth, two other factors are necessary: (a) flexible, multi-functional workers and (b) layouts for flow and flexibility.

Workers should be capable of moving from station to station, and they should be able to trade elements of work between stations. This is essential for assembly lines and often important for fabrication areas. Cell layouts lend themselves to this, and trade-off flexibility is an outstanding feature of a well-developed U-line layout.

In addition to the obvious inflexibility created by a workforce segregated into castes by constricted job descriptions, the demands of flexibility on operator skill is often underestimated. The ability to operate all machines in a cell or take any one of the several positions on a complex assembly line taxes operator skill.

Likewise, the problems of layout are generally underestimated. One reason for using small, standard containers at assembly is to load many different part numbers at each line station. Another is to provide ability to quickly change layout by shifting parts between line stations. If assemblies have several unique parts, the objective may be more easily attained by pre-kitting all unique parts to ride down an assembly line next to the unit to which they are to be attached.

In the non-repetitive case, the level loading of a true job shop is likely to be best attained by loading the total labour force. If extra equipment is present and if workers are flexible enough, they can move to a different machine for work that obviously needs to be done at that time. Workforce skill and flexibility is a big factor in preventing bottlenecks in job shops producing custom-designed products.

Layouts for flow and flexibility frequently require trial and error to develop, and no layout is satisfactory forever. To the maximum extent, a plant should be able to quickly and easily change layout. Some shops with light equipment have developed the capability to change layout overnight if necessary.[2] This requires ability to easily reconnect utilities in different locations—a layout concept something like a laboratory—a production laboratory. (With heavy, fixed equipment, this is obviously not practical.)

Fixed Work Cycle Operations (Usually Machines)

The work cycle of a machine often cannot vary much and still produce a quality part. Induction heat treating is one example. A curing cycle for a polymeric part is another. And even when varying the work cycle is technically possible, the adjustment time adds to setup time.

The solution is to have each piece of equipment stand idle while the work cycle is not in progress. Process a workpiece only when one is present and necessary to be processed. Rigging a machine to do this is usually very simple. The difficulty is managerial tolerance for idle time.

The belief is that cost per part is reduced when a high speed, expensive machine is used to the full. This leads to machines which are stand-alone work centres processing many parts. Then machines with apparent lowest costs are favoured for routings even if other equipment is available. The consequence is the creation of bottlenecks in a job shop environment, and the creation of a job shop (stand-alone work centres) when one does not need to exist. However, if a machine is capable of quality production and can be modified for little operator attention, the work cycle need only be short enough to meet the necessary output rate. Sooner or later, the remaining time on a machine would not be needed anyway.

The difficulty of actually doing this lies more in the acceptance of a different philosophy of operations than in any understanding of technique. Machine design and development is different for machines used in cell arrangements than if standing alone, and similar considerations apply to rate-balanced operations, even if machines are not juxtaposed in cells.

Companies attempting to transform independent operations into a set developed for both flow and flexibility discover that their thinking must radically change. Existing machines to be linked have greatly differing work cycles. Setups on them are difficult in a close layout. Configurations do not lend themselves to cells. Operator skill to manage a variety of machines is underestimated.

Another difficult idea to accept is that neither a total operation nor any of its suboperations should run at full capacity. Some slack time should be allowed for three reasons:

1. A little slack time allows any operation which falls behind to quickly catch up. Then any production delays are for reasons other than intrinsic machine capacity, and these reasons can be addressed. The term "bottleneck" takes on a different meaning.
2. Time should be allowed for regular maintenance. Preventive maintenance and predictive maintenance are preferred to the reactive kind.
3. Time should be allowed for improvement of the operations. That time is slack capacity of both people and machines. If the time is well-spent, both can be greatly improved, so extra capacity is a far better investment than extra inventory. (Five to ten percent of the total available time spent on improvement is common for managements who think this way.)

Products also need to be designed with this approach to production in mind. Product families can be designed so that options are interchangeable, and so that they are built up step by step. Then products with different options can still flow through the same operations sequence with similar cycle times.

A similar idea is the development of the same machine or supplier to produce a family of parts. If setup times are short, the overall production rate can continue without disturbance even though the mix of specific parts required sometimes changes on short notice. With suppliers, this greatly simplifies communication of changes. The same supplier changes the mix of output. Requirements are not cancelled from one supplier while rush orders are expedited from another.

The accounting system must also go through a metamorphosis. Most accounting systems assume that operations are independent, and therefore that total costs are the sum of a series of independent, direct costs with other costs pooled and allocated as overhead. This system creates far too much emphasis on "direct" costs, and far too little emphasis on the overhead required to manage the independent operations. A change more toward a process form of costing is a subject in itself, but there is no question that costing methods profoundly affect the thinking of management.

The schedule for any operations must deal with them as they are at the time, so the method of scheduling evolves as the operations evolve. If the process can be rapidly transformed, so can the scheduling approach. In fact, in the repetitive manufacturing case, development of a uniform-load lead schedule is one of the earliest changes to work on. Schedule and process must be developed symbiotically.

SCHEDULE DEVELOPMENT

Schedule development must consider the specific nature of the total process to be scheduled. The process includes both production operations through several tiers of suppliers, and the process of identifying customer demand and conveying product to the customers. Some of the major characteristics of the production process which affect schedule development are: size of product, number and complexity of parts, cycle time (rate of production), are standard routings (flowpaths of material) possible?, and are long delays (as for testing) necessary?

On the marketing and distribution side, the issue is whether the product is made to order or made to stock. To be sure, many companies have the goal of making to order rather than to stock if their lead times can be reduced for it. Some products are made both to order and to stock. Some products are made for both to order and to stock. Some products are also made for other manufacturers, and depending on the nature of their process, that may be regarded as make-to-order, make-to-stock or as production synchronized with the customer company's schedule (or demand pull signals).

A simple way to think about initiating this is to consider how short a production period would be adequate for a production process to cycle through every product in the product line. Reduce lot sizes to shorten this time, producing only what is needed to cover demand during the schedule period.

Given all the possibilities, a good way to describe how a schedule is developed is with examples. In each case the lead schedules receive major attention, and the materials plans for fabrication and supply operations derive from those.

Large, Complex Products Manufactured Repetitively
Examples in this category are automobiles and large appliances. The lead schedules are normally mixed-model assembly schedules. Auto assembly plants everywhere normally operate by mixed-model assembly schedules. That is, instead of assembling the same model in a long run and then switching to another, different models are interspersed one after another:

A-B-C-D-A-B-C-D

In an auto assembly plant this is most commonly done to run a variety of models with a near-constant line balance. The sequence is developed to provide a mix of major components that neither overcycles a particular line station with too much work several cycles (autos) in a row, nor undercycles the station. Overcycling is normally considered the most serious problem since either the line must stop to complete the work or operations are missed.

The same concept can be extended to provide a level pattern of parts usage which converts to a uniform load for supplying operations also. Some of the most common components which are considered in developing an auto assembly line sequence are:

• body type: two-door, four-door, front wheel or rear wheel drive, etc.
• engine type (and type of emissions control equipment)
• transmission
• air conditioning
• seat types
• colour (paint); special problem is two-tone
• special trim packages

Most autos have many possibilities for combinations; some are common and some are rare. Creating a uniform load for all the components is virtually impossible. If the assembly sequence provides balanced spacing for major components, some of the lesser ones "fall where they may." One of the more common difficulties is with paint colours, for instance.

A difficulty here is the setup time for a different paint colour. If paint system lines must be blown clear of one colour before starting another, the paint loss is a cost to consider. Then it is desired to sequence a number of vehicles all of one body colour before switching to another. This grouping of vehicles by colour decreases the possibilities for good mix of cars based on other major considerations. If the system can change colours with every car, that is no longer a restriction.

Auto trim items also present special problems. Suppose there are 20 different wheel types for one car model. If one wheel type comes from only one supplier, the demand on that supplier may not be uniform load. A low-volume option cannot be perfectly spaced in the schedule if the spacing is to remain acceptable for major items.

The answer to these kinds of problems is not scheduling brilliance. Companies seem to consider 10-25 major components in devising assembly sequences. Many more than that begins to create interferences between components which cannot be resolved anyway. The answer is in process flexibility: one-unit lot sizes for paint, family-of-parts sourcing from one supplier which has quick setup capability, etc.

The degree to which a uniform load schedule affects any supplying operation depends on how closely it is linked to assembly—how frequently it delivers. If a supplier delivers once per day, then it needs to see a somewhat level load by day. Variations within the day do not matter much to it. However, if a supplying operation delivers parts in sequence (often done with auto seats, for instance), the ability of the supply operation to closely track the final assembly sequence is vital. If either the uniform load or the process flexibility can be established, transmitting the assembly sequence to a nearby supplier is generally the least of the problems.

In assembly operations, much depends on size or unit and on the cycle time. Autos may assemble with a cycle time of 1 minute or more. As cycle time decreases, the ability to space units decreases. Units may be sequenced in groups of four or five, which is sometimes done with motorcycles or appliances. On the other hand, a smaller, simpler unit may assemble in a mixed model sequence by unit at a cycle time of 15 seconds or so. The specific physics, geometry and timing of a particular situation must be worked out on its merits.

Small Items With Short Cycle Times

This example is 1/2-in. VHS American recording tape. It comes in about 100 different variations in final cassette form, not including the labels which may be applied for different customers. Of this number only half are commonly demanded, and only 20 or so within any given week. Most production is to order with some common types carried in stock (which is kept small).

The outer configuration of a tape cassette is nearly uniform so it will fit in the recorder. The variations are inside: different speeds, tape lengths and so forth. A consideration is also the packing box volumes. Producing less than one shipping container is confusing so "mixed model" in this case is at least one full packing container. The lead schedule which pulls everything to it is the packing schedule.

This company at first decided on a two-week schedule period. About 30 or so different variations of the 1/2-in. VHS tape were requested by customers every two weeks, and after layout changes and setup time reductions, 30 to 40 different variations could be produced in two weeks. After further process improvements, the schedule period was reduced to one week.

The process has been developed to run this way. All the variations of tape are cut from a coated substrate made in the same way at the beginning of the process. The operations downstream from this; slitting, cutting to length, moulding parts, winding and so on; are all laid out and refined to allow material to flow into assembly and then packing. A simple form of Kanban system is used for downstream shop floor control.

The schedule rules are simple. If the volume of a variation allows production of one or more final shipping containers per day, it is run every day during the schedule period. If the volume is less, it is run once during the week. Less-than-full container special orders are run as needed. A portion of each daily schedule is set aside for small orders telephoned in by morning and shipped by evening, just as if removed from stock. Finally, a little time is allowed during each average day for both people and process to be improved—through education or through devising and trying new ideas.

Performance to this schedule is very good. Completions are always as scheduled except when the customer's label does not arrive in time to be placed on the material. Customer lead times have been reduced from weeks to a week or less. Lead time through the downstream process is hours, so customer lead time for a small order is one day.

This simple example is real, and it illustrates two points:

1. The production process operates in the service of every volume customer to some extent each day, and it serves every customer in the backlog within at least a week. The larger customer orders are not run all at one dedicated time thus preventing the use of capacity for other customers. That is the cause of big backlogs and long customer lead times.

2. The process does not run at full capacity. A few common varieties are run to stock during weekly schedules when customer orders are down, but if stock is at a sufficient level to cover customer service for these items, the schedule time per day is reduced. (The company might also increase cycle times when this happens, but they have not yet developed to that point.)

LINEAR PERFORMANCE TO SCHEDULE

In the case of the uniform-load schedule, the goal is not only to complete units to ship on schedule, but to also maintain a steady cycle time so that all the operations keying from a lead schedule can stay together. This is seemingly simple to accomplish if an assembly line is set on rate and never stopped—a paced line. The matter is not quite that simple. Stops occur for various reasons—machines break or jam, critical parts are not in place when needed, or for other reasons. In the United States, the term "paced assembly line" just means that the *worker* cannot stop the line, not that a line never stops.

Line stops or process stops by workers are desirable. The stops are better than correcting botched work at line's end or having an unuseable unit produced. Many of these preventive line stops can extend beyond avoiding an obvious catastrophe. The stops are both a training and improvement method.

Assembly lines in well-coached JIT companies have line stop time built into the schedule as part of the improvement—an allowance of 5% of total assembly time or thereabouts. In fact, if a line subject to worker runs uninterrupted through a shift, little learning or improvement is taking place. Perhaps the line is overmanned or perhaps the workers are not paying attention to opportunities for improvement.

Hour	Schedule	Cumulative schedule	Actual (cumulative)	Notes
1	60	60	56	
2	45	105	99	15 min. break
3	60	165	157	
4	60	225	217	
5	30	255	248	30 min. for lunch
6	60	315	306	
7	45	360	350*	15 min. break
8	40	400	400*	20 min. "improvement allowance"

* The line ran 10 minutes over to catch up at end of shift. Of the 20 minutes allowed for daily improvement, the workers on this day used 10 minutes in line stops during the day. The other 10 minutes was used for end-of-shift discussion.

Nominal cycle time = 1 minute/unit

Average cycle time = $\dfrac{480 \text{ min/shift}}{400 \text{ units}}$ = 1.2 minutes/unit

Linear performance to schedule.

Linear performance to schedule means a higher level of accomplishment than just maintaining a paced rate assembly line. Finished units—after all repair and testing—are completed at a steady rate. Very important is that the lead operations closely maintain set schedules while also providing time for improvement. The illustration in the Table shows an allowance of 20 minutes per shift for improvement, and the line also has scheduled stops for worker breaks. In the American JIT plants, end-of-shift time for improvement is quite commonly scheduled; allowance for impromptu downtime is less common. Downtime allowance is common in Japanese plants.

In measuring performance, it is important to keep the purpose of the lead schedule in mind. Linearity in the value of shipments, which some companies use, is no indicator that a lead schedule is providing the tempo for cycle times.

LINKING THE SCHEDULE TO THE MARKET

There are two major cases: (a) make-to-stock, and (b) make-to-order. The objective is to match production cycles with marketing and distribution cycles. Many companies have both make-to-stock and make-to-order, so the total situation can become complex. However, the matching process should seek to simplify the existing arrangements. Doing so implies not just developing a different scheduling approach, but also revising the marketing and logistics cycles in addition to production. Many JIT companies belatedly conclude that marketing and distribution changes are necessary.

Make-to-Stock Case

The planning cycle for distribution inventory should be of the same length as the planning cycle for production. That is, the appropriate length of a segment of uniform load schedule depends on the need to match production to the market.

Production planning should use the most current possible estimates of need from the distribution system. If the production planning period is two weeks, the inventory replanning should be done every two weeks just prior to the production plan. The lot sizes coming from inventory should cover demand for a specific period of time, the same length period as the production period or a multiple of it. Every item in stock may be produced in each schedule period, but this is not always done for low volume products.

This reasoning is the opposite of reorder point systems. A reorder point system with EOQ lot sizes is a disaster when trying to develop uniform load schedules. Orders are triggered at random times, and lot sizes cover different time periods of demand. With numerous products in a product line, the law of large numbers will help smooth this, but the potential is ever present for an irregular demand pattern to upset the capability to uniform load a production schedule. Such a system also automatically adds to lead time. Orders triggered during a production period must wait until at least the next period to be produced—or break into the current schedule.

If the methods of production are made flexible enough to accept this irregularity, they are flexible enough that they should simply react to the market as directly as possible. The inventory system then passes through the demand with a minimum of buffering.

The volume of an item to be made in a period is:

(Forecast of demand for that period)+(Any change in inventory level)

The amount of stock to keep in finished goods or distribution stock is mostly safety stock and pipeline stock. If the production process completes production of most items at a steady rate throughout the period, very little working lot size stock is needed. Most companies are able to reduce the amount of finished goods stock carried while retaining or improving the customer service level once everyone has gained confidence in this approach, which is no small feat.[3]

Methods for estimating the amount of safety stock to keep are well known. Safety stock should cover the lead time until the production system can regularly schedule an increase in output to cover an increase in demand. The psychological problem is the comfort of believing that a higher level of inventory should ensure a higher level of customer service. However, true customer service is provided by the one unit that a customer needs and not by all the rest that no one wants, no matter how inventory levels are calculated.

Equal or better customer service is obtained by developing very flexible production capability so that the market can be traced with much shorter lead times, and with less risk of obsolescent stock. The production system should be capable of making great changes in the volume and mix of production from one period to the next. This is obtained through short setup times, flexibility to change layouts, flexibility of workforce and all the rest. An incorrect impression of JIT is that the market should be in thrall to a rigid production system. That is the reverse of the intention.

What about seasonal demand? If production is flexible enough, and peak capacity is high enough, production can increase in season in stepped segments, and decrease in the off season, likewise in stepped segments. However, if the capability is not adequate to cover the peak, or if it is feared to be inadequate, there is little choice but to build stock ahead of the peak. Stock built ahead is that with the best chance of selling, and the capacity at peak is reserved to react to late-developing changes in the demand mix. The strategy for building ahead of a season is also well-known, including discounts to persuade customers to share the risk of a forecast. Short lead times and flexibility may decrease the risks, but they do not eliminate them, especially for weather-related or fashion-trend products.

Another source of demand irregularity is the marketing practices of the company itself, or of its customers. Marketing specials or discounts for huge volume buys create major blips in the sales pattern. The question is whether actual deliveries need also be in large quantities. Marketing can contract large sales quantities without all being delivered at once, as with annual contracts. Deliveries distributed over the time that the product will be used also saves a storage problem for the customer—but again the psychological problem is customer unease whether the producer will actually deliver as promised.

Inventory system dynamics may distort demand as seen by a factory. Management at various stages of a distribution chain over-order when a small sales increase is seen. If sales do not continue to rise, that stage is left with stock that will not move for a while. The result is boom-and-bust order patterns often seen in low volume parts such as spares.

If a company has control over distribution one solution is to order at each stage by demand replacement. Each stage should order primarily to replace stock actually sold. This policy prevents minor fluctuations in actual users' demand being amplified by the distribution system itself.

Other sales practices also create irregular demand patterns. One is the cycles for sales quotas or sales report deadlines. Sales personnel tend to save up orders and present them in a rush at the end of such periods. The solution is to shorten the cycles for closing sales management activity, and attempt to match the production schedule periods with them. However, sales cycle lengths depend on the time required to actually make sales development work materialize into booked orders.

Customer payment systems may also unbalance demand. One company had customers pay by the tenth of the month following to receive a discount. By no accident regular customers wanted delivery on the first of the month by this system. It maximized the time they could delay payment.

Such issues with respect to development of a uniform load schedule require a company to rethink its approach to sales management. Many sales managers prefer to decouple selling and delivery from the uncertainties of production using as much inventory as possible. Persuading them to have confidence in a new, flexible manufacturing capability is no small accomplishment.

Make-to-Order Case

The type of make-to-order production synchronized by a uniform load schedule is typically assemble-to-order. A product line with many standard options makes forecasting which ones to stock infeasible. Most non-JIT companies keep components and options in stock and assemble the desired customer combination for shipment. With the JIT philosophy, they press the inventory to as low a level in the production process as possible. Product lines having a core of custom-designed engineering content usually cannot be made by a synchronized process, but rather by asynchronous job shop methods.

Customer orders enter a backlog from a variety of market sources. In the classic case, a unit order comes from the user of the product, and the nature of the product requires make-to-order. However, some make-to-order situations are really make-for-another-company's-stock, as in the case of contract production for major retail chains.

Unit orders in a backlog must be slotted into a uniform load schedule. The matching process is basically matching the acquisition and management of a backlog with the production process. In such a company, marketing "sells unfilled spots on a moving train," each spot eventually occupied by a customer.

The backlog is unbuilt inventory, but managing it is costly. Orders in the backlog change in quantity, specification and delivery. Some orders are cancelled. Managing the backlog is another phase in the total process of obtaining and defining the order, but at some point a firm order must be slotted into a segment of uniform load schedule. The larger the backlog, the more expensive to manage, and the longer the average lead time to the customer. The longer the lead time, the more time to create and manage changes.

One reason for a large backlog is an inflexible rate of production. Another is production of orders in long runs, but that can be ameliorated by mixing orders in a uniform load schedule. However, a company with a uniform load schedule can still have a large backlog if the overall rate of production is not flexible, period to period.

The overall rate of production (and cycle time) for a segment of level schedule is based on the total number of orders for that period smoothed throughout the period. The longer the schedule period, the less variation in cycle time due to short term variations in desired customer delivery. (Long-term business cycle conditions are another matter.) Taken to an extreme, several years' orders could be used to develop the world's most perfect uniform load schedule, but that is ridiculous. The process of developing segments of uniform load schedule should consume no longer than a competitive lead time for the customer, and it should ideally take a shorter time.

Marketing should marshall orders into delivery time slots that correspond with segments of uniform load production schedule. They should confirm the orders for specification, quantity and delivery, but this is never done perfectly for each customer. Firm orders are then slotted into an upcoming segment of uniform load schedule. No orders are ever completely "frozen," but with discipline the amount of change can be held to a level which can be accommodated by the flexibility of production. (A common misunderstanding is that JIT demands schedules inviolate for extended periods. Shorter process lead times should take companies in the other direction—toward more flexibility with customers.)

The figure roughly diagrams the process by which marketing gathers, marshalls and confirms orders, then transfers them to a production process which sequences orders in the schedule segment according to the needs for uniform load. How precisely delivery time is promised to the customer makes a difference. Suppose a schedule period is one week and calls for 100 units. If customers expect delivery any time within the week, orders can be sequenced however best promotes a uniform load throughout the week. If delivery is specified to the day, sequencing is more constrained, and daily production more varied. (In such a case, a mixed-model schedule with "empty slots" may be preplanned. Marketing then sells "delivery dates" to match the slots.)

Obviously many considerations affecting the customer are involved in determining how to develop a uniform load schedule in the make-to-order case. If the uniform load schedule is attempted without giving thought to the readiness of the production process for it, the result is apt to be a long lead time for customers and poor delivery performance besides. In any case the long-term objective should be to develop product design and production processes so that operations can remain synchronized while still having flexibility to produce what a customer wants when it is wanted. The objective is not to create a complex order entry and scheduling procedure. Order processing for something complex as an automobile will of necessity be complex anyway. The complexity should not be compounded by trying to systematize around production constraints rather than eliminating them whenever possible.

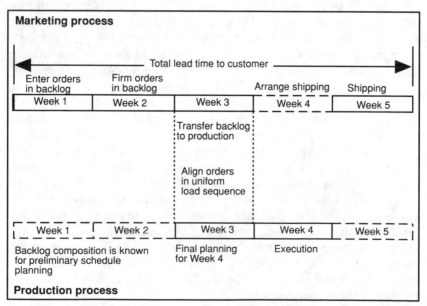

Overview of example situation: Development of uniform load schedule, make-to-order case.

256

The intent is to maintain meshed cycles of production activity, not to limit the combinations of product available. Meshing cycles of sales and customer activity are also important. Customer lead time may be filled with sales and customer activity as well as production activity. For instance, a site for a product must be prepared. Customer training conducted. Shipping must be arranged, and perhaps installation also.

A customer lead time short as possible may not be desired for a complex product because of concurrent customer preparation activity. Some companies try to maintain a constant lead time to the customer by adjusting the production levels each schedule period. (Mainframe computers are an example of this). However, there are inevitably some schedule changes originating from the customer, if not from difficulties with production or suppliers. Therefore an objective is to reduce all supplier lead times to less than the lead time for the customer.

The benefits of meshed cycles of activity extend from the order management process to the supply management process. If the coordination of suppliers can also take place within regular, repeating cycles, the possibilities for improvement multiply, but that can be explained from the viewpoint of a supplier.

Make-for-Another-Manufacturer

Suppose the customer is another manufacturer. The orders from that customer really derive from its production schedule. The ideal is for the production cycles of the customer to coincide with the supplier. However, most supplier companies have more than one major industrial customer. One may send irregular orders quantities at irregular times. Another has a monthly planning bucket, replanning at the month's start, while a third customer replans at midmonth. Still another may provide a rolling weekly replan.

From the viewpoint of a supplier serving all four customers from the same production process, no clear planning cycle meshes with all customers. The supplier might come closest with a weekly plan, but then the selection of the length of its uniform-level period must also consider the characteristics of its own production process.

In general, buffer inventories can become smallest and backlogs the shortest when customer, producers and suppliers can all march along using production cycles of the same length. An enormous amount of effort is required to sustain development toward such an ideal—which is closest to reality in some Japanese industries—but one of the major foundations of this progress is the concept of cyclic scheduling for improvement and for synchronization.

FOOTNOTES

1. The author has visited well-counselled Japanese plants beginning JIT. In assembly operations, an important difference observed was that the assembly cycle time is set and posted, boundaries of the line stations are clearly marked, and the operators are busy with cycle time analysis and the change work which follows from that. In Western plants, effort is more limited to only that necessary to achieve a line layout for mixed-model flow. Less experienced Westerners think of JIT more as a materials management programme than as a total improvement programme.

2. A Japanese example is the Tokai Rika Otowa Plant.

3. For example, Black and Decker reduced finished goods inventory by half in some lines with no decrease in customer service. However, managements with lack of confidence actually increase finished goods until assured that service from production is reliable.

21

A LESSON IN SMED
WITH SHIGEO SHINGO
PER JOHANSEN AND KENNETH J. MCGUIRE

The benefits of reducing lot sizes and inventory are becoming increasingly recognized by most manufacturing professionals. The Japanese have proven with a vengeance that smaller lots and inventories can lead to (1) reduction of waste and rework, (2) quality improvement, (3) enhanced worker involvement, (4) better process yield and productivity, and (5) increased awareness of causes of errors and delay.

It is, therefore, not an exaggeration to say that just-in-time or stockless production represents a revolution in manufacturing thinking. For the victors, that revolution leads to continuous cost reduction and increased market share.

It is well known by now that one of the necessary steps to achieving successful just-in-time performance is driving towards stockless production. Reduction of setup time is often the first and biggest "rock" to appear as the proverbial inventory (the water) is lowered in the stream. The Japanese have really excelled in this area, particularly Toyota and its major suppliers. With tremendous ingenuity and persistence, Toyota and other top Japanese manufacturers have driven setup costs down to the bare minimum. When setup times are measured in minutes instead of hours, the logic of the economic order quantity (EOQ) approach is dissolved. The blind-spot of EOQ logic has always been that setup costs are both fixed and high. Accepting the premises as givens is an attitude problem that fulfills itself.

Among the many stories coming out of the "war on waste" fought on the factory floor of top Japanese companies over the past decade, a large number are about how the setup times on particular machines were reduced from many hours (sometimes days) to a few minutes. These remarkable results were achieved primarily by challenging the root cause of the problem: attitude. Instead of accepting the givens, management asked: Why do setups have to be so high?

Reprinted from *Industrial Engineering,* October 1986, vol. 18, no. 10; Norcross, GA: Institute of Industrial Engineers, 26-33.

The authors recently observed a demonstration of how setup time can be reduced dramatically through improved management practices. Shigeo Shingo, one of the principal figures behind the development of Toyota's "stockless" production system, visited a large midwestern manufacturer of aerospace and defense products. Through lectures and demonstrations, he taught the brilliant yet simple approach to setup time reduction he developed at Toyota: the SMED system (single-minute-exchange-of-die, referring to changeover done in less than ten minutes; i.e., single-digit time).

Don't be misled by the use of the word *die*. Setup reduction efforts were initially aimed at stamping machines which use dies, but the methodology developed was carried over to all types of equipment which require setup. The principles, however, are perhaps demonstrated most dramatically in the changeover practices on dies.

A DRAMATIC DEMONSTRATION

Shingo's lecture and demonstration were scheduled to begin on a Monday morning. But, having arrived on a Sunday morning, Shingo requested a plant visit that afternoon with the key managers and engineers. His purpose was to observe how changeovers were done and how they could be improved. As he interacted with his hosts and observed a particular 45-ton press, he learned that the setup time on this machine was about two hours, and he learned why. He then made a series of recommendations which the engineering manager agreed to perform prior to the demonstration scheduled for the following afternoon.

Shingo's visit to the factory that Sunday afternoon was perhaps the most important incident of the entire seminar/consulting event. With his unusual request, Shingo demonstrated to the management that setup reduction is a serious enough matter to require time even on a Sunday afternoon. A big attitude problem is overcome when management views setup reduction as an important issue. This represents a major first step because when management demonstrates real commitment to setup reduction, everyone else will take the issue seriously. The required technical actions then tend to follow quite naturally.

On that Sunday afternoon visit, Shingo emphasized many waste eliminating principles. One was to avoid adjustments while the press was down. For this, he suggested various remedies such as putting L-shaped pieces of metal to hold the die in correct position. Another principle he stressed was the need to have all tools correctly organized. This may require appropriate movable tables located within easy reach of the setup people. To successfully streamline the operation, he emphasized the need to meet with the operators involved to:

- coach them
- teach them the simple principles involved
- get their ideas pertaining to procedures
- provide an environment that allows operators to practice the procedures

There is sound logic behind Shingo's emphasis on getting input from operators. Though setup reduction is a management responsibility, operators are the real experts, by virtue of their intimate familiarity with all the practical day-to-day details of the situation.

GET OPERATORS INVOLVED

Establishing an environment that allows operators to contribute their expertise and to practice continuous improvement requires "management by walking around" as well as support for SGIA (small group improvement activities). Managers can no longer sit in their offices and direct from a distance through memos alone. They must provide day-to-day guidance and coaching. They must constantly remind operators of the tremendous importance of reducing setups, how the success of the entire company depends on it, how it helps cut costs, how it contributes to the overall drive toward stockless production.

This means being seen and heard on the floor at least once each day. It also means checking results and listening to input from operators at key moments. This requires sensitivity to the all-important human aspects of the improvement process. Management must gain the trust of workers so that mistakes are not hidden but instead are thought of as starting points for improvements ("a mistake is a gem"). Finally, management must recognize the efforts and achievements of operators through personal praise as well as financial rewards.

In all this, personal contact is essential. Managers must not think of themselves as a breed apart from workers. Instead, the interdependence of everyone involved—i.e., team-spirit—needs to come much more to the forefront. This, like the EOQ logic, presents a major attitude obstacle. It is another large "rock" to remove.

On Monday afternoon, after his lecture, Shingo went to the press machines with a group of managers, supervisors, engineers and operators to demonstrate how much time could be cut from the setup as a result of the approach he had taught them. All the adjustments and minor technical changes he had suggested had been carefully followed, including a meeting and practice session. The meeting and the practice session clearly reinforced how seriously management was actually taking the setup reduction issue.

With stop watch in hand, Shingo gave the signal: "Go!" Two operators performed the changeover. They went to work unbolting the old die. All the necessary tools were laid out within easy reach, at the right height, in the appropriate order. The men worked efficiently in a rehearsed manner. When the old die was unbolted, it was swiftly slid directly onto a waiting cart of the appropriate height. From an identical cart, the new die, which had been moved from storage in advance, was pushed directly into place with a minimum of movements. It fit directly against the L-shaped pieces of metal, and no adjustments were necessary. Some bolts were tightened with a few turns, and the press was ready to go. The time for the setup: two minutes and 33 seconds. The real experts were showing management what was possible when they were asked to use the most important tool, their heads. The combination of involvement, recognition and a challenge that is clearly important to management is the most powerful tool box in any factory.

BRAIN-POWER

After this dramatic demonstration, Shingo spent the rest of the afternoon interacting with the key engineers and operators in the plant. There was a noticeable increase in their interest level after what they had just seen. Although often tempted to say "No, it can't be done," these engineers and managers generally resisted. They instead asked technical questions geared to finding out how improvements could be achieved. Shingo made a number of suggestions:

1. Develop "visual control" in die storage area. Make it easy to find correct die through color-coding, floor marking, etc.
2. Standardize size of fixtures, dies, and tooling.
3. Have a specialized transportation person to get dies to and from storage.
4. Make tightening changes and tools uniform. (This makes it unnecessary to search for the right bolt and the right tool.)
5. Do all "centering" as external setup.
6. Make all "measurements" external, and then reduce the time of these operations, too.
7. Drive adjustment and other (usually) internal operations outside (external).
8. Have the operators themselves, not specialized setup people, perform the setup operations.
9. Get input from operators and hold guided practice sessions.

Shingo had a number of ideas pertaining to technical issues. For example, he suggested putting an extra washer in the die to avoid problematic friction and wasted time of adjustment and tightening. This extra washer works like an extra pair of socks to keep our feet from getting blistered by friction against tight shoes. Instead of the friction occurring between the sock and the foot, it occurs between the two layers of socks. The same thing happens between the two layers of washers.

Chapter Twenty-One

IMPROVEMENT EFFORTS

The next attitude obstacle Shingo had to overcome was the notion that only huge cost buys dramatic improvements. That attitude provides a rationale for procrastinating, waiting for some "gee whiz" technological breakthrough. While that waiting goes on, costs pile up, causing loss of ground to competitors who take immediate action toward improvement. It doesn't matter if that action takes the form of very small steps, as long as they are steps in the right direction. The key to long-term growth is persistent day-to-day improvement efforts.

To the great surprise of some of us present at the session, the cost of permanently installing the improvements Shingo had just demonstrated that afternoon was only about $200. The improvements made in this one instance also could be applied to hundreds of similar jobs done on this machine for the same small cost. This clearly illustrates that SMED does not require high capital investment. In fact, where companies approach reduction in setup through costly investments, this usually fails to bring the type of dramatic results we had just observed. It is brainpower that is important in SMED, not fancy machinery.

The last attitude issue to overcome was the priority for attacking setup reductions and getting the time to begin the attack. The problem is real if the purpose of the setup reductions is viewed only as a way to reduce costs and not as a facilitator of better, more flexible flow. If the lot sizes are dramatically reduced, the priority is obvious. And if time is scheduled, say, the first hour of each day before production runs are begun for the experts to work on the setup reductions, the cumulative impact of achieving real setup reductions soon provides more than enough time to work on fixing the setups which are most annoying.

This attitude obstacle is the "just-in-case" syndrome. That is, just-in-case management is not really serious about reducing setups, lot sizes are left the same and the effort on setups is left for when time is available, and when production is slack. This is a self-fulfilling failure. Time never becomes available, and even if it did, no one would know what to work on. Management clearly gives the message that it is either not serious or not confident the method will work and doesn't believe it is worth investing in with a little lost production until it does succeed.

SMED AND MANAGERS' WORK

As Shingo's hosts were setting up for his last lecture on Tuesday, which included the use of overhead transparencies, there were some problems in getting the projector located and focused properly. Shingo immediately used this incident as a way to illustrate the importance of standardization in setup operations. He pointed out that at the Japan Management Association, all operations pertaining to the projector are standardized so that speakers can begin without delay. "At the JMA," he said, "there are markings on the floor for the projector stand, markings on the stand for the projector itself, markings for how to focus, where the screen should be located, and so on."

The markings referred to could all be made in advance, as "external setup," or "outside exchange of die" (OED). The distinction between "internal" or "inside exchange of die" (IED) and external setup is extremely important to ensure dramatic reduction in setup time. Internal (IED) refers to setup operations performed while the machine is down. External (OED) refers to operations that can be performed while the machine is running.

SMED is accomplished in three stages. Stage 1 is to separate internal and external setup. Here we distinguish between (1) what is done while the machine is running and (2) what is done while it is shut down. Everyone agrees that preparation of tools, parts, maintenance, etc., should be done while the machine is running, yet it is astonishing to see how much time is usually wasted in looking for parts and tools while the machine is down. Usually, treating as much of the setup operation as possible as external setup will cut setup time by about 30-50%.

In Stage 2 of SMED we convert internal setup to external setup. Here, we reexamine operations to see whether any steps are wrongly assumed to be internal, and find ways to convert these steps to external setup. (For example, elements that have previously been heated only after setup has begun might be preheated.)

In Stage 3, all aspects of the setup are streamlined. A detailed analysis of each elemental operation is performed, both internal and external, and each operation is made as efficient as possible. (For example, it might be discovered that even after an operation has been successfully changed from internal to external, there was still time wasted due, say, to the way tools were arranged to be used during setup.)

CONCLUSIONS

In the demonstration Shingo gave that morning, we saw the power of following the stages of SMED and of involving operators in a team effort to solve setup problems. We learned that managers must develop an attitude of the expectation of continuous improvement as opposed to an attitude of "we've always done it that way and it can't be done differently because...." Armed with a continuous improvement attitude, managers must then learn to "coach" by providing guidance, teaching, support and listening, as opposed to directing and controlling every action of workers. This requires an openness to fact-finding and novel solutions as well as a willingness to listen and learn from others. Most importantly, the operative principle is trust.

With genuine trust and through careful application of the SMED principles, SMED capitalizes on the specific information and suggestions gained from the people closest to the situation (the operators themselves). Their intimate knowledge of actual production problems provides input on all levels of waste that might be eliminated. It is the leverage of thousands of days of experience that enables setup times to be cut to the bone.

By making it possible to abandon the traditional EOQ approach, SMED is a major key to the achievement of stockless production. With quick setups in place, one-piece flow can become a reality, provided plant layout is changed to follow the process, all unnecessary handling is eliminated, and other necessary adjustments are also accomplished.

Shingo's demonstration and the results of his work with the Toyota group companies, coupled with the constant drive for improvement evidenced throughout all the top companies in Japan, suggest the need for American manufacturers to move with extreme urgency, yet with infinite patience and perseverance, toward implementation of SMED and other stockless production techniques.

The Shingo Methodology

1. *Non-cost-principle—cost not price determines profit.*
   Origin of profit = reduction of cost = elimination of wastes.
2. *Non-stock principles—first pillar of waste.*
   Inventory is large "visible" waste to be eliminated.
3. *One-piece flow operation.*
   Establish network linkage of manufacturing processes.
4. *Shorten setup times for small lot production.*
   Adopt "single minute" then "one touch" exchange of dies.
5. *Elimination of breakdowns and effects.*
   Total preventive maintenance and defects equal to zero methods.
6. *Uniform production loading.*
   Leveling and balanced mix of product reduces shocks of change.
7. *Overall integrated one-piece flow operation.*
   Remove factory walls and then network suppliers into flow.
8. *Reduction of man-hours—second pillar of waste.*
   Mechanization of man's action (machines do physical work).
9. *Convert "brainwork" of man to automation.*
   Pre-automation phase-mechanized load, unload, clamping, problem detection.
10. *Maintain and develop process as standard operation.*
    Completely document detail of operation for constant improvement potential.
11. *Develop "Kanban" system.*
    The cards can aid the clerical and administrative tasks.

22

REDUCTION IN LEAD TIME DOES MAKE THE DIFFERENCE IN PROFITABLE OPERATIONS
RICHARD MARTEL

American discrete lot (batch) manufacturing companies which amount to over 70% of all manufacturing companies, are focusing their manufacturing lead time reduction efforts not only on the smallest, but the wrong element of total lead time. There does seem to be a concerted effort to reduce actual manufacturing lead time and labor by automating, computerizing and robotizing manufacturing processes, but considering that historically 80% or more of total manufacturing lead time is time in which the product, its components, and sub-assemblies are not being worked on, the emphasis is on the wrong thing.

An extreme example of a batch processing manufacturing environment which has proliferated the use of lead time generating non-manufacturing steps are the many aerospace and defense companies whose manufacturing lead times now extend from two to three years cumulatively.

American manufacturing companies should concentrate their efforts by reducing or eliminating nonmanufacturing steps that interrupt the direct flow of material to the manufacturing work center, create bunches of needless paperwork, require a significant amount of computer transactions to record and report status, help create departmental empires and wrongfully add valueless cost to the product. Everything must be done to eliminate material issue, receipt, receiving inspection, stocking, kitting and staging activity. Out on the shop floor, a manufacturing/material process flow needs to be created that eliminates work-in-process planned queues, in transit and set up time. It should also support the elimination of unplanned manufacturing interruptions such as equipment and tooling breakdowns.

It is not necessary to add more lead time as a contingency to soften the blow of unexpected operational breakdown surprises. It is a proven fact: the longer the lead time, the greater the inventory investment. Another proven

Reprinted from *Industrial Engineering,* October 1989, vol. 21, no. 10; Norcross, GA: Institute of Industrial Engineers, 25-30.

267

fact: the longer the lead time, the more difficult it is to ensure the predicted outcome of manufacturing plans.

Questions that can not be accurately answered by setting up these kind of contingencies are:

- Which products, sub-assemblies, components and raw materials will be impacted by business operational problems?
- How big will the problems be?
- Are the manufacturing lead times and safety stocks large enough to offset the problems?

The natural reaction when things go wrong is to add more contingencies in the form of more inventory or lead time. When things still don't substantially improve, additional contingencies are again added, and so on. This becomes a never ending, vicious, self-defeating loop!

The answer for all discrete manufacturing companies is to pressure their manufacturing operations to utilize as many of the philosophies and procedures as are inherent in the "process flow/repetitive" manufacturing operation:

- The manufacturing environment is more simple, direct and uninterrupted.
- Manufacturing process/material flows are planned in detail and physically set up for each product, in advance of actual manufacturing.
- The manufacturing work center is product line driven, with the flow of all product line raw material, components, sub-assemblies and finished goods regulated and synchronously manufactured simultaneously and sequentially, in an uninterrupted process.

Using these process flow operating philosophies as a model for reducing non-manufacturing lead time steps, the following strategies are recommended for implementation.

The strategies for reducing non-manufacturing lead time in the internal operation and creating uninterrupted manufacturing/material flow throughout the process, are the following:

1. Eliminate bill of material (BOM) levels. Every manufactured item requires a bill of material (BOM). With the exception of Phantom BOMs, every BOM manufactured item requires a work order to have it fabricated or assembled. Releasing a work order generates a need for physical material issuance and kitting, completing the issue document and entering the issue transactions into the inventory computer database. Once the work order is complete and the item is ready to proceed for use in the next level BOM, it must first have a work order receipt and stocking transaction, and be issued to the next level work order. Each of these transaction steps is normally supported in the system with lead time. By broadening the BOM and eliminating lower level BOMs, weeks of non-manufacturing lead time can be eliminated.

2. Eliminate manufacturing material stores areas. With the exception of material required for field service support, customer spares and manufacturing scrap, and yield and rework replacement, do not warehouse manufacturing material in a stores area. In order to implement this strategy, the original concept of MRP (Material Requirements Planning) emphasizing a discrete lot sizing rationale must be used. No longer can this original concept be muddied by lot sizing techniques that do not recommend purchase order and/or work order quantities based on the simple "one-for-one" calculation. The excess inventory generated by these lot sizing techniques will no longer exist, and therefore, storage space will not be needed. By implementing this strategy, material will flow directly to the work center of use. The lead time associated with related receipt, storage, issue and computer transactions will be eliminated.

3. Revise the MRP process. Implement product line MRP that clearly ties demand to a specific product. This requires the following MRP process changes to also take place:

- Change the MRP calculation so that material on hand *is not considered as available inventory to satisfy requirements.*
- Place purchase orders and work orders for specific product line requirements to get a complete product supply picture.
- Individual MRP management reports should be provided for each product line.
- Purchase orders and work orders must indicate the next work center of use in order for the material to be delivered directly to the appropriate work centers.

Specific benefits received by implementing these steps are:

- The reduction of difficult time consuming analysis associated with schedule changes, delays, material shortages and other manufacturing schedule impact problems on the end product.
- The advantages of spending the time to ensure that a clearly defined product schedule can be supported as planned.

4. Create manufacturing product work centers that group sequential work flow together. The majority of today's manufacturing plants have manufacturing work centers consisting of grouped similar manufacturing resources, capable of performing exact duplicate operations and accepting interchangeable tooling. For instance, a work center may consist of a group of five axis, multi-spindle, fully computerized machine centers; or a group of electronic test equipment used for performing functional or systems tests on electronic equipment; or a group of plastic injection molding machines having equal pressure, heat and speed settings and physically capable of utilizing all designated molds.

A change in manufacturing process flow and floor layout must take place! Rather than the described work center concept, the manufacturing work center has to have the capability of manufacturing complete products. The resources within the work center have to be arranged so that the manufacturing process creates a natural flow for converting raw material into component parts by processing those parts through various sequential fabrication and finishing operations. As a result, the completed component parts will travel uninterruptedly to the assembly areas for sub-assembly, final assembly and test operations. In an electronic assembly manufacturing environment, the work center might include various sub-assembly and test operations such as harness assembly, PC board sub-assembly, and functional test. The output of these sub-assembly and test operations will flow uninterruptedly to a final assembly and test operation.

Those manufacturing resources that normally cause bottlenecks because of scarcity must be mobile and able to travel from one work center to another. This will guarantee that these scarce resources will be fully utilized. If size or weight do not permit this mobility, additional resources have to be obtained and placed in the work center. Supporting steps for implementing the concept are:

• The manufacturing routing documents for each complete product have to be stripped of all non-manufacturing lead time other than "set-up time" and "in-transit time" for travel in and out of plant for completing outside manufacturing and processing operations. Doing this reduces lead times to basically the actual manufacturing time required to complete the manufactured item.

• Perform a capacity requirements plan for the anticipated daily, weekly and/or monthly time demand for manufacturing finished product, sub-assemblies and components. You start by extending scheduled quantities for the combined demand by the manufacturing operation time standards for all of its manufacturing components, sub-assemblies and finished product; and time phased by operation sequence. This will indicate the amount of each manufacturing resource required to completely manufacture the specific products. Once this step is completed for every product, the company will have a clear picture of the manufacturing resource requirement profile for each product, how many work centers will be required to support manufacturing demand, and what manufacturing resources will be required in each work center. It may be that a work center may totally support the entire manufacturing process for one product or a group of products, depending on demand volume.

- With all unnecessary non-manufacturing lead time removed from all product routing documents, a product critical path analysis must be performed to identify those parts that have both long lead time and manufacturing operations requiring the use of historically scarce manufacturing resources previously discussed. Once the critical path is determined, the BOM may be restructured and the routing document re-sequenced to ensure that critical path items are given just priority and are started in the product specific manufacturing process first.

5. Expand manufacturing router document capability. Eliminating Bill of Material levels and increasing the number of items per Bill of Material requires that the manufacturing router be expanded in content and detail. The router that was previously used only for the final assembly of the product, now becomes the master router and represents the entire manufacturing process for a given product. Internally manufactured component parts and sub-assemblies will have their own sub-routers and their part numbers will be referenced at the master router operation sequence in which they become part of the finished product.

When a product line work order is released in support of a schedule, finished product, component and sub-assembly work orders will all have the same work order control number. Finished manufactured component parts will flow directly to the sub-assembly and final assembly work center without having to be received, stored, issued, kitted and transacted on the computer with the support of the various completed inventory transaction documents.

6. Employ the use of multiple manufacturing resource set ups. Manufacturing lead times can be further reduced by employing the use of excess multiple manufacturing resources to complete a manufacturing operation faster. A minor additional investment in tooling or other complimentary resources may have to be made in order to utilize the excess major resource. This is especially effective when trying to reduce very long lead time manufacturing operations.

7. Provide excess resource capability for each work center. The manufacturing scheduling strategy must provide excess resource capability for each product work center. At no time should every resource be scheduled for maximum utilization. Excess capacity needs to be provided to accommodate absenteeism, vacations, holidays, preventive maintenance, minimal machine and tooling breakdowns, etc. As stated earlier, with the exception of critical resources, all work center resources will be dedicated to a single product work center! The major benefit is that, like a finely tuned athletic team, the manufacturing team needs fully prepared, ready to go, highly trained primary and secondary manufacturing resources to successfully execute the manufacturing plan.

8. A preventive maintenance program becomes essential. A comprehensive manufacturing operations preventive maintenance program must be fully implemented to greatly reduce the risk of not meeting schedules. The maintenance program should support manufacturing, test, material handling and inspection equipment, tooling and facilities. Like an automobile service program, the preventive maintenance program has to be completely scheduled, in detail, with service, repair and/or part replacement intervals clearly understood. Even if parts do not look worn, they must be replaced if it is time to do so according to schedule!

9. Daily manufacturing schedule reviews must take place. A daily schedule review must take place between the production planning/scheduling, purchasing and manufacturing functions. The meeting will encompass a review of current manufacturing schedule performance to ensure that schedules are being met as planned. Also, proposed manufacturing schedules are set for the following two or three manufacturing days. Contingency product schedules are discussed, finalized and incorporated into the overall schedule. The contingency policy must state: "If a product schedule breakdown and timely recovery cannot be made, the entire work center must be stripped and set up with a total new product schedule (work order)." This policy is consistent with process flow/repetitive manufacturing management practices.

10. The master production schedule will have variable product line time fences. Rather than having a single time fence for all master schedule products, each product will have its own time fence according to its individual cumulative manufacturing and procurement lead time. Those products with a shorter lead time will have "close-in" time fences. Those that have longer cumulative lead times will have time fences that are frozen further out. This will provide the opportunity to make Master Production Schedule changes for those products with shorter lead times without negatively impacting subsidiary manufacturing and vendor schedules and inventory levels.

Chapter Twenty-Two

STEPS TO REDUCING NON-OPERATION LEAD TIME

The strategies for reducing nonoperation lead time in the external vendor based manufacturing operation and creating uninterrupted manufacturing/material flow directly to the internal manufacturing work centers are the following:

1. Reduce quantity of vendors. The fewer purchase material sources a company has to deal with, the greater control it will exert over its vendor base in delivery, quality and cost performance. The assumption is that the vendor selected to be the major supplier of a given commodity group of items will eagerly cooperate and try to please its manufacturing customer, knowing that it has the "lion's share" of its customer's purchases for that commodity group. Depending on the volume of material purchases that a manufacturer makes, it should have no more than two to three vendor sources for each commodity.

2. Make heavy use of release type blanket purchase orders. The manufacturing company should place 80% to 90% of its material and outside processing purchase orders on "release type" annual blank purchase orders. These purchase orders should state the anticipated annual buy quantities and the release agreement in detail for each purchase order line item. They are reviewed and releases made frequently. The higher dollar volume items and the higher unit cost items will have the most frequent review/release cycles. This is because they generally have the largest impact on schedule, inventory and cash flow. With purchase orders placed once a year, lead time is reduced by the amount of time it takes to complete the review and release cycle. This normally amounts to one to two weeks. Administrative costs associated with constantly releasing new purchase requisitions, negotiating new purchase orders and releasing new purchase order documentation are significantly reduced. The buyer can now concentrate on successfully executing the purchase plan.

To further reduce administrative costs, a purchase order change document is not generated every time a blanket purchase order release is made. Instead, a multiple part summary release report is printed immediately at the time the manufacturing company/vendor blanket purchase order release meeting is concluded and the purchase order computer database is updated with the agreed to release quantities and schedules. Both buyer and vendor sales representatives sign their company's respective copies of the summary report as an indication of schedule acceptance by both vendor and manufacturer.

3. Set up bills of material for product purchased material kits. Once vendor sources are established, the manufacturing company should develop product line specific commodity BOMs for all those component/raw materials that are to be purchased from one vendor source and are to be used in a specific product. The quantities per item on each BOM are to represent the actual quantities required to complete one unit of the finished product. Having one part number on the purchase order representing potentially many different product line parts will greatly reduce the number of purchase orders, purchase order line items, vendor invoices, accounts payable vouchers, purchase order receipts and inventory issues. This technique is especially effective when dealing with low cost, high volume hardware and electronic component items.

4. Support/emphasize vendor internal quality assurance/control programs. The manufacturing company needs to shift its purchased material incoming inspection responsibility back to the vendor. Rather than having a staff of receiving inspectors, it will require quality assurance engineers charged with the responsibility for developing vendor quality assurance/control programs that will ensure receipt of quality acceptable purchased material with no auditing/ sampling required at the manufacturing customer plant. When purchasing industry standard parts such as hardware, electronic components, etc., the vendor's quality acceptance certification documentation is to be kept on file at their location. This will eliminate requiring someone within the customer manufacturing operation to establish and maintain a physical file for these documents.

With receiving inspection eliminated, purchased material should go directly to the manufacturing work center it is required for next level use.

5. Combine material planning and buying functions. Material planning, as a separate function, should be eliminated. By doing so, the document known as the "Purchase Requisition" will be done away with. With the buyer placing the majority of his/her purchase orders once a year via the release type blanket purchase order system, he/she needs to be trained to review material requirements from the MRP report and respond with the required blanket purchase order releases. This will eliminate between two to five planning days for the processing of purchase requisitions for each item purchased.

PREREQUISITES TO SUCCESSFUL IMPLEMENTATION

The manufacturing lead time reduction implementation strategies described above require that certain foundational prerequisites be established before some of the strategies can actually be implemented and/or maximum benefit can be received. Those prerequisites are:

1. Computer BOMs and manufacturing routers must be 99% + accurate and complete.

2. Technically strong industrial, manufacturing, tool and facilities engineering functions must exist. These functions must be capable of performing the required product manufacturing flow analysis, work center layout, equipment selection, tool design and manufacturing, BOM and manufacturing router development and maintenance.

3. A vendor base that is truly considered an external manufacturing resource. Like the internal manufacturing operation, it must continuously be kept apprised of schedule changes, new requirements, etc. This vendor base must have in place the same manufacturing lead time reduction philosophies and strategies that will ensure unfailing schedule performance and maximum flexibility.

4. A "new product introduction" process must not only address product design issues, but include the complete product line manufacturing process planning described above for each new product.

5. A company philosophy that safeguards manufacturing performance, not by establishing reserves of inventory and lead time contingencies, but by eradicating the underlying conditions that cause manufacturing performance uncertainty and lead to setting up those contingencies in the first place. If contingencies are to exist, they will exist in alternate manufacturing plans, additional manufacturing resources and in practices that greatly reduce or eliminate the risk of manufacturing breakdowns.

THE BOTTOM LINE EFFECT

Some of the techniques recommended for reducing manufacturing lead time are independent of each other—others require a prerequisite technique be implemented. Some are simple to understand and implement, others are complex and require more time to fully plan and implement.

Individually and cumulatively, they all will have a positive effect on the company's bottom line.

• Work-in-process and stores inventories will be reduced by more than 50% and have a significant one time cash flow contribution. In addition, interest expense will drop proportionately to the reduction in inventory dollar value. If current interest rate is approximately 10%, a $3 million drop in inventory in the first year will result in a minimum of $300,000 savings on interest expense in the second year.

• Administrative costs associated with non-manufacturing steps will be greatly reduced. A streamlined manufacturing operation which has rid itself of

275

much of these lead time contributors no longer requires the people, facilities, equipment and routines that heavily add to manufacturing indirect costs.

• The need for additional facilities can be delayed as materials storage areas are freed up for more useful company purposes.

• With up to 70% to 80% of the manufacturing lead time eliminated, the company can develop greater capability and flexibility to respond to close-in customer demand variables, without having to support this capability with inventory and/or lead time contingencies.

The bottom line is that company fiscal performance will be positively affected, not only by reductions in operating costs, but by company revenue, profit and growth increases as a result of its ability to meet market demand more satisfactorily than the competition.

ABOUT THE EDITORS

F. Robert Jacobs is associate professor of operations management, Graduate School of Business, Indiana University, Bloomington. He holds B.S.I.E., B.S.C.I.S., M.B.A. and Ph.D. degrees from Ohio State University.

Dr. Jacobs has published in *Industrial Engineering, Management Science, Decision Sciences,* and other academic and professional journals. His current research interests focus on the design of manufacturing systems and cellular manufacturing. He has served as a consultant to many manufacturing companies and often leads management seminars on such topics as total quality management, materials management, and cellular manufacturing.

Dr. Jacobs is the chairman of the Indiana Manufacturing Excellence Roundtable, an organization sponsored by the Operations Management Department at Indiana University and composed of the leading manufacturing companies with plants in the Midwest region of the United States.

Vincent A. Mabert is professor and chairman of the Operations Management Department, Graduate School of Business, Indiana University, Bloomington. He also has held teaching positions at Ohio State University, Purdue University, and Bowling Green State University. He received his B.S., M.B.A., and Ph.D. degrees from Ohio State University.

Dr. Mabert has authored and co-edited other publications for the Institute of Industrial Engineers. He has also published extensively in academic and professional journals in the areas of forecasting, material control, job scheduling, and work force planning. He has served as a consultant for both service and manufacturing firms, and leads management seminars on such topics as material requirements planning, forecasting, and master scheduling.

Dr. Mabert is a senior member of the Institute of Industrial Engineers and a past director of the Banking and Financial Services Division.